Microcomputer Programming Languages

Jeffrey Hsu

Hayden Book Company

A DIVISION OF HAYDEN PUBLISHING COMPANY, INC.
HASBROUCK HEIGHTS, NEW JERSEY

Acquisitions Editor: LES PURIFICACIÓN
Production Editor: ALBERTA BODDY
Developmental Editor: KAREN PASTUZYN
Design: JIM BERNARD
Illustrations: YVONNE BUCHANAN
Cover Photo: RON MORECRAFT
Composition: McFARLAND GRAPHICS AND DESIGN, INC.
Manufacturing: THE MAPLE-VAIL BOOK MANUFACTURING GROUP

Library of Congress Cataloging-in-Publication Data

Hsu, Jeffrey.
Microcomputer programming languages.

Bibliography.
Includes index.
1. Programming languages (Electronic computers)
2. Microcomputers–Programming. I. Title.
QA76.7.H78 1986 005.26 86-293
ISBN 0-8104-6288-5

Copyright © 1986 by HAYDEN BOOK COMPANY. All rights reserved. No part of this book may be reprinted, or reproduced, or utilized in any form or by any electronic, mechanical, or other means, now known or hereafter invented, including photocopying and recording, or in any information storage and retrieval system, without permission in writing from the Publisher.

Printed in the United States of America

2 3 4 5 6 7 8 9

86 87 88 89 90 91 92 93 94 YEAR

This book is dedicated to my parents, Henry and Irene Hsu, who gave me not only my first computer, but also continuous love, support, and encouragement. In addition, I would like to make a personal dedication to M.L.J.C.

PREFACE

WHEN MICROCOMPUTERS BECAME widely available to the general public at affordable prices, they opened up the power of computers to hundreds of thousands of users. Never before had this technology been so readily available to so many businesses, schools, and personal users.

The world of computer languages is also now available to this vast group of users. Everyone from the casual hobbyist to the serious professional micro programmer can now learn and use a wide variety of programming languages. New implementations of almost all major languages either are already on the market or are currently being developed. This profusion of languages, books, and language software has created the need for a comprehensive handbook describing and evaluating the languages and programming aids available for microcomputer users.

Can I get Pascal for my Commodore 64? What are APL and Forth? What COBOL compilers are available for my CP/M system? What's the best language for writing an accounts receivable program? How much memory do I need to run Ada on my IBM PC? These are just a few of the questions this handbook is designed to answer.

This book will acquaint you with the many programming languages and direct you to the various software packages/books available. Detailed language descriptions help you select the right one for your interests and needs.

The Meet the Language chapters, which describe in detail specific languages, are not intended to teach programming but rather to give you a "feel" for the character and capabilities of each. An extensive bibliography follows each chapter, outlining books that provide a more in-depth study of a particular language.

If you are not familiar with programming languages, I suggest that you first read Chapter 1, which serves as a concise introduction to languages in general, starting with machine code, and briefly but thoroughly covering the field from compilers to arrays and files. It discusses the need for languages and the uses of compilers, interpreters, and assemblers. Finally, the major components common to all programming languages are covered.

The language overview chapter is followed by the language chapters, which are grouped into four Meet the Languages sections. The four sections cover the Familiar Four, Specialized, Statistical, and Other languages. The first covers the most commonly used micro languages—BASIC, COBOL, FORTRAN, and Pascal. The second section includes 11 other languages less widely used yet powerful and versatile in their own way. The third section is designed for more specialized users who are interested in statistical analysis languages such as SPSS and SAS. Finally, the last section covers other microcomputer languages.

The Reference Section is designed to direct you to the right language software package for your particular computer or operating system. Each product's features and limitations are discussed, as well as memory and hardware requirements. Pertinent information such as firm names, addresses, and telephone numbers are included. Since modem and telecommunications services (timesharing) are so widely used today, I have included a comprehensive list of companies that offer language timesharing, usually from mainframe or minicomputers.

Finally, to tie the language and reference sections together, I have included charts which describe languages in capsule form and compare languages to access availability.

I welcome any suggestions, comments, or questions you may have about this book or about programming languages in general. Please write to me at the address below or through my CompuServe account 71106, 1467. I hope you will find this book useful and will come to discover, as I have, how fascinating programming languages can be!

Jeffrey Hsu
5 Tristam Place
Pine Brook, New Jersey 07058

ACKNOWLEDGMENTS

I am indebted to the following people for their help in making this book a reality.

Les Purificacion, my editor at Hayden Book Company, for working closely with me in developing this book. I am grateful for his support of my project from the very beginning. I also thank the others on the editorial staff at Hayden who have worked on producing this book.

Raymond Ga Côté, for his role as consulting editor on this book. Mr. Côté is the editor and publisher of *Robot Experimenter* magazine, and was Editor-in-Chief of *Byte* magazine.

Connie Saxon, who spent many hours of her time reviewing and editing my manuscript as well as providing ideas, support, and encouragement. Thanks also go to her husband, Andy, and her daughter, Adrienne.

Dave Stuehler of Montclair State College, who reviewed and offered suggestions on my Introduction and BASIC chapters.

Stephen Hsu, who reviewed several chapters and made valuable suggestions concerning them.

Susan Tamson, who first encouraged me to write.

Patricia Gartenberg of Rutgers University, who, together with her husband, Max, offered valuable advice on my proposal and contractual arrangements.

Joseph Kusnan, for information on the Lisp language.

David Touretsky of Carnegie-Mellon University, for information on Lisp.

Harold J. Bailey of Bloomsburg University, for information on the Logo language.

Simon Chang, who offered advice and encouragement.

I am also grateful to all who offered their support, encouragement, prayers, and time to help me.

I am also thankful to those publishers and software companies who generously provided me with information and review copies of their products for inclusion in the reference section of this book. I would like to mention them individually:

Book Publishers

Barbara Friedman, Computer Science Press
Delores Wright, Que Corporation
John Willig, Harper & Row
Terrell Anderson, Brady Communications
Frank Rugirello, Wadsworth Publishing
Reston Publishing Company
Osborne/McGraw-Hill
Wm. C. Brown Co.
Dilithium Press
Cambridge University Press
McGraw-Hill
Science Research Associates (SRA)
Blackwell Publications
PWS Publishing
Mitchell Press
Benjamin-Cummings Co.
Little, Brown & Co.
Howard W. Sams & Co.
W.W. Norton & Company
Chilton Book Company
Plum Hall Inc.
Petrocelli Books
Sybex Inc.
Warner Books
Hayden Book Company
Springer-Verlag
Prentice-Hall, Inc.
Allyn & Bacon
New American Library
Holt Rinehart Winston
Society for Computer Simulation
Anaheim Publishing Co.
Dell Publishing Co.

Software Companies

Microsoft Corporation
The Software Toolworks
Supersoft Inc.

BD Software
Pro Code International
Laboratory Microsystems
Summit Software Technology
Northwest Computer Algorithms
Hippopotamus Software
Lattice Inc.
Mark Williams Corp.
Rational Systems
ExperTelligence
Watcom Corp.
IBM Microcomputer Software Division
MicroSparc
Harvard Softworks
Ecosoft
Portable Software
Manx Software Systems
Interface Technologies Corp.
Sunburst Communications
Megamax
Voice Operated Computer Systems
STSC
Abacus Software
Blaise Computing
C-Source
Sensible Software
Chalcedony Software
Mountain View Press
Solution Systems
Computer Innovations
M.E.C.C.
Integral Quality
Expert Systems Int'l.
M.E.C.A.
New Classics Software
Micro Focus
Network Consulting
XOR
Chalcedony Software
Terrapin Inc.
Krell Software
Volition Systems
Logic Programming Associates
Logitech
Logo Computer Systems
Software Dynamics
Absoft Corp.
Sally A. Roberson, SAS Institute

The Alternate Source
Texas Instruments Inc.
Kaypro Corp.
Tandy/Radio Shack
Apple Computer Company
6502 Program Exchange
D.I.S.C.
Media Materials
Sterling Swift
Microway
Southwestern Data Systems
Systat Inc.
Kyan Software
Bellesoft Inc.
R R Software
The Byte Works
Softsync Inc.
Mitek Inc.
C Ware
Loki Engineering
Computer Software Design
Microrim Inc.
Phoenix Computer Products

Other Organizations

C User's Group
New Jersey Educational Computer Network
Educom
Computer Sciences Corporation
Datapro Inc.
Susan Wulf, Korsmeyer Electronic Design
Ted White, IP Sharp Associates
Frank Triplett, Control Data Corporation
TSR Inc.
Delphi
IBM Information Network
Infopro Systems
Programmer's Journal

CONTENTS

Part I

Introduction *1*

1 A General Introduction to Languages *3*

Part II

The Familiar Four:
BASIC, COBOL, FORTRAN, Pascal *17*

2 BASIC *19*

3 COBOL *38*

4 FORTRAN *64*

5 Pascal *78*

Part III

Specialized Languages *103*

6 Ada *105*

7 APL *127*

8 Assembly and Machine Languages *142*

9 C *163*

10 Forth *185*

11 Lisp *198*

12 Logo *212*

13 Modula-2 *227*

14 PILOT *241*

15 PL/1 *246*

16 Prolog *262*

Part IV

Statistical Languages *273*

17 SPSS *275*

18 SAS *284*

Part V

Other Languages *293*

19 Past, Present, and Future Languages *295*

Part VI

Reference Section: Language Availability *301*

20 Language Software *303*

21 Telecommunications, UNIX, and Other Systems *364*

Appendix *378*

Index *395*

Part I

INTRODUCTION

CHAPTER 1

A GENERAL INTRODUCTION TO LANGUAGES

COMPUTER PROGRAMMING LANGUAGES are tools which allow you to instruct computers. Contrary to the popular notion that computers are dangerous because they can make decisions on their own, computers are just "dumb" machines that can do many tasks much faster and more efficiently than people. What a computer can do is determined only by the instructions given to it by programmers.

MACHINE LANGUAGE

The first computer languages were made up of long rows of ones and zeros called *Binary Machine Language.* Machine Language programs were difficult to write since people are not very good at reading and remembering long strings of digits. However, it was the only language available. Since binary numbers are simply not readable or easily understood by people, it was very difficult to write or correct the code. Errors were the rule rather than the exception, even for short programs. Also, each kind of computer had different hardware and needed different instructions, so the machine language for each was also different! A program written for one system had to be completely rewritten in order to be run on another.

Solutions to these problems were not long in coming. One of the most obvious was the use of a more convenient way to represent the binary codes. For this purpose, number systems such as octal, decimal, and hexadecimal were used—with a base of 8, 10, and 16, respectively—rather than 2 (binary). With hexadecimal, for example, there are 16 digits: 0-1-2-3-4-5-6-7-8-9-A-B-C-D-E-F. Now a 16-digit binary instruction could be reduced to four, more easily remembered digits, and the contents of an eight-bit register could be represented by only a two-digit hexadecimal number. See Table 1-1 for a comparison of different number systems.

ASSEMBLERS

The problem still remained of breaking down a problem into simple machine-level operations, determining the right instructions to use, and then converting the entire algorithm to

Table 1-1. Number Systems: Binary, Decimal, Hexadecimal

Binary	Decimal	Hexadecimal
0000 0000	0	00
0000 0001	1	01
0000 1010	10	0A
0001 0000	16	10
0010 0000	32	20
0010 0111	39	27
0100 1010	74	4A
0111 0100	116	74
1000 1111	143	8F
1011 1110	190	BE
1110 1111	239	EF
1111 1111	255	FF

numerical codes. Finally, a program known as an *assembler* was created to make this task easier. Now, instead of binary or hexadecimal numbers, programmers could use mnemonic (easy to remember) operation codes or *op-codes* such as LDA for load or STA for store when they wrote their programs. Labels could be used to identify places the program was to branch to, and operands were listed with the instructions. Such programs were relatively easy for humans to understand and correct. When the program was completed, the assembler would translate or assemble it into correct machine code.

Assembler listing for a program

```
0300:  A9 C4      LDA $C4      ; load $C4 into accumulator
0302:  8D 25 3A   STA $3A25    ; store into location $3A25
```

Assembly Language, the name for this method of machine programming, was a great improvement over straight machine language. However, it merely simplified many of the tedious details of dealing with machine code. The programmer still had to deal with each problem from a machine-level, instruction-by-instruction perspective.

HIGH-LEVEL LANGUAGES, COMPILERS, AND INTERPRETERS

In the mid-1950s the first "high-level" language, FORTRAN, was developed. It is called a high-level language because the user can write programs without worrying about the "low-level" details of how the computer hardware will carry out the instructions. For the first time, programming tasks could be considered on a much simpler, problem-oriented basis without concern for the operation of the computer itself. However, before such a high-level program can be run on a computer, it must be translated into the specific system's machine language. Here is a FORTRAN program that adds two numbers and prints the result.

```
C PROGRAM TO ADD TWO NUMBERS
      I=4
      J=5
      K= I + J
      WRITE (5,100) K
100   FORMAT (I3)
      END
```

Two main methods of translation are used: compilation and interpretation. Each method has its advantages and drawbacks, and each language we will cover usually uses only one or the other. One exception is the language BASIC, which is usually interpreted but can also be compiled.

A *compiler* takes a program (called *source code*), evaluates it, and produces an equivalent machine language program (called *object code*). Errors are recorded during the compilation process, and a listing of the original text with relevant comments and error messages is produced along with the object code file. This object code file can be executed directly. COBOL, Pascal, and FORTRAN are examples of compiled languages.

Interpreters, on the other hand, examine, translate, and execute each line of the program separately. If any errors are found during the examination of each line, the line is not translated, and an appropriate message is sent to the screen. The error must be corrected before translation can continue. This method helps create a friendly, interactive environment in which you can follow the creation of your program line by line. The main limitation with interpreters is speed. Because of the time needed to evaluate, translate, and execute every line separately, an interpreted program runs much more slowly than an equivalent compiled program. Examples of interpreted languages include BASIC, Lisp, and Logo.

With the use of compilers and interpreters, we can "talk" with the computer and give it instructions in a form that is easy for us to understand. Like every good thing, however, this advantage has its price. Because of the enormous complexity of compiler and interpreter programs, it would be impossible to write one language suitable for all needs. Instead, languages were created that have strengths in certain areas. For instance, COBOL is strong in business data processing and FORTRAN excels at handling mathematical formulas. Helping the microcomputer user to select the right language for his or her needs is one of the main objectives of this handbook.

Despite the fact that most languages have significant differences in syntax and form, all share many features and capabilities. The next section describes these common features.

CHARACTERISTICS OF LANGUAGES

Some human languages, like English, Chinese, and Arabic, are very different in alphabet, vocabulary, grammar, and use. The same is true for computer languages, such as COBOL, APL, and Forth. However, computer languages are much more limited since computers, being machines, cannot deal with any ambiguity, abstract concepts, or generalizations. Every aspect of a program must be specific, clear, and logical, and programming languages are designed to reflect this requirement. The following discussion will take us from data types to operations, loops, and other important concepts.

Data Types

Since the purpose of our using computers is to manipulate data (information), it is important to know what kinds of data a particular language can handle. For instance, in a space shuttle or other advanced mathematics application, most of the data would be in numerical form, perhaps requiring scientific notation and high precision. An inventory program, on the other hand, might require only whole numbers and character data.

Although numerical information is most closely associated with computers, the powerful languages available today feature not only numbers, but characters, arrays, graphics, pictures, files, and many other useful types. First we shall discuss numerical data.

Numerical Data Types

Integers Integers are used whenever decimal places or more complex notation is not required. Integers are suitable for simple calculations in arithmetic, counting lines on a page, or counting the number of records in a file. Microcomputers can handle both positive and negative integers in the range of −32678 to +32767. Examples of integers: 45 −393 12 495 66.

Real Numbers Real numbers are numbers that include decimal points or scientific notation (exponents). This very wide range of numbers is used for most calculations: business prices ($4.98), fractions (0.25), and very large or small numbers (3.45E5 or 2.41E−6). Some languages distinguish between real numbers by designating those without exponents as *fixed point*, and exponentials as *floating point*. Examples of reals: 16.25 4.44E6 −2.3 .467356.

Double-Precision Numbers Double-precision numbers are used for calculations requiring a greater number of significant decimal places. For complex problems requiring a high degree of accuracy, double precision can be used to handle round-off errors and lost digits by putting off the error further down in the decimal digits where they have less impact on the numbers being computed.

Boolean Based on the concept of Boolean algebra, an algebra of two values, "true" and "false," a Boolean data type can take only one state or the other. Generally, this data type is used either for Boolean operations on binary numbers, or for indicating the state of something. For instance, if we wanted to know if a grade was passing, we could make "PASS" a Boolean variable. If the score is above 60, we set PASS to "true"; otherwise, it is "false."

Binary Numbers Some languages allow the user to set a condition based on a binary number string. For instance, "00" could be programmed as a flag to continue looping, while "01" would terminate the loop. This data type is also useful when binary numbers must be used as data. The PL/1 language, for example, supports both a binary data type and a special "binary function."

Character Data

The need for manipulating characters (letters, symbols, and numbers without regard for their numeric value) is just as important in today's society as the need for handling numerical data. Names and addresses are used heavily in data processing. Computer-assisted instruction (CAI) relies on textual data. Word processing is one of the major uses of microcomputer systems today. However, although so much of the information used by computers is textual, there are only two main character data types, character strings and single characters.

Character Strings Although human languages deal with characters in words, sentences, and paragraphs, computers work with character strings. These are simply sequences of keyboard characters terminated by carriage returns. Although numbers are stored in an equivalent form in the computer, characters are stored internally as numbers in a code such as

ASCII or EBCDIC. See the appendix for a chart of ASCII codes. Examples of strings: 'hello' '44.568' '$&&$%#()'

Single Characters Some languages such as Pascal offer a single character data type. This is useful when you accept a choice from a menu or for multiple choice input. Functions for manipulating strings and single characters are described in the separate chapters on each language.

Special Computer Data Types

Lists Instead of a single number or character string, some languages are equipped to deal with complete lists of items, such as a list of words or even a list of lists! One language that we will discuss is specially designed to handle this data type—Lisp.

Logic In the Prolog language, data can take the form of a logical relationship. An example might be:

```
loves (Bill,Jane)
```

This represents the logical relationship "Bill loves Jane." Operations can be performed on these kinds of relationships. Consult the Prolog chapter for more detailed explanations of this special type of data.

File and Records One very important way of organizing data is to group them in some way. A widely used method, especially in data processing, is to put related information together in a record. Related records are then collected into a data file. The records can be compared to file cards in a manual filing system. A single mailing list record, for instance, might contain a name, address, and phone number of a customer. Each item in the record is called a *field.* For our mailing list record, the fields might be these:

Last name (character string)
First name (character string)
Middle initial (character string)
Address (character string)
City (character string)
State (character string)
Zip code (character string)
Phone number (character string)

Our mailing list file is a collection of these records, each containing the same fields but different information. Languages that support file and record data types provide means of inserting, deleting, and updating information in the files and of merging records.

Pointer Pointers are used to create dynamic (changing) types of data structures. We usually think of pointers as "arrows" or "links" between the parts of a linked list or tree, but in actuality a pointer contains the address of the location where the next piece of "linked" information exists. Such linked lists are widely used in application programs. For example, an airline reservation system may use a linked list to store all the bookings for each flight. The pointers make it possible to find each reservation, making it easy to insert, delete, or change them.

User-Defined Type Some languages allow the programmers to define their own data types, a handy feature when you have nonstandard yet related data items. For instance, if we wanted to create two sets of favorite classical and rock musicians, we could define one set as data type COMPOSERS (Bach, Beethoven, Chopin) and the other as type ROCKERS (Elvis, Beatles, Stones). These are also called *enumerated data types,* since you must specify all acceptable values for each type you declare.

Understanding which data type to use in a particular situation is important to effective programming. Knowing which language is best suited to processing the data types you want to use is also important.

Variables

Computer programming wouldn't be very useful if every value that we needed had to be spelled out exactly in the program. Take the simple problem of adding two numbers. If we had to modify the program every time we wanted to add a different pair of numbers, it would be simpler to use pencil and paper. However, if a general program could be written and the data changed from outside the program, the computer would be much more efficient.

We can do this with the concept of a variable. As in high school algebra, a variable is a symbol or name that can take on different values. However, in a computer, the variable actually represents a place in the computer's memory where we can store numbers or characters. Variables are simple to use. In some languages, they must first be declared and given a type (integer, real, etc.) In others, assigning a value to a variable name creates that variable in memory. In general, a variable is like a little "cell" in memory where information is kept. A value is stored in that cell until something else is put there, after which the first value is gone forever.

Operators

Operators are used to manipulate data and variables in a program.

One of the most important operators in any language is the assignment operator for assigning a value to a variable. Many computer languages use the symbol "=" to indicate assignment. This symbol should not be confused with the algebraic concept of equality. Because of the potential confusion, some programming languages use a different symbol. For example, Pascal uses the symbol ":=" for assignment.

For the operators that perform standard mathematical calculations, special symbols are defined. In languages such as BASIC, Pascal, and PL/1, arithmetic symbols are used (+ − / *). A more English-like language like COBOL allows the use of either English words (ADD, SUBTRACT) or the standard arithmetic symbols (+,−). Assembly languages, on the other hand, use machine-level instructions (ADC for add with carry, or SBC for subtract with carry).

Another type of operator is used to compare different data items or variables in order to make decisions. Operators for equality (=), larger than (>), smaller than (<), larger than or equal to (>=), smaller than or equal to (<=), and logical operations such as AND or OR are available in all programming languages.

Data Input/Output

A computer would be useless without provisions for putting data into the program and then getting back the output that is needed.

Input The three methods of data input are interactive communication, DATA statements, and data files. In *interactive communication*, data are typed into the program from the terminal or CRT in response to prompts from the program. A language like BASIC allows the use of *DATA statements*, in which lists of data are included as a part of the program itself. The third, the most complicated but often most useful method, involves first entering information into a *data file*, then reading that file into the main program.

Output Output from a program can be sent out from the computer to a number of peripheral devices—the terminal screen, a line printer or plotter, a disk file, or even another computer or terminal via modems and telephone lines or through cables.

For both input and output, special statements must be used. Input most often takes a form similar to READ, READLN, or INPUT, while output is usually done using a WRITE, PRINT, or PUT.

Making Decisions (Conditionals)

After data are read into a program, decisions must often be made about what to do next on the basis of certain conditions. For instance, if a salesman sells 30 dolls, he gets 5% commission. Above 30 dolls, the commission is 8%. Since computers cannot make decisions by themselves, the programmer must have some way to tell the computer how much commission to pay the salesman on the basis of the number of dolls sold. Every language makes some provisions for decisions. Although commands vary from language to language, the most common ones are the IF..THEN and the CASE structures. Whereas the first makes its decisions based on the truth or falsity of a condition, the second determines a branch by a "matching" method:

```
.
.
.
IF (SALES > = 30 ) THEN
      COMM = SALES * 0.08              IF..THEN Structure
ELSE
      COMM = SALES * 0.05;

CASE A OF
      1 : A=A + 1;                     CASE Structure
      2 : A=A - 2
END
```

Repeating Yourself (Loops)

Most of the power of the computer lies in its ability to efficiently and continuously repeat a selected group of instructions. These structures are called *loops* and are very important in programming. For loops to be used effectively, the program must know exactly how many times to repeat and when to stop. There are several types of loops:

Counted Loop The number of times around the loop is set before execution. For example, BASIC features the FOR loop, and FORTRAN and PL/1 have DO loops.

Conditional Loop Continued execution of the loop depends on a condition that is tested either at the start or the end of each repetition. For instance, a DO WHILE loop is tested at the beginning, whereas a REPEAT loop is tested at the end.

```
FOR I= 1 TO 5
                                    Counted
NEXT I                              For..Next Loop (Basic)

DO K=1 TO 5

END DO;                             Counted Do Loop (PL/1)

DO WHILE (A > 10)

END DO;                             Do While Loop (PL/1)

REPEAT

UNTIL (A > 10);                     Repeat Loop (Pascal)
```

String Handling

In an application that requires much character string input and output, the ability to manipulate these strings is important. For instance, we may have input a string

"John A. Smith"

but want to print the name out in a report as

"Smith, John A."

Most languages include functions for finding the length of a string, finding a substring, taking a substring, searching for a string in a larger one, and pasting together (concatenating) two separate strings. See the individual language chapters for specific details on string functions available.

Programs in a Program

Often when a program is being written, the need arises to perform the same set of instructions at different points in the code. Rewriting this code repeatedly can be very time-consuming and tedious, especially if it is a long routine. In addition, it is often difficult to understand long programs that are not segmented into manageable sections.

Subprograms are very useful since they break longer programs into modular units, each performing a specific function. They also help to maintain some understandable structure in the long program. There are three types of subprograms that are commonly used: subroutines, procedures, and functions.

Subroutines Subroutines are generally found in BASIC and FORTRAN. In general, they are invoked by using the name of the subroutine in the main program segment, or by using a GOSUB command. After completion of a subroutine, control reverts back to the line immediately following the subroutine call. BASIC does not support parameters or local variables, those used and accessible only within the subroutine. FORTRAN subroutines support parameters and local variables, and they resemble procedures, which are described in the next section.

Procedures Procedures, which are found in languages such as Pascal and PL/1, are similar to subroutines. They usually allow the passing of values from the main program to the subprogram, using arguments and parameters. Local variables are available in most procedures, and unlike global variables, are not accessible outside the procedure. This helps to prevent the confusion of dealing with the same variables both inside and outside of procedures.

Functions Functions differ from subroutines and procedures in that they are used primarily in some kind of calculation. The results of a function are returned immediately to the calling statement and are used to complete the operations there. Functions can either be defined by the user or used from a "library" that is built in or prewritten.

Organized Data

Data in a program can be stored more efficiently than as a single integer, real number, or character string. Arrays and files are two structured ways data are often organized and stored.

Arrays Arrays allow you to store and retrieve a large amount of similar data under one variable name with a numerical subscript. An array can be compared to a row of mailboxes, each with the same name but with a different "address" or subscript. Arrays can be either single dimensional or multidimensional, depending on the needs of the user. A two-dimensional array can be visualized as a table. The variable name will have two subscripts, corresponding to rows and columns in the table. You can retrieve any item of data simply by specifying the variable name and the subscript that indicates its position or address in the array.

The problem of adding 100 test scores and finding an average offers a good example of the use for an array. To assign the score values to 100 different variable names would be tedious and time-consuming. With an array, each value could be read into a different element of the array, after which they could be summed and the average found. One limitation of arrays is that they are fixed data structures and, once declared, will take up the same amount of memory space regardless of how many elements actually contain data. Another is that all the data must be of the same type. Arrays are very powerful tools that can be used to create advanced data structures such as stacks, queues, and lists.

Files Because files are so widely used on large amounts of information, several kinds have been developed. These differ in the way they are accessed, searched, and stored in the computer. The three main types are sequential, random (or relative), and indexed files.

Sequential files must always be read from beginning to end, regardless of the position of the records we are looking for. For instance, if there are 500 recipe records in Mary Jean's file and she is searching for Brownies (which happens to be #499), the computer must search through all 498 preceding records before it finally locates Brownies. This type of file is usually easy to program but is less versatile and takes more time to use. However, for files that are usually read from start to finish (such as a mailing list) it is probably the best type to use.

Random access (or *relative*) *files* permit fast access to file records; thus any record can be found without accessing previous records if its record number or position in the file is known. This is a useful feature if updates of certain records in the file are needed frequently, as in a customer transaction file. However, the record number or position must be known in order to perform random access.

Indexed files allow searching on a key field. This type of file is found in data processing languages such as COBOL. Without having to know the exact record number, a user can search on a selected "key" or "index" field in the record. For instance, on a general mailing list record, surname might be selected as the key field. A search could be made for "Hsu" and all records with a corresponding key would be found and made available for use. On a large customer file, for instance, account numbers could be set up as a key field, so access to any record would be quick and easy. Although indexed files are very useful, they are not found on most microcomputer languages. Exceptions are some of the business-based languages (COBOL, business BASIC, etc.). Indexed files can be simulated on the other file types if appropriate search routines are written.

OTHER FEATURES OF LANGUAGES

Many languages for micros have special capabilities such as graphics, sound, and other unique functions. They will be covered in detail in the individual language chapters.

This ends our concise introduction to languages. Most languages are built to have some, if not all, of these capabilities. For more advanced information on languages, see the Appendix, which lists several textbooks on programming language design and structure. Advanced books on compilers, data structures, and files are also included.

Part II

THE FAMILIAR FOUR

BASIC
COBOL
FORTRAN
Pascal

CHAPTER 2

BASIC

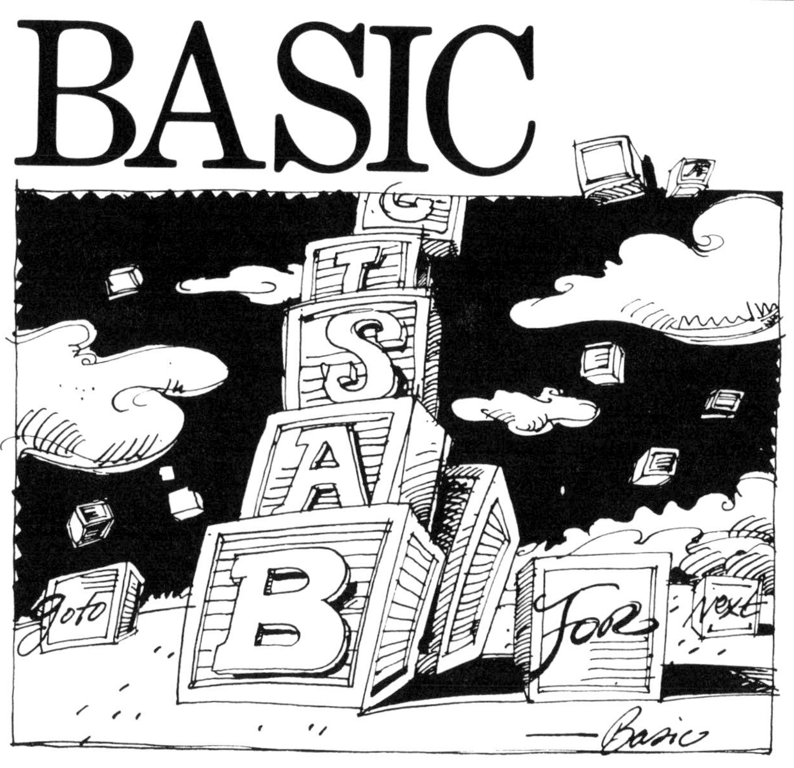

OF ALL THE programming languages available, BASIC is probably the most widely known, since so many of the popular systems are sold with some form of this language. It is also the language most commonly taught in the schools and in the many adult computer literacy courses.

Developed in the mid-1960s by two Dartmouth College professors, John Kemeny and Thomas Kurtz, BASIC was designed to help students learn programming without having to deal with the rigid syntax and detail common to other languages existing at the time. The acronym BASIC stands for Beginner's All-Purpose Symbolic Instruction Code, but the word "BASIC" is very descriptive in itself, since in many ways the language is just that—simple and easy to use.

BASIC is usually an interpreted language, and on many systems the interpreter itself is built into the computer's ROM (read-only memory). Turning on the computer or loading the operating system is all that is needed to start programming; the BASIC interpreter is right there, ready to accept commands. On systems that don't have BASIC in ROM, the interpreter program must be loaded in from a disk or cassette.

BASIC can be classified as a general-purpose language since it is equipped to handle a wide range of applications from business and science to education. The language has no clear standard since it has been widely modified and extended by various computer manufacturers and software companies. At the present time, there are dozens of different "dialects" of BASIC, each with its own syntax and special features. This creates a problem of portability; a BASIC program written for one computer often cannot be run on another system without extensive changes.

One very widely used dialect is Microsoft BASIC, which has added many powerful extensions to the original version. Most of the examples in this chapter were written in Applesoft BASIC, a variant of Microsoft supplied with the Apple II computers. Some other popular dialects are TRS-80 BASIC, TI BASIC, Pet BASIC, CBASIC, and GBASIC. The first three come with their respective computers; CBASIC is a compiler (more about this later); and GBASIC offers graphics commands under CP/M and MS-DOS.

Despite its wide availability and popularity, BASIC has a few serious limitations. One is its slow execution speed. Because it is an interpreted language, BASIC runs very slowly and is often slowed down even more by documentation (REM statements) included in the programs to make them understandable. In an effort to remedy this problem, compiler/interpreter dialects and BASIC compilers have been developed. Compiler/interpreter dialects, like CBASIC, compile a BASIC program created with a word processor or line editor into an intermediate type. At run time, this intermediate program is translated into machine code by the interpreter. Although programs are more difficult to write since errors are not detected until the program is compiled, CBASIC offers several advantages, such as the use of labels for subroutines and greatly increased execution speed. BASIC compilers, on the other hand, take a regular Applesoft or MBASIC program and compile it directly into an executable binary file, which will run much faster.

A second problem with BASIC programs is that they can so easily be made unreadable. Very short programs present little difficulty, and so do longer ones that work well. However, long programs that require some modification or correction can defy attempts to trace the way they are supposed to work. Even the original programmer can find it almost impossible if any time has gone by since the program was written.

Two characteristics of BASIC contribute to this situation. The first is the inability in most dialects to form long, descriptive variable names. For example, in Applesoft only the first two characters of a variable are significant. In a large program with many variables, this is a serious limitation.

The second aspect of BASIC that can cause unreadable programs is its lack of any requirement for structure. A *structured program* is one that is divided into clearly defined segments, each responsible for a separate aspect of the program's overall functioning. Many languages, such as Pascal, are structured. Subroutines are labeled and called by name, and local variables can be defined and used within them. Through careful use of the GOSUB statement and other programming techniques, it is possible to write a structured BASIC program, but it is temptingly easy not to.

The ease of use of the built-in interpreter encourages programmers simply to turn on the machine and begin programming without having carefully worked out all the problems beforehand. One of the most widely used (and abused) control statements in BASIC is the GOTO. Excessive use of GOTO for branching causes the flow of control quickly to become impossible to follow in programs of any size. The subroutine commands supplied are not as useful and versatile as those in languages such as Pascal or PL/1. Parameters and arguments are not supported, nor are local variables. BASIC is therefore not as suitable for large-scale or advanced programming.

However, BASIC is useful and valuable as a first language. It makes programming easy and friendly, especially for novices, and its interactive nature makes it ideal for the development of short programs. More books are available, more courses are given, and more programs can be found in magazines and other sources for BASIC than for any other language. A simple BASIC program follows.

Program Structure

BASIC programs consist of a sequence of language statements, usually preceded by line numbers. Line numbers, usually starting in the first column of the line, are required in the most commonly used versions, such as Microsoft or Applesoft BASIC. They direct the sequential flow of control somewhat like a "label" in other languages. Statements follow the line

```
10 REM    BUBBLE SORT PROGRAM
20 REM    SORTS UP TO 100 NUMBERS IN AN ARRAY
30 DIM B(100)
40 INPUT "HOW MANY NUMBERS ?" :N
50 REM INPUT DATA
60 FOR I = 1 TO N
70 INPUT A(I)
80 NEXT I
90 REM   SORT NUMBERS
100 FOR J = 1 TO N-1
110 LAST = N-1
120 FOR L = 1 TO LAST
130 IF A(L) > A (L+1) THEN GOSUB 300
140 NEXT L
150 NEXT J
160 REM   PRINT SORTED LIST
170 FOR S=1 TO N
180 PRINT A(S)
190 NEXT S
200 PRINT "ALL SORTED"
210 GOTO 999
299 REM EXCHANGE SECTION
300 TEMP = A(L)
310 A(L) = A(L+1)
320 A(L+1) = TEMP
330 RETURN
999 END
```

A Bubble Sort Program sorts a list in ascending order

numbers in a free form. Multiple statements can be used in program lines as long as they are separated by colons. The final line of a program may have an "END" but that is not required. A REM statement after a line number indicates that the line contains comments; these lines are not executed.

Data Types

BASIC supports an adequate number of data types including integer and real numbers, characters, and records/files. Real numbers can be either fixed point or floating point (scientific notation). Some extended dialects feature double-precision, hexadecimal, and octal numbers. The limited number of data types helps to simplify the language and makes programming easier if not more flexible.

Variables and Assignment

Variable names can be long or short, depending on the particular implementation, although short is the rule. The data type of the variable is defined by an indicator that follows the name. For instance, "A%" is an integer variable, "A" (no indicator) a real number variable, and "A$" a character string variable.

Assignment is performed with the "=" symbol, as in A$ = "abc" or B% = 256. Most variables do not have to be predefined; simply using one in the program allocates memory to it. It is good programming practice, however, to initialize at least number variables before use. The number of variables that can be used in a program is limited only by the amount of memory space available.

Mathematical Operators

The standard mathematical operators are provided in BASIC. The operators are indicated by these symbols:

addition	+
subtraction	−
multiplication	*
division	/
exponentiation	ˆ or ↑

Expressions containing these operators are evaluated first by the grouping of parentheses and then the operations are executed in the order: multiplication, division, addition, subtraction.

Comparisons

Comparisons are accomplished in BASIC through the use of comparison operators (> larger than, < smaller than, >= larger than or equal or, <= smaller than or equal to). They are the same symbols used in mathematics, and they can all be used to compare both numbers and character strings. Character strings are compared by character code precedence (the letters that come earlier in the alphabet are of smaller ASCII code and consequently have a smaller value).

Boolean Operators

Boolean operators, like Boolean data, are designed to detect the truth or falsity of an expression. In BASIC, expressions with two or more parts can be evaluated with AND, OR, and NOT. For an AND, all of the different parts must be true in order for the expression to be true. In the case of OR, at least one must be true for the entire expression to be true. In the case of NOT, the negation of the expression must be true for the expression itself to be true. Commonly used symbols for AND and NOT are "&" and "< >".

Built-In and User Functions

Built-in functions are written into the language in order to make certain frequently used tasks easier. For instance, you do not need to write a routine to calculate such things as cosine, sine, or absolute value. Simply calling the function name, SIN(x), for instance, returns the value from a function written into the interpreter program. Besides mathematical functions, hardware functions such as support for game paddles and ports, and machine functions like PEEK (examine a portion of memory) or POKE (insert code or values directly into memory) are often included. Each dialect has its own set of built-in functions.

Besides the built-in functions already described, you can define your own functions using the DEF FN command followed by the function name and formula. The primary limitation to such user-defined BASIC functions is that they can be only one line long.

Input/Output

Input and output are relatively simple in BASIC. Data can be input into a program from DATA statements, interactively from the CRT terminal, or from files. Input from files will be discussed in the file section. Output to the screen or printer is done with the PRINT statement.

The DATA statement is a handy way to store data in the program itself. The information is included on separate program lines preceded by the line number and the word DATA. All information following the word DATA is nonexecutable program data and is "read in" to the main program through the READ statement. The type (integer, real, character) of the variables in the reading statement must match the corresponding data exactly. If the computer reads data of the wrong type, a "mismatched type" error will result. In most cases, DATA statements are read only once in the execution of the program, but they may be reread if the RESTORE command is executed first.

Interactive input is programmed through INPUT statements. There are two ways of using INPUT: one uses just the variable name itself; the other includes a message string in quotes before the variable. The first method merely prints a question mark on the screen and waits for you to enter the appropriate information. The second prints out the specified message string before waiting for your response. The interactive method of input is very useful for conversational programs such as adventure games, educational programs, and so on.

Output to the screen or printer is controlled by means of the PRINT statement. The word PRINT is followed by the data that are to be printed, either in constant or variable form. Both numeric/character variables and character strings "in quotes" can be PRINTed.

Applesoft BASIC does not support controlled and formatted output, but some dialects do. Controlled output PRINT can specify which device to send the information to. For instance, PRINT might send output to the screen whereas LPRINT sends it to the printer. Formatted output is most needed for business applications and is controlled with the PRINT USING ####.## command, which will force output to take the form specified by the symbols following the command. A simple kind of formatting is available on all BASICs: a semicolon between variables or character strings will provide for spacing between items printed on a line, and the comma provides for field spacing. In other words, in order to print out two adjacent items, you simply insert a semicolon between them; to separate items by fields (there are several fields in a text screen), you use the comma. Some examples of input and output are shown here.

Conditional Statements

Most programs will not be executed entirely in the order of the statement numbers. Any time a decision needs to be made, flow of control must branch off into one or another direction.

BASIC has one conditional structure, the IF [condition] THEN statement. When this statement is used, branching can

Input in BASIC (Applesoft):

```
10 INPUT "YOUR NAME IS ?" ;N$
20 INPUT "YOUR AGE IS ?" ;A%
30 INPUT "YOUR WEIGHT IS ?" ;W
```

READ/DATA INPUT:

```
10 READ N$,A%,W

100 DATA JOHNNY,44,135.25
110 DATA MARIE,32,112.0
```

OUTPUT:

```
10 PRINT N$
20 PRINT N$,A%
30 PRINT N$;A%;W

JOHNNY
JOHNNY          44
JOHNNY44135.25
```

Input and output in BASIC

occur on the basis of the included condition. IF the condition is true, the instructions following the THEN will be executed. If not, the next line in the program will be executed. Some dialects allow an extended form of this statement: IF [condition] THEN..ELSE. In this case the program will branch either to the statements following THEN or to those following the ELSE, depending on the truth of the included condition. The IF..THEN statement can direct control to an imperative statement, a GOTO, or a GOSUB (branch to subroutine, which will be covered in the section on subroutines).

Control Statements ON and GOTO

Control can also be directed on the basis of a special variable's value. The ON statement will transfer program execution according to the integer value of the ON variable:

```
30 ON X GOTO 100,200,300,400
```

The next line to be executed will be 100 or 200 or 300 or 400, depending on whether X has the value 1, 2, 3, or 4. The ON variable must have a value from 1 to the maximum number of line number branches. Use of ON can direct flow either to a line (GOTO) or to a subroutine (GOSUB).

Subroutines

Larger BASIC programs can be broken into smaller, more manageable parts with subroutines, although the facilities for doing this are not as flexible as in some other languages. Subroutines in BASIC must use the same variables as the main program (global variables). Local variables are not available, nor are such other features as the ability to pass values through arguments and parameters.

Subroutines are called with the GOSUB statement followed by the line number of the beginning of the subroutine. The following example illustrates the general structure:

```
200 GOSUB 440
210 . . .
    . . .
440 REM this is the start of the subroutine
450 . . .
    . . .
490 RETURN
```

When execution of the subroutine is completed, the RETURN command sends control of the program back to the line immediately following the calling line.

Loops

The loop construct available in BASIC is the FOR loop. This is a counted loop—the number of repetitions or trips through the loop is controlled by a loop variable. Extended forms may include a form of the WHILE loop known as the WHILE..WEND loop. The format of the FOR allows you to specify the beginning value, the ending value, and the loop counter increment. The loop counter can count either up or down, depending on the sign of the STEP constant. Some examples of loops follow:

```
30  FOR I = 1 TO 10
40  PRINT "A";
50  NEXT I                          run: AAAAAAAAAA

30  FOR I = 12 TO 1  STEP -2
40  PRINT "A";
50  NEXT I                          run: AAAAAA
```

String Handling

String manipulation is accomplished with several built-in functions used to take apart and put together strings and substrings.

The LENGTH function returns the length of a given string. LEFT$ takes a substring starting from the beginning of a given character string, and RIGHT$ takes a substring of a specified length terminating at the last character. The MID$ function extracts a substring beginning and ending inside the given target string. For example, if A$ = "Ruth Burke Johnson":

LEFT$(A$,4) will return "Ruth"
RIGHT$(A$,7) will return "Johnson"
MID$(A$,6,5) will return "Burke"

The use of the addition operator (+) on character strings or string variables concatenates them. "BA" + "SIC" will yield "BASIC." Any program using substantial character input would be highly difficult to write without such string functions.

Arrays

BASIC supports both single-dimensional and multidimensional arrays, although different dialects vary in the number of dimensions allowed. One- and two-dimensional arrays are most frequently used.

For arrays of more than ten elements, the DIM statement must be used to specify the DIMension, or size, of the array. This allocates space in memory for the array. For arrays of ten or fewer elements, such declaration is not usually necessary. Accessing individual elements of an array is done simply by means of the array name followed by the appropriate subscript in parentheses. The subscript can be either a constant or an integer variable. The number of array elements allowed is limited only by the amount of memory space in the computer system. An example of the use of arrays follows:

Small Array	*Larger Array*
10 FOR I = 1 TO 9 20 A(I) = 0 30 NEXT I	10 DIM B(15) 20 FOR I = 1 TO 15 30 B(I) = 0 40 NEXT I

Records and Files

BASIC has provisions for records and files; however, it does not have a separate record structure. Records must be created as a set of fields and then stored, one by one, into the file. Because every system has its own set of commands and syntax for file processing, only a general description will be given here. For instance, in Applesoft, a special control character (control-D) must precede any file processing statements, while another system will require the use of a device number (such as WRITE(#2)).

In Applesoft BASIC, before information can be placed in a file, it must be made available for use by means of the commands OPEN and WRITE. Records then can be read into the file with a PRINT statement followed by each of the field variables. To get records from the file, the INPUT command is used instead of WRITE. Then an INPUT followed by the field variables will retrieve the record. After all processing is completed, the file is CLOSEd.

Sequential files are simple to program but must be read from beginning to end. Each group of fields is put into the file sequentially, without any identifying record number or key. When an existing file is reopened for additional records to be added, the APPEND command adds new records to the end of the file. Random access files allow the referencing of records by record number; hence the number of bytes in a record must be specified and a count must be kept of the records saved in the file.

Files and records are an advanced topic, and many good books are available on the subject. Check the reference section in this chapter for books on BASIC files. The following example illustrates the use of files on the Apple II microcomputer:

```
10 D$=CHR$(4)                 --sets up the file control character.
20 PRINT D$;"OPEN CHAR-FILE,L20"      --opens up a file of record
                                       length 20.
30 M$="MY NAME IS JOHNNY A."          --defines value for M$.
40 PRINT D$;"WRITE CHAR-FILE"         --prepares file for writing.
50 PRINT M$                   --prints M$ into the file.
60 PRINT D$                   --stops the write process.
70 PRINT D$;"CLOSE CHAR-FILE"  --closes the file.
```

Graphics

Because of the graphics capabilities of many popular micros, machine-specific dialects may offer graphics commands as a part of the language. Applesoft, for instance, offers low-resolution, high-resolution, and shape graphics. Low-resolution offers graphics in the form of "blocks" of color, which are useful for very simple drawings or for creating block letters. High-resolution graphics uses a large number of small points of light, enabling much finer graphics displays. In Applesoft, you can define a rather complex shape as a *shape table.* These "shapes" are defined as a single entity and can be manipulated rather easily on the screen.

Many microcomputers that include graphics capabilities allow you to access the graphics screen through special BASIC commands. If you have a color monitor, you can easily create multicolor designs using the COLOR command, since several colors are available when you use the graphics screen. Check your reference manual as well as books on graphics for more information.

Assembly Language Interface

Often you will need to use a speedy machine code subroutine from within a BASIC program. BASIC features a CALL statement that allows the program to call such an external routine, which functions just like regular intraprogram subroutines. For instance, sorting is often done via a called machine code subroutine when faster execution is required. These machine code subroutines are usually written in assembly language, assembled, and then separately loaded into memory before the main program is run. Of course, they can also be loaded by the program itself.

SUMMARY

BASIC is a simple language that is best suited for fast development of short programs. It is also ideal for the beginning programmer because of its user friendliness. It will remain a popular language, especially in light of the efforts made to improve its weaknesses. The original designers of the language have recently released a revised form of BASIC known as True BASIC. It features long, descriptive variable names, compiled speed, a structured format, and even optional line numbers. The next section covers True BASIC in more detail.

TRUE BASIC

In the introductory segment on BASIC, the problems of portability and unstructured programming were discussed. In response to these problems, the originators of BASIC, John Kemeny and Thomas Kurtz, along with four computer professionals, teamed up in 1983 to form True BASIC Inc., a firm that developed an entirely new version of BASIC known as True BASIC.

True BASIC is much more powerful and versatile than the forms of BASIC currently in use. It is a complete development system, including a screen-oriented program editor, compiler/interpreter, and windows which will show the source code and output simultaneously. The compiler/interpreter system is developed to be both easy to use and fast. For a typical program, the source code is first developed through the editor, then submitted to the interpreter through the "RUN" command. Next the compiler takes over the job of compiling the text and producing the object file. Errors are displayed in a "text editing" window. After a successful compile, the interpreter takes control again and executes the program. True BASIC has the speed of a compiler and the convenience of an interpreter.

Some of the new features of True BASIC are optional line numbers, long variable names, longer strings, array-handling statements, DO loops, a SELECT case structure, independent subprograms, and graphics.

One of the notable aspects of old BASIC's program structure was that of line numbers. Every line had to have a number, and if you numbered lines too closely and wanted to insert a line later, you'd have to renumber the whole program. True BASIC is written in a free-form format, with the option of using line numbers.

Variable names and strings are also improved. Variable names, which could be as short as 2 characters (in Applesoft) can be up to 31 characters long, and underscores can be used for readability. Strings can be as long as 32,000 characters instead of the previous 255 or so found in many dialects.

Powerful statements for manipulating arrays are available, including the following:

MAT READ	read data into an array
MAT INPUT	put keyboard entry data into an array
MAT PRINT	print an array
MAT PRINT USING	print an array (formatted)

In regular BASIC, only the FOR loop was available. In True BASIC, the WHILE loop is supported. The WHILE loop can be tested either at the top or at the bottom:

```
DO WHILE (condition)
{loop commands}
LOOP   (end)                DO WHILE..LOOP—test at top

DO
{loop commands}
LOOP (condition) (end)      DO..LOOP—test at bottom
```

The SELECT case structure makes multiple conditions easy. Instead of using a list of IF..THENs, the SELECT structure is designed to handle an unlimited number of conditions and results:

```
SELECT CASE A

CASE 1
    {COMMAND}

CASE 2
    {COMMAND}

CASE 3
    {COMMAND}
```

```
CASE ELSE
     {COMMAND}       --IF ABOVE CASES FAIL

END SELECT
```

This is a very powerful structure and is designed to be clear and easy to use.

Finally, there are subprograms (procedures and functions) which can be called by name and declared separately from the main program body, and graphics commands which can be used to draw graphics pictures much more easily than with a standard BASIC dialect.

In conclusion, True BASIC is a great improvement over the standard BASIC, which has been around for about 20 years. In a sense, it is no longer the BASIC we know, but a new type of language that reflects the thinking and improvements of the present computer age.

True BASIC is currently available for the IBM PC and will soon be available for the Apple Macintosh and other 16-bit microcomputers. It is available from Addison-Wesley Publishing Company. *Back to BASIC*, a book by Kemeny and Kurtz covering True BASIC, is available from the same company.

Despite the fact that True BASIC is included in this chapter on BASIC, it is neither a "true" form of BASIC, nor does it have any relationship to BASIC as we know it. It is an entirely different language, based on new approaches to programming.

REFERENCES—BASIC

Because of its great popularity and availability, there is an enormous amount of material on the BASIC language. There are general (nonmachine-specific) books, books for a specific computer or operating system, and others on a specific application (files or graphics, for example). Although this listing is by no means complete, it is an attempt to give a comprehensive list of books available. For certain books of particular interest, there are some brief comments and observations.

General Books on BASIC (Introductory)

BASIC Programming (latest edition), by Kemeny & Kurtz. An introduction to the language by the language's creators, this book features the language in relation to specialized applications. (John Wiley)

BASIC and the Personal Computer, by Dwyer & Critchfield. A colorful, friendly introduction to BASIC, loaded with drawings, cartoons, and photos. (Addison-Wesley)

Programming in BASIC, by Tom Logsdon. Textbook style yet a simple beginning book. (Anaheim)

Your First BASIC Program, by Rodnay Zaks. A colorful, profusely illustrated "fun" introduction to programming in BASIC. (Sybex)

Apple Backpack, by Kamins & Waite. (Byte)

BASIC: A Hands On Method, by Peckman. (McGraw-Hill)

BASIC: Fundamental Concepts, by Giarratano. (Sams)

BASIC Fundamentals and Style, By Quasney & Maniotes. (Boyd & Fraser)

BASIC from the Ground Up, by Simon. A clear, beginning guide for novice users. (Hayden)

Basic BASIC, by Coan. A beginning book with many examples and programs. (Hayden)

Instant BASIC, by Brown. An interesting and entertaining approach to learning BASIC. (Dilithium)

Beginning BASIC, by Chirlian. (Matrix/Dilithium)

Introduction to BASIC, by Morton. (Matrix)

BASIC for Home Computers, by Finkel/Brown. Self-teaching guide. (John Wiley)

BASIC, 2/E, by Albrecht, Finkel, & Brown. Self-teaching guide. (John Wiley)

Learning BASIC Fast, by De Rossi. (Reston)

BASIC Programming Self-Taught, by Hirsch. (Reston)

General Books on BASIC (Advanced)

BASIC: Advanced Concepts, by Giarratano. A continuation from his "Fundamentals" book. (H.W. Sams)

Secrets of Better BASIC, by Mau. Contains helpful information on how to create better and more efficient programs. (Hayden)

Advanced BASIC, by Coan. Advanced techniques and applications for serious programmers. (Hayden)

Beyond Beginning BASIC, by Vickers. Advanced topics including assembly language with BASIC. (Dilithium)

Data File Programming in BASIC, by Finkel & Brown. An introduction to data files. (John Wiley)

Apple II Series (II+, IIe, IIc)

Apple II BASIC Handbook, by Hergert. A reference-type handbook to Applesoft Basic. (Sybex)

Hands on BASIC, by Peckman. (McGraw-Hill)

Advanced BASIC for Apple IIE, by Coburn. (H.W. Sams)
Applesoft for the IIE, by Blackwood & Blackwood. A reference-type resource for IIe owners. (H.W. Sams)
Applesoft Language, by Blackwood/Blackwood. (H.W. Sams)
Your First Apple II Program, by Zaks. A BASIC language primer, with illustrations. (Sybex)
Our Second Apple II Program, by Lippman. A sequel to the preceding book. (Sybex)
Basic Apple BASIC, by Coan. Includes files and graphics in its complete coverage of Applesoft. (Hayden)
I Speak BASIC to My Apple, by Jones. A very basic "computer literacy course" for the Apple. (Hayden)
BASIC for the Apple II, by Brown, Finkel, and Albrecht. A self-teaching guide. (John Wiley)
Apple BASIC: Data File Programming, by Finkel & Brown. Advanced programmed instruction on files. (John Wiley)
Golden Delicious Games on the Apple Computer, by Franklin, Koltnow, & Finkel. How to program games in Basic. (John Wiley)
Better BASIC for the Apple, by Hume & Holt. (Reston)

TRS-80 (Radio Shack) Computers

TRS-80 BASIC, by Albrecht, Inman, & Zamora. Self-teaching guide. (John Wiley)
More TRS-80 BASIC, by Inman, Zamora, & Albrecht. Continuation of the above. (John Wiley)
Structured Program Design with TRS-80, by Dwyer & Critchfield. Teaches style and structure in programming. (John Wiley)
Hands-On with the TRS-80 Color Computer, by Peckman. Includes applications for the Color computer. (McGraw-Hill)
TRS-80 Color BASIC, by Albrecht. Self-teaching guide to the Color computer. (John Wiley)
Top Down BASIC for the TRS-80 Color Computer, by Skier. (Byte)

Atari Computers

Hands-On BASIC for the Atari 400/800, by Peckman. (McGraw-Hill)
Atari BASIC Tutorial, by Peck. A beginner's guide to Atari programming. (H.W. Sams)
Advanced Atari BASIC Tutorial, by Peck. Continuation of the above. (H.W. Sams)
Your First Atari Program, by Zaks. (Sybex)
Your Second Atari Program, by Lippman. (Sybex)
Atari BASIC Programs in Minutes, by Trost. Features examples in many applications. (Sybex)

Basic Atari BASIC, by Coan & Kushner. Adapted from the Apple version, this includes both simple and advanced techniques. (Hayden)
I Speak BASIC to My Atari, by Jones. (Hayden)
Atari BASIC, by Albrecht, Finkel, and Brown. Self-teaching guide. (John Wiley)

Timex/Sinclair Computers

BASICS: A Guide to Programming the Timex Sinclair 1000, by Mullish. (Byte)
Timex Sinclair BASIC Primer, by Waite & Chapnick. (H.W. Sams)
Times Sinclair 1000 Programs in Minutes, by Trost. (Sybex)
The Timex Sinclair 1000 BASIC Handbook, by Hergert. (H.W. Sams)

Commodore Computers (64, Vic-20, Pet)

Hands on BASIC for the Commodore 64, by Peckman. (McGraw-Hill)
Hands on BASIC for the Pet, by Peckman. (McGraw-Hill)
Learn BASIC in 14 Days on Your Commodore 64, by Schecter. Fourteen chapters, one to be learned each day. (H.W. Sams)
Your First Commodore 64 Program, by Zaks. (Sybex)
Your Second Commodore 64 Program, by Lippman. (Sybex)
The Commodore 64/Vic 20 BASIC Handbook, by Hergert. (Sybex)
Basic Commodore 64 BASIC, by Coan. (Hayden)
I Speak BASIC to My Pet, by Jones. (Hayden)
I Speak BASIC to My Vic, by Jones. (Hayden)
I Speak BASIC to My Commodore 64, by Jones. (Hayden)

Texas Instruments Computers

Hands on BASIC for the TI/99A, by Peckman. (McGraw-Hill)
Programming in BASIC with the TI Home Computers, by Peckman. (McGraw-Hill)
Learn BASIC: Texas Instruments Compact Computer 40, by Thomas. (Byte)
Your First TI 99/A Program, by Zaks. (Sybex)
Intro to TI BASIC, by Inman, Zamora, and Albrecht. (Hayden)

IBM PC and PCjr Computers

Data File Programming on Your IBM PC, by Simpson. Explores creating records and files in IBM BASIC. (Sybex)
Hands on BASIC for the IBM PC, by Peckman. (McGraw-Hill)
BASIC Programming with the IBM PCjr, by Willen. (H.W. Sams)

Beginning Programming on the IBM PC, by Olsen. (H.W. Sams)
Advanced BASIC:IBM PCjr, by Coburn. (H.W. Sams)
Your First IBM PC Program, by Zaks. (Sybex)
Your Second IBM PC/PCjr Program, by Lippman. (Sybex)
IBM BASIC from the Ground Up, by Simon. Includes not only skills, but files, graphics, tricks, and useful appendices. (Hayden)

Microsoft BASIC (MBASIC)

MBASIC Handbook, by Ettin. (Osborne/MGH)
Microsoft BASIC Made Easy, by Ettin. (Osborne/McGraw-Hill)
Using Microsoft Compiled BASIC, by Lesser. For intermediate to advanced programmers. (Byte)
Basic Microsoft BASIC, by Coan. For Apple softcard users. (Hayden)
Microcomputer Programming with Microcomputer BASIC, by Crawford & Barnard. (Reston)

CBASIC

CBASIC Users Guide, by Osborne, Eubanks, and McNiff. (Osborne/McGraw-Hill)

BASIC on Other Systems

BASIC: The Time Sharing Language, by Wu. Written for timesharing system users. (William C. Brown)
VAX BASIC, by Weiman & Kurshan. Written for DEC VAX Systems. (Reston)
BASIC for Business for the VAX and PDP-11, Silbey and Parker. Written for these two minicomputer systems. (Reston)

3 CHAPTER

COBOL

COBOL IS ONE of the most widely used languages in the United States and the world. The majority of data processing centers for corporations, banks, and other finance-related operations use COBOL for accounting, bookkeeping, and report/statement preparation. You can find the COBOL language supported on mainframe, mini-, and microsystems.

The language is not suitable for general-purpose applications, since it was designed specifically for data processing. The extremely detailed DATA division, sort/merge facilities, file commands, and report writer were all designed for storing and manipulating large amounts of business data. COBOL is also very strict in format, requiring four separate parts for every program. The code was designed to be very English-like and thus understandable to noncomputer-oriented users. In addition, COBOL source code is generally portable, allowing a program written on one machine to be run on another with little or no changes.

COBOL was developed by a committee of computer manufacturers and users, including the U.S. Department of Defense. The language was designed in 1959, and about a year later corporations such as Remington-Rand-Univac and RCA had already developed working compilers. Although different versions of COBOL are available, there is a standard specified by the American National Standards Institute, and COBOL following this standard is known as ANSI COBOL. The two versions of ANSI COBOL used today are the ANSI 1974 and the older ANSI 1968 standards, with a revised version known as ANSI 1980 presently under development. The language was widely accepted throughout the computer community, and since the 1960s the majority of data processing programs written have been done in COBOL. There are now quite a number of microcomputer compilers on the market, some as powerful as mainframe implementations.

COBOL's strength is in data processing. It is ideally suited for handling business data by virtue of its detailed data descriptions, file capabilities, and powerful sorting and merging functions. The organized four-part structure adds clarity to the source code and supports structured programming. COBOL code is easily understandable and self-documenting. Since sorting and file merging are so important in business data processing, COBOL includes these capabilities in the language itself; most other programming languages do not have this ability.

On the negative side, COBOL is considered by some to be wordy and repetitive. Generally, you must write much more code to perform some task in COBOL than in a more general-purpose language such as BASIC. Also, COBOL statements must be coded in certain columns in your source file. In order to write a very simple program, you must first state all details about the type of computer, author, installation, and type of data used before you can use any executable statements. COBOL cannot be used as a general-purpose language or for mathematics and science. All the commands available are geared toward the type of computing done in commercial data processing.

In general, COBOL is the language of choice for most programs that handle data processing tasks. Despite its long source code, it is effective because of its readability, power, and availability to users. Microcomputer versions, such as CIS COBOL, Level II COBOL, and COBOL-80, are just a few of the ones available today. An example of a simple COBOL program follows.

```
IDENTIFICATION DIVISION
PROGRAM-ID. OUTPRINT.
AUTHOR. JOHN DAVIS.

ENVIRONMENT DIVISION
CONFIGURATION SECTION.
SOURCE-COMPUTER. APPLE II WITH SOFTCARD.
OBJECT-COMPUTER. APPLE II WITH SOFTCARD.

INPUT-OUTPUT SECTION.
FILE-CONTROL.
FD   IN-FILE   LABEL RECORDS ARE STANDARD
               VALUE OF FILE-ID IS "FILER.DAT"
01   IN-REC    PIC X(80).
FD   OUT-FILE LABEL RECORDS OMITTED.
01   PRINT-REC.
     03    NUMBER PIC 9(5).
     03    FILLER PIC X(75).
WORKING-STORAGE SECTION.
77  LIN          PIC 99  VALUE 99.
77  SEQUENCE PIC 999 VALUE ZERO.

PROCEDURE DIVISION.
OPEN-FILER.
     OPEN INPUT IN-FILE,OUTPUT OUT-FILE.
GET-RECORD.
     READ IN-FILE, AT END GO TO FINI.
     ADD 1 TO SEQUENCE     MOVE SEQUENCE TO NR.
     IF LINES > 56
          MOVE ZERO TO LIN.
          WRITE PRINT-REC AFTER ADVANCING PAGE.
     ELSE
          WRITE PRINT-RECORD AFTER ADVANCING 1.
     ADD 1 TO LIN.
     GO TO GET-RECORD.

FINI.
     CLOSE IN-FILE,OUT-FILE.
     STOP RUN.
```

A Simple COBOL program prints out the data stored record by record in a data file. The program is written in Microsoft COBOL-80.

Program Structure

The COBOL language has a highly organized structure. Every program written in COBOL must conform to this structure, which includes column restrictions and a four-part general format.

COBOL code is column-sensitive. Different levels of code (such as divisions, paragraphs, and statements) must be coded in their correct columns. For this reason, COBOL programmers often use special printed coding sheets that mark off the different sections by columns. A source code line in COBOL is divided into the following sections:

Sequence Number (col. 1-6)
Continuation Column (col. 7)
A Section (col. 8-11)
B Section (col. 12-72)
Identification Code (col. 73-80)

The sequence number is used to keep track of the numerical sequence of program lines. This was used more often in the days of punched cards. However, anything coded in these columns will not be compiled or affect your program in any way.

The continuation column is used either to indicate a continuation of a previous line or to indicate a comment line. For instance, if you had a program statement that was too long to fit on a preceding line, putting a special character into column 7 on the following line informs the compiler that the remainder would be found there. An asterisk (*) in this column makes the remainder of the line a comment, which would not be compiled.

The A section is where all division, section, and paragraph headers must begin. In other words, these statements must all start in column 8 but may continue past column 12. An error results if any of these were coded in the wrong column area.

Most of the executable statements and nonheader commands must start in Section B, which begins in column 12. The majority of the code will be contained in this section, which extends to column 72. The columns 72–80 are known as the Identification Code section, and anything coded there is ignored by the COBOL compiler. Generally, a name or code for the program is put there for program identification purposes.

The most characteristic aspect of COBOL's structure is the four divisions. Each program must consist of four divisions, each of which has a specific function. They are the Identification, Environment, Data, and Procedure divisions.

The Identification division identifies the program and helps to document its origin. Although not all the entries are required, with most compilers only needing the PROGRAM-ID, the following are available:

```
IDENTIFICATION DIVISION.
PROGRAM-ID.              (program name)
AUTHOR.                  (author of the program)
INSTALLATION.            (where the program was created)
DATE-WRITTEN.            (date the program was written)
DATE-COMPILED.           (if coded, the compiler will
                            insert date)
SECURITY.                (security level of the program)
COMMENTS.                (any additional comments desired)
```

The first line, "IDENTIFICATION DIVISION", is a division header and starts in section A. The entries to follow (such as "PROGRAM-ID") are paragraph-names and must also start in section A. The data following each paragraph-name should start in column B or wherever the paragraph-name ends. All the statements in the Identification division do not affect the program in any way but help to document the origin, name, and function of the program following. Although the amount of code required for the Identification division may seem excessive, the developers of COBOL did this purposely so that all COBOL programs would be fully self-documenting and understandable to nontechnical people.

The second division is the Environment division, where the computer system and hardware used to compile and run the program are specified. The Environment division consists of two sections, called the CONFIGURATION and INPUT-OUTPUT sections, each of which has its own function.

The Configuration section specifies the computers used and the special variables defined for this particular program. The entries available are:

```
SOURCE-COMPUTER.    (the compilation computer)
OBJECT-COMPUTER.    (the execution computer)
SPECIAL-NAMES.      (used to specify names for special
                       hardware features, ex: top of form,
                       special characters)
```

The Input-Output section specifies the files used in the program for input and output. Using SELECT and ASSIGN commands, you can relate a file name (such as IN-FILE or PRINT) to the name of a hardware device (such as DOT-MATRIX or DISK-A) as in the following example:

```
SELECT IN-FILE ASSIGN TO DISK-A.
```

The other two divisions, the Data division and Procedure division, are the heart of the COBOL program. They are exceedingly more complex than the two divisions described above and so will be described in separate sections.

Data Division

In data processing, as opposed to scientific or mathematical programming, there are generally a great deal of data to be processed, although the complexity of such processing may not be great. Therefore, the program should be able to handle a large amount of data accurately and in precisely the way needed.

COBOL's Data division is one of the largest portions of any COBOL program and specifies the format and composition of the input, output, and internal processing data. There are two main sections to this division, the FILE section and WORKING-STORAGE section. The first details all the data to be read in or printed out from this COBOL program. There are two generally similar parts to this section, one for the input data and one for the output data. The files, equipment, and record structures are all described in detail. The WORKING-STORAGE section outlines the variables that are to be used while the data are being processed but that are not involved in input/output.

For any COBOL program that uses data, an FD (file description) and corresponding record formats must be specified both for input and output. Here is a typical FD section:

```
FD  DATA-IN
    BLOCK CONTAINS 5 RECORDS
    RECORD CONTAINS 80 CHARACTERS
    LABELS RECORDS ARE OMITTED
    DATA RECORD IS DI-RECORD.

01  DI-RECORD.
```

After writing the division and section headers, you next define the file description (FD). The FD specifies the file record corresponding to the input data. The name placed to the right of the letters FD is the file name, which must be the same as the file name you specified in the Environment division in your SELECT statement.

The next few lines give important information about certain aspects of your file. The example above includes a number of the major statements, including the BLOCK, RECORD, VALUE OF, and DATA RECORD statements, or clauses. For some systems, records are grouped together physically on a storage device, and so

```
BLOCK CONTAINS 5 RECORDS
```

indicates that there are five records per block. The number of characters in each logical record (group of fields) is specified by the RECORD clause:

```
RECORD CONTAINS 80 CHARACTERS
```

If you are using a mainframe compiler and are reading data from a tape, you need to use LABEL RECORDS when reading in data. If instead the data are from cards or some other storage device, labels would not be necessary. Thus there are two different ways to read in information:

```
LABEL RECORDS OMITTED
LABEL RECORDS STANDARD
```

Although there are other optional clauses, the ones just mentioned are usually ended by a DATA RECORD clause, where the FD is related to its record description entry. These record descriptions usually follow the FD entry. The name indicated in this clause must be the same as the record name.

There are three important concepts to understand in regard to record descriptions: level numbers, data (field) names, and description clauses. With the details coded in this section, the exact structure of any input or output record is specified down to the very last character. Because of this, COBOL has often been branded as being "tedious, wordy, and repetitive." However, it is this quality that is COBOL's main strength. COBOL must be tedious and wordy if it is to be self-documenting, readable by nontechnical people, and English-like.

The COBOL record structure allows you to divide your records into logical levels or "hierarchies." For a "name" field, there could be two subfields containing "first name" and "last name," and for a "date" there may need to be "month," "day," and "year" subfields. In COBOL, the level of any field or subfield is indicated by a level number. The hierarchy is as follows:

01	main record level (coded in Area A)
02-49	subfields, with a higher number indicating a lower level. A number of equal-depth fields may have the same level number.
66	Fields described by a RENAMES clause.
77	Independent item found in Working-Storage
88	For conditional choice fields known as CONDITION-NAME entries.

The highest level, 01, must always be used to declare the record name. In other words, the record as a whole is of level 01. All record fields, except those that are part of RENAMES clauses, independent items, or CONDITION-NAME fields, must have a level number between 02 and 49. Fields that are on the same hierarchical level must have the same level number, with deeper nesting indicated by higher level numbers.

The 66 level number is used when you wish to create a new "pseudo-record" from certain fields or records. In other words, you can create three fields in the exact format of an existing five-field record, give it a new name, and work with it as a unique data item. For example:

```
01      OLD-REC.
        02  FIRST           PIC XXX.
        02  SECOND          PIC XXXX.
        02  THIRD           PIC 9999.
        02  FOURTH          PIC 999.
        02  FIFTH           PIC 9.

        66  NEW-REC RENAMES THIRD THRU FIFTH.
```

creates a new "record" which is named NEW-REC but has only the last three fields of OLD-REC. In the above example, you use the 66 level number to declare a new record, which has the name NEW-REC and consists of the fields THIRD, FOURTH, and FIFTH. The structure of each of these three fields is exactly the same as that in OLD-REC. NEW-REC can be accessed as a unique data item.

The second special level number, 77, describes independent items which are not a part of any larger record. These are like special "variables" which are used for temporary storage and are found only in the Working-Storage section.

Sometimes you may need conditional choices within records. For instance, suppose you wanted to indicate the sex of an employee in a record. Instead of coding a number or letter, you can use a condition variable and condition name. Later, in the Procedure division, you can use the condition name as an indicator of the current state:

```
03  SEX          PICTURE 9.   (one integer digit).
    88  MALE        VALUE 0.
    88  FEMALE      VALUE 1.

procedure division:

IF SEX = MALE THEN PERFORM MALEROUTINE.
ELSE
   PERFORM FEMALEROUTINE.
```

After level numbers, we come to field names and specifiers. Field names can be of any length from 1 to 30 and can consist of letters, numerals, and the hyphen character. You must give each field a different name for each record. After assigning a name, you can also use various specific clauses to describe the data in more detail. These are the REDEFINES, BLANK WHEN ZERO, JUSTIFIED, OCCURS, PICTURE, SYNCHRONIZED, USAGE, and VALUE clauses.

In cases where the data in a field need not be moved, manipulated, or altered, the general designation FILLER is given instead of a field name. This is used for title records or other nonchanging data.

The REDEFINES clause allows you to specify a different name and data definition for a certain memory storage area. For instance, in the following example the field SALARY is redefined as PAY:

```
03    SALARY   PICTURE 9(7).
03    PAY REDEFINES SALARY, PICTURE X(7).
```

The BLANK WHEN ZERO clause is used together with the PICTURE clause, which will be described shortly. In short, a numeric picture, which usually will return a zero for every zero value, in this case will return a blank space.

Whenever data are moved from one location to another, and the field sizes are unequal, the information would be justified according to a default setting. Numeric data are justified to the right, and alphabetic information is justified left. In order to override this preset justification, you need just add this to the field specification:

```
JUSTIFIED LEFT
JUSTIFIED RIGHT
```

Sometimes, on specific machines, it is necessary for the programmer to ensure that certain data start on certain word boundaries. An example is the need to have numbers always start on even-number words in memory. Because of specific hardware dependencies, this arrangement can increase the speed with which calculations are performed. In COBOL, the statement SYNCHRONIZED RIGHT will align the data item to the right side of a word boundary, while SYNCRONIZED LEFT will align the data to the left boundary. The data can be synchronized either left or right.

The *picture clause* is one of the most important of the data description statements. Here, we can specify data in a format suitable both for the input data and for business report output. Unlike the case in other languages, where a variable name is declared by type and perhaps by length, in COBOL every number or character string must be defined character-by-character. For example, let's say that you wanted to print the title "REPORT" on top of a printout page. Using another language, it may be a short one-line affair. In COBOL, however, you must define the spaces before the heading, the heading itself, and the spaces after the heading down to the exact character count.

Although this may be somewhat tedious to do, it leaves nothing to chance and in the case of numbers creates very organized and accurate reports. Coming back to the PICTURE clause itself, in a sense we are putting down an actual picture of the data format, as in the following:

```
03  ACCOUNT-NUM    PICTURE 99999.
```

In our example, we are indicating that ACCOUNT-NUM consists of five integer numeric characters, each of which would default to "0" if there was no value present in any one location. As you may have noticed, "9" is one picture character. In fact, COBOL has a whole set of characters, which are combined to form the proper format for each data item. The characters are as follows:

Nonedited PICTURE characters (for input and output)

X Alphanumeric character—letter or number.

A Alphabetic—same as above but no numbers.

9 Decimal digit.

S Sign digit, to show as minus or plus.

V Assumed decimal point.

P Scaling factor which positions the decimal point away from the number itself. In other words, each P stands for an assumed zero. Inserting "35" into a 99PPV picture clause would produce a result of 3500.

Edited characters (for printer output only)

Z Zero-suppression character. Will return a blank in place of the default zero.

. Decimal point. Used for printing amounts.

* Asterisk, used for check security.

CR
DB Prints out the indicated figure only if the value of the number is negative. These credit and debit symbols are used for business reports. CR and DB are used separately, and the actual symbols will be printed when the value of the data item is negative.

$ Used for printing dollar amounts.

, Used for printing large amounts.

– Printed only if the value is negative.

\+ Printed only if the value is positive.

B Space.

With these PICTURE characters, the exact type of data item required can be defined, and any data that are moved into that location will conform to its structure, as shown below:

Nonedited PICTURE

number	picture	result
3201	99V99	32.01
456	9V99	4.56
234	999PP	23400.
4XS	XXX	4XS
AW4	AAA	error !
34	S99	34
−56	S99	−56

Since nonedited pictures are generally used for input data, the values given in the right columns are interpretations of the data rather than what would be printed. Edited characters are much more interesting:

Edited PICTURE characters (output) for source picture 99V99

data	picture	result (printed)
9564	−ZZ,ZZ9.99	95.64
0000	−ZZ,ZZ9.99	0.00
0044	$**,**9.99	$******0.44
2861	+++++++.99	+28.61
0445	ZZZZZ.99CR	4.45
−2351	ZZZZZ.99DB	23.51DB

Most of the entries are self-explanatory. The long strings of PIC characters, such as minuses, pluses, or dollar signs, are known as *floating strings*. The sign or asterisk will float in or out, depending on the value of the number.

Although a bit tiresome to code, picture clauses are one reason why COBOL is so popular in the business data processing field. It shows clearly the number format needed and has provisions for dollar signs, asterisks, CR, DB, and other useful business symbols.

The final section of the DATA DIVISION, the Working-Storage section, can hold either records or single (elementary) items. Data put here are usually intermediate values from computations or report headings, or any other data that are used internally.

The Procedure Division

Of all the divisions of a COBOL program, the Procedure division is the most important. Program logic and instructions for all calculation and processing take place in this division. There are four classes of commands available, each one containing action statements or "verbs" which perform a certain type of processing. Since COBOL is such an English-like language, we commonly use English-language terms such as "verbs" and "clauses."

The four classes of verbs are input/output, arithmetic operations, control structures, and data manipulation. Each command verb will be discussed individually after we cover the general structure of the Procedure division.

The Procedure division is composed of program statements segmented into individual "paragraphs." When you look at a COBOL program listing, the PROCEDURE DIVISION header and paragraph names are easily distinguished by their presence in Area A. All regular program statements must begin in Area B. The only other coding requirement is that the final statement of both the procedure division and the entire program must be "STOP RUN."

```
PROCEDURE DIVISION.

MAIN-TITLE.
    {STATEMENTS}
```

```
COLUMN-HEADINGS.
   {STATEMENTS}

COMPUTE-FIGURES.
   {STATEMENTS}

STOP RUN.
```

In many cases, one of the paragraphs would function as the "main procedure" and call other paragraphs, while statements in these called paragraphs could call others. In other words, the COBOL Procedure division is a group of paragraph "procedures," each of which can be interrelated by a group of calling statements.

Input/Output Statements

When you perform input/output in COBOL, you must deal with files, whether or not disk or tape data files are used. Data from punched cards or output to a printer are all considered to be part of files when using COBOL.

The commands, or "verbs," that we will cover in this category include OPEN, READ, WRITE, and CLOSE, as well as ACCEPT/DISPLAY, MOVE, and PERFORM. The last three are not strictly file commands, but rather are used to display, input, or alter data or execution control.

Any files used in COBOL must be OPENed before use. In most cases, both the input and output files should be opened, via the names declared in the Data division FD declarations.

```
OPEN INPUT CARD-IN OUTPUT PRINT-OUT.
```

In this example, we open the input file "CARD-IN" and the output file "PRINT-OUT." The READ and WRITE commands are used to obtain information from an input file (as from a tape, disk, or cards) and send data to an output file (such as the printer or disk), respectively. Since the number of records in a file is usually unknown before program execution, often a kind of conditional loop is set up. With this type of structure, another record is read each time around until the EOF (end of file) condition is reached. The COBOL code is similar to the example below:

```
MOVE 0 TO EOF.
OPEN INPUT CARD-IN OUTPUT CARD-OUT.
READ CARD-IN
     AT END MOVE 1 TO EOF.
PERFORM MAIN-ROUTINE
     UNTIL EOF=1.
CLOSE CARD-IN CARD-OUT.
```

Here, we first open the files needed, then read cards one-by-one, after which a flag variable (found in Data division Working-Storage) is set to a value of 1. The following perform statement, which will be discussed in detail later, will execute only while there are still records left (EOF=0). If the EOF condition is reached, we close the files using CLOSE followed by the file names.

For WRITE, things are a bit simpler. The command WRITE must be followed by the file name, and the record name if applicable. Specifiers appended to the WRITE can implement specific printing formats. There are two methods of using the WRITE command, one using the record descriptions located in a file section, the other using a very simple record description, with the description located in Working-Storage. The two methods are given below:

```
DATA DIVISION.
FILE SECTION.
01    FILE-OUT.
      02  FIRST     PIC XXX.
      02  SECOND    PIC 999.

PROCEDURE DIVISION.

WRITE FILE-OUT.
```

This method defines the record structure in the file section and can be printed using the command shown. The alternate method uses record descriptions stored in Working-Storage:

```
FILE SECTION
01    PRINT           PIC X(132).

WORKING-STORAGE SECTION.

01    PRINT-REC.
      02  FIRST     PIC X(60).
      02  SECOND    PIC X(72).
```

```
PROCEDURE DIVISION.

WRITE PRINT FROM PRINT-REC.
```

This method keeps the record description in Working-Storage, enabling the writing of several different output records using the same general file name. The following variations will cause output to be spaced in a particular format:

```
WRITE PRINT FROM PRINT-REC AFTER ADVANCING 2 LINES.
WRITE PRINT BEFORE ADVANCING 1 LINE.
WRITE PRINT AFTER ADVANCING PAGE.
```

The first two commands above will print data either after or before moving forward a number of lines. The final example will write the output record after advancing to the top of a new page.

The ACCEPT and DISPLAY are used to enter or print data interactively from a computer terminal. The following examples will illustrate the use of these commands:

```
ACCEPT PERSON-DATA FROM CONSOLE.
DISPLAY 'PERSONAL DATA BELOW: ' UPON CONSOLE.
DISPLAY PERSON-DATA UPON CONSOLE.
```

These three commands will accept data, display a prompt, and then print out the data to the terminal console. On many microcomputer compilers there is a facility to expand this feature, making the language more interactive than it was previously on large systems. You can program messages to the screen, do screen input/output, and route both the program listing and the output to the terminal for display.

The MOVE statement functions much like an assignment statement in other languages. Data from one memory location can be moved to another, provided the two locations are at least partly compatible.

The MOVE command performs the action of moving data values from one variable or data location to another. The statement

```
MOVE FIGURE TO AMOUNT.
```

will put a copy of the value in FIGURE into the AMOUNT location. They now both will have the same value, since the old value in amount is now gone. If the move is valid (such as alphabetic to alphanumeric), then the moved value will conform to the new field's PICTURE clause. If it is an illegal move, then an error will result (such as a move from numeric to alphabetic pictures). Entire records can be moved, as well as individual data items.

The PERFORM statement is used to branch to a procedure or group of procedures. The branch points are labeled by paragraph names, so it is possible to jump only to another procedure, not to a place within a procedure. The branch, using the PERFORM command, is shown in the following example:

```
PERFORM NEW-PROC.
PERFORM NEW-PROC 5 TIMES.
```

With a slight variation, with the addition of a repeat factor, a procedure can be repeated a set number of times. PERFORM statements effect a return back to one line past the previous calling line.

Arithmetic Verbs

In business computing, calculations are essential for accounting, bookkeeping, and finance. Although many of the commonly used languages use mathematical operators exclusively, in COBOL's case there is a choice between an English word or a concise symbol. For the basic mathematical operations, the following statements are available:

English	***Symbol***
ADD	+
SUBTRACT	−
MULTIPLY	*
DIVIDE	/
COMPUTE	formula or expression
no equivalent	** (exponentiation)

The basic operations ADD, SUBTRACT, MULTIPLY, and DIVIDE work in the usual ways, and the symbols and word commands can be used interchangeably. Some examples of usage are as follows:

```
ADD A TO B.
SUBTRACT C FROM D.
```

In the first example, you add the value in A to that in B, storing the value in B. The SUBTRACT command subtracts the value of C from D, storing the final result in D.

You can write more complex equations using the GIVING OPTION:

```
ADD A,B,C GIVING D.
MULTIPLY C BY D GIVING E.
```

In these two examples, values are added and multiplied, respectively, with the result going to a GIVING variable. The first adds three variable values, A, B, and C, putting the result in D. The multiplication example performs C * D and puts the results in E.

Two other important options available are the ROUNDED and ON SIZE ERROR statements. The ROUNDED option will round off numbers in order to depict numbers more accurately in a limited picture clause. If the PICTURE is S99V9, 3.44 will return 03.4 while 3.45 will return 03.5. The ON SIZE ERROR statement is used where there is a possibility of a number's being too large for its memory location. In this case, the existence of the error would cause the program to execute the "emergency condition" that you have specified, as in ON SIZE ERROR PERFORM A-ROUTINE.

The COMPUTE statement is used in situations where a more complex formula is needed. In this case, you can define your own formula, as in

```
COMPUTE A = (A + B)/(C ** N)
```

The options mentioned previously also apply to COMPUTE. In conclusion, COBOL has the arithmetic operations necessary for data processing applications while still maintaining an English-like source code.

Program Control Structures

The COBOL language has one main control structure in the IF..THEN..ELSE, as well as the more minor structures GO TO, PERFORM, and STOP. There are a number of ways to use the IF..THEN..ELSE structure.

```
IF PRICE = 0 THEN PERFORM SALE-ITEM
ELSE
NEXT SENTENCE.
```

In this example we use the simplest form of the IF..THEN.. ELSE. This format is common to several programming languages. More than one statement can be coded for the IF..THEN and the ELSE condition. You may have noticed that we used a relational operator for our condition, equals (=). The conditions available include the following, and again we have a choice between words or symbols:

GREATER THAN >
LESS THAN <
EQUAL TO =
NOT
AND
OR

Depending on the type of data, comparisons are made in different ways. For instance, numbers are compared according to value whereas alphanumeric characters are compared logically according to the characters' collating sequence within the computer. There are also special conditions available in COBOL called the Class and Sign conditions.

Class conditions are concerned with whether a data item is numeric or alphabetic. For instance, the following are valid class conditions:

```
IF PRICE IS NOT NUMERIC THEN
PERFORM ERROR-ROUTINE.

IF NAME IS ALPHABETIC THEN
PRINT ROSTER-LINE.
```

The *sign condition* works in the same way. Here, we wish to determine whether a data item is positive, negative, or zero. Some examples are as follows:

```
IF FINE IS ZERO THEN
PERFORM AWARD-ROUTINE.

IF FINE IS POSITIVE THEN
PERFORM PRINT-BILL.
```

The final control structure is the dreaded GO TO. It performs an unconditional branch to the procedure-name indicated and provides no way to return. An example is GO TO PROC-A. The use of the GO TO in programming is a controversial subject and will not be debated here. The control structures available in COBOL are applicable to the uses for which COBOL is best suited.

Data Manipulation Statements

The data manipulation statements available in COBOL include EXAMINE, INSPECT, STRING, and UNSTRING. Since these commands are not used widely in basic COBOL programs, but are more specialized, they will just be mentioned briefly. The EXAMINE and INSPECT statements are like extensions of MOVE. They take a data field, examine each character in turn, and then either count or replace certain characters. The INSPECT is a more powerful form of EXAMINE. The STRING and UNSTRING are used to concatenate or break apart data fields. The STRING statement takes two or more fields and joins them into one data field, whereas UNSTRING takes apart a selected data field and puts segments into several selected locations. These two statements could be compared to concatenation and substrings in other languages.

ADVANCED FEATURES OF COBOL

The topics of table handling, sort/merge, report writer, and files are vital to the development of professional COBOL programs. They are both powerful and complicated, with some of the topics requiring an entire textbook in order to be covered fully. Since the purpose of this chapter is to give an overview of the language from the beginner's viewpoint, the coverage of these topics will be brief but will touch on the important and necessary points.

Table Handling

In COBOL, both tables and arrays are available. In general, they are similar in that they both handle large numbers of data items in an ordered fashion. However, while most languages have only arrays, COBOL has as its main structure the table, with arrays being more of a subset of the table concept. Tables usually contain both elementary and group items, each of which must be referenced by a "lookup" or "keyword." Arrays are generally referenced as a whole at one time and do not use the key lookup command.

A table (which will be the term given to tables and arrays) is defined using the OCCURS clause. For a simple table consisting of a numerical value, the declaration would be as follows:

```
03  PRINT, PICTURE 999V99 OCCURS 30 TIMES.
```

This is a single-dimensional table, which will have 30 elements, each of the type specified in the picture clause. Tables with more entries can be defined as follows:

```
03  STUDENT    OCCURS 100 TIMES.
    05  ST-NUM        PIC XXXX.
    05  NAME          PIC X(40).
    05  GRADE         PIC X(2).
```

In order to set up a table "index" for data searching, you must use the KEY and INDEXED BY options. Then, with the PERFORM and SEARCH commands, tables can be searched for the right information. In this way, large amounts of information can be narrowed down to the facts needed for a particular application. An example of an indexed table follows:

```
01  SPEC-TABLE.
    04  SPEC-ELEMENT OCCURS 30 TIMES
            INDEXED BY SPEC-INDEX.
            08  SPEC-NUM        PIC 9(5).
            08  SPEC-PRICE      PIC 999V99.
            08  SPEC-QUANT      PIC 999.
```

This sets up the table called SPEC-TABLE, which is indexed by SPEC-INDEX and has three fields called SPEC-NUM, SPEC-PRICE, and SPEC-QUANT. The SEARCH command is used to search through the table for items to process, as in the Procedure division statement below:

```
SEARCH SPEC-TABLE
WHEN SPEC-NUM(SPEC-TABLE) IS LARGER THAN
SPEC-QUANT(SPEC-TABLE)
PERFORM PROCESS-ROUTINE.
< rest of program >
```

Sort/Merge

Sorting and merging are important for dealing with business information. Wouldn't a phone book be difficult to use if the names were in a random order or if there was a separate book for every single town? In other languages, sort and merge routines had to be written by the programmer and then incorporated into the program in which it was needed. One of the most useful features of COBOL is its built-in SORT and MERGE statements.

Although the details are somewhat more complex than shown here, in the Procedure division sorting a file based on a certain field can be done very easily as follows:

```
SORT BANK-FILE ON ASCENDING KEY NAME.
SORT BANK-FILE ON DESCENDING KEY NAME.
```

The choice of which statement to use depends on the order in which you want your data sorted (small to large or vice versa). Merges can be done just as easily:

```
MERGE BANK-FILE ON ASCENDING KEY NAME
   USING INPUT-FILE-1,
    INPUT-FILE-2
   GIVING OUTPUT-FILE.
```

Here you need two files, which are merged together, forming the new merged file, OUTPUT-FILE. The SORT and MERGE statements make normally complicated programming procedure simple and painless.

Report Writer

Since much of business computing involves the preparation of detailed reports, the COBOL language features a Report Writer facility. Using the Report Writer, you can specify a report's format based on its appearance rather than on the mechanical details of the printing. In a manually prepared report, a large amount of code is used to control the printing, line counting, and headings. These are usually coded in the Procedure division. However, when you use the Report Writer, these are handled by a RWCS (Report Writer Control System); you provide the specifications in both the Procedure division and the Report section of your Data division. The general format is as follows:

```
DATA DIVISION.
FILE SECTION.
   {STATEMENTS}
WORKING-STORAGE SECTION.
   {STATEMENTS}
REPORT SECTION.
RD   {REPORT NAME}
     {RD SPECIFICATIONS}

     {VARIOUS RECORDS &
        TYPE SPECIFICATIONS}

PROCEDURE DIVISION.

DECLARATIVES.

{REPORT GENERATION COMMANDS}
```

To write a report through the Report Writer, you must first declare an RD (report description) in your REPORT SECTION paragraph. Then, after specifying through record and type entries the appearance of the report, you can actually generate this report using statements in the DECLARATIVES section of the Procedure division. The statements include OPEN INPUT, INITIATE, GENERATE, TERMINATE, and CLOSE. Although the Report Writer is a very useful feature for report generation, it was not as well accepted as was originally anticipated. See the Book Reference Section for Report Writer textbooks.

Files

Throughout our coverage of COBOL, we have dealt with files: the input card files, printer files, sort files, merge files, and report writer files. These are adequate where the data is input to the system from an input device (such as cards or terminal) and output to a printer. However, in cases where the input data are stored on tape or a disk, or where output must be stored on these same devices, special file statements must be used.

For disk or tape storage, there are several forms of organization. These are sequential, indexed, and relative. *Sequential files* must be read from start to finish, so it is suitable for instances where all the data can be processed together. *Indexed files* have an "index" where a particular record can be found quickly by means of a certain "key" field specified by the programmer. Finally, *relative files* allow retrieval based on the record number of the particular data sought.

In order to specify files of the types just mentioned, you must specify details in the Environment division file control, Data division FD, and Procedure division. Several books are listed in the Reference Section that cover files in great detail. Most COBOL programming textbooks also cover files to some extent.

CONCLUSION

Although reports have been rumored of COBOL's imminent demise in the computing world, currently there are more people using COBOL for business data processing than all the other languages combined. Its specialized orientation toward business computing has helped to maintain its popularity and strong user support.

REFERENCES—COBOL

The following books are grouped into several categories, including beginning books, advanced books, and titles related to more specialized areas (report writer, files, etc.). Each listing includes the full title, author(s) names, publisher, and a brief description. The books I have been able to examine and evaluate are distinguished by more extensive descriptions.

I. Beginning Books on COBOL

Fundamentals of Structured Cobol Programming (fourth edition), by Carl Feingold. A well-designed textbook, featuring flowcharts, program listings, and a complete set of appendices. The coverage begins with detailed coverage of each division, then moves on to tables, files, and the Report Writer. Includes ten major problems, with solutions provided in the instructor's manual. (William C Brown)

Structured COBOL Programming (third edition), by Stern & Stern. A textbook for beginners to COBOL, it includes numerous examples in the language, and a self-evaluating quiz after each chapter. Printer charts are included in the back. (John Wiley)

Structured Cobol, by Gerald Paquette. This book starts at the basics of computing and moves on to the four divisions. Some special topics covered include accumulators, control breaks, lists, and sort/merge. (PWS Publishers)

ANS COBOL, by Ruth Ashley. A basic guide to COBOL, presented in a programmed, self-teaching format. (John Wiley)

Structured COBOL, by Philippakis & Kazmier. An introductory book, emphasizing basic programming techniques. (McGraw-Hill)

Structured COBOL, by Chai & Chai. A beginning textbook on COBOL programming. Second edition to be released soon. (Academic)

COBOL, by George Jackson. A popular-level book on the language. (TAB)

Introductory Structured COBOL, by H. Weiner. A textbook emphasizing skills rather than the mechanics of the language itself. (William C Brown)

II. Advanced COBOL Books

Advanced COBOL, by Philippakis. After reviewing the major aspects of the language covered in most beginning texts, the book goes on to some less common aspects of each division, and also covers report generation, tables, sort/merge, and sequential, indexed, and relative files. (McGraw-Hill)

Advanced ANS COBOL, by R. Ashley. Advanced COBOL concepts such as files and Report Writer. (John Wiley)

Advanced Structured COBOL, by Gary Popkin. This books covers advanced topics such as the Report Writer, tables of multidimensions, files (sequential, indexed, relative, VSAM), debugging, string processing, and sort/merge. (Kent Publishing)

Advanced Structured COBOL, by Shelly & Cashman. Files are covered in detail along with various other topics. (Anaheim)

Advanced Structured COBOL, by T. Welburn. Includes intensive coverage of files and file maintenance, report generation, logic, variable-length records, on-line processing, and database concepts. (Mitchell)

III. Specialized Topics

COBOL with Style, by Chmura & Ledgard. A supplemental book, describing various aspects of COBOL programming style. (Hayden)

File Processing with COBOL, by Beil. A complete coverage of the different types of files and how to implement them in COBOL. (Reston)

Structured COBOL Report Writer, by Schecter and Yvkoff. A comprehensive book on how to use the Report Writer feature effectively for different applications. (Reston)

IV. Microcomputer COBOL

Microsoft COBOL, by K. Seidel. Describes how to program in COBOL using the Microsoft COBOL-80 compiler, available for many CP/M microcomputers. Its emphasis is on compiler-specific topics such as files, subprograms, screen functions, and special features. (Dilithium)

COBOL on Microcomputers, by Alan D. T. Fryer. A book covering COBOL using the Micro Focus CIS and Level II compilers. Begins with installation and proceeds to features found in these compilers. (H.W. Sams)

4 CHAPTER

FORTRAN

FORTRAN HAS THE distinction of being the world's first high-level language. Prior to the development of this language, all programming had to be done in machine language, limiting computer use to only highly trained computer scientists. With the development of FORTRAN—an acronym for FORmula TRANslation—mathematical programs could now be developed using English-like statements.

In 1954 Jim Backus began work on a compiler that would take a high-level source code (FORTRAN program) and translate it into machine-executable object code. Three years later, in 1957, the first FORTRAN compiler was available for use.

One of the goals for FORTRAN was to make it portable, so it could be run on different computers with little or no modification. The first standard version, ANSI FORTRAN 66, was a basic implementation of the language; after that followed more powerful versions known as FORTRAN IV and FORTRAN 77. Most of the improvements were in the area of conditional statement structures and input/output.

One widely used nonstandard compiler series, developed by the University of Waterloo, features a very fast in-memory compiler and extensive diagnostic error messages. The major compilers in this series are the WATFOR (wat-four), WATFIV (wat-five), and WATFIV-S. These are currently being used on many university computer systems, since their fast compilation speeds and diagnostic listings are very helpful to computer science students. The main reason for WATFIV'S speed is that the compiler is maintained in core memory and need not be loaded into the system for each run.

The differences between WATFIV and standard ANSI FORTRAN are in the ways input/output, output list expressions, character variables, and assignments are handled. Details of these will be noted in the following sections.

FORTRAN's major strength lies in its ability to handle numerical information. You can write algebraic formulas in a form very close to standard mathematical expressions. In addition, a great number of prewritten functions and routines can be used from large "libraries" developed by FORTRAN programmers over the years. You can program everything from simple arithmetic to calculus and differential equations using FORTRAN.

The language can also be said to enjoy "strength in numbers." This does not mean strength in handling number data, but strength in the sheer number of FORTRAN users. There is a version available for almost every computer system, and some are now available for microcomputers as well. Even after 30 years, it is still popular in scientific, business, and academic circles.

Since the language itself hasn't really changed much since its creation, it still suffers from some irritating weaknesses. For instance, most FORTRAN statements and variables are evaluated according to context rather than a strict keyword definition, so small errors can cause erroneous results to be produced. Also, when FORTRAN was invented, there wasn't yet the concept of structured programming, so with the exception of the RATFOR system, most FORTRAN programs do not have a well-organized structure and may be difficult to follow.

Years ago, everyone used mainframes and typed programs on punched cards. One drawback of FORTRAN is that it is card oriented and requires that every line be coded in specified columns. This requirement may be annoying to those who are used to modern free-form source programs. Other criticisms involve the appearance and development of FORTRAN programs. The language does at times look cryptic and difficult, and since FORTRAN is compiled, the usual procedure of edit-compile-execute must be used.

Despite these shortcomings, FORTRAN is well established as a major programming language and is well suited for scientific and technical software applications. A sample FORTRAN program follows.

FORTRAN Program Structure

FORTRAN programs generally have no predetermined structure and are simply long sequences of program lines. The structure of each line itself must be column-oriented, though, and is a throwback to the days when programs were written on punched cards.

Each line of FORTRAN source code must be coded in specific columns. Column 1 either may contain a "C," meaning that the rest of the line contains only comments, or it may contain the first digit of a line number. In the first case, it tells the compiler that everything on that line should be ignored, whereas in the latter, it is specifying a line number label. One sure way to identify a FORTRAN program is to look for the

```
C   A FORTRAN PROGRAM
C   THAT FINDS THOSE NUMBERS WHICH ARE
C   CONSECUTIVE AND SUM TO 100
       DO 15 N=1,100
       ISUM = 0
         DO 20 K = N,100
         ISUM = ISUM + K
         IF (ISUM .EQ. 100 ) GO TO 25
         IF (ISUM .GT. 100 ) GO TO 15
   20    CONTINUE
   25    WRITE(5,26) N,K
   26    FORMAT('0','INTEGERS FROM',14,'TO',14,'SUM to 100')
   15    CONTINUE
         STOP
         END
```

A FORTRAN program finds the consecutive numbers that sum to 100. For example: 9+10+11+12+13+14+15+16 =100

"C" comment indicator, since no other major language uses this notation.

Actually, the first five columns can be used to code a line number, and anything put in this area will be considered a line label. Although line numbers are written only where needed, they are very important in FORTRAN, since most loops and formatting are controlled by means of these numbers.

FORTRAN program statements are found in columns 7-72 of each line. If the need ever arises to write a longer line than the 65 characters allotted, you can continue on the following line if you insert a nonblank, nonzero character in column 6, the CONTINUATION column.

Columns 73-80 are usually ignored by most programmers. They were used years ago to label cards sequentially in a program deck.

Another special feature of FORTRAN is the use of FORMAT statements. Each input or output command must have a corresponding FORMAT specifier line. A FORTRAN program would have a form similar to this:

```
C   program #1
C   FORTRAN LANGUAGE
C
    INTEGER declarations, etc.

    SUBROUTINES

    {MAIN PROGRAM STATEMENTS}

    Write (3,60) J
3   FORMAT (I3)

    STOP
    END
```

Data Types

As you might expect, FORTRAN is strong in the area of numeric data types. It supports real, double-precision, integer, complex, and "logical" numbers. With the exception of complex numbers, all of them should be familiar. *Complex numbers* are used in science and math and consist of both a real part (such as 3.8) and an imaginary part (such as square root of −1).

In its original standard form FORTRAN was very weak in the area of character data. FORTRAN IV, for example, didn't feature any character data types, but in later implementations (such as FORTRAN 77, WATFIV, MICROSOFT) this type was created to suit the needs of business and general users.

Variables and Assignment

Variable names can be defined with lengths of up to 6 characters, consisting entirely of alphabets and numbers. The only stipulations are that the first character must be a character and that no special characters be included in variable names.

Glancing at a FORTRAN source text, you may think that there is no way to distinguish between integer and real variables. However, depending on the first character of the name, the compiler can determine the type:

Name begins with	*Type*
I,J,K,L,M,N	integer
A-H or O-Z	real

You can also declare a variable to be of a certain type, thereby overriding the preset designations.

FORTRAN uses the equals sign (=) to denote assignment. For example, L=6 assigns the number 6 to variable L.

Math Operators

FORTRAN uses standard computer/math symbols as operators:

**	Exponentiation
*	Multiplication
/	Division
+	Addition
−	Subtraction

The normal rules of precedence are in effect (**,*,/,+,−), with parentheses taking precedence over all. For example:

```
J=5     K=3     L=2
```

without parentheses	J + K * L = 30
with parentheses	(J + K) * L = 16

Comparisons

In FORTRAN, unlike in many other popular languages, comparisons are done with special words instead of symbols. They are written with words, but the words work just like the usual symbols:

FORTRAN	***General Symbol***	***Meaning***
.eq.	=	equality
.ne.	none	not equal
.gt.	>	greater than
.lt.	<	less than
.ge.	>=	greater than or equal to
.le.	<=	less than or equal to

In addition, Boolean logic operators can be used the same way:

FORTRAN	***Symbol***	***Meaning***
.and.	&	AND two values
.or.	OR	OR two values
.not.	none	NOT (negate a value)
.xor.	XOR	true if one true, one false

The operator is usually arranged between the two operands, and the entire expression must be parenthesized:

```
IF (A.EQ.B) THEN GOTO 50          --if a=b then goto 50
```

Built-In and User Functions

The FORTRAN language has available a large set of library functions that were prewritten into the language itself. These make programming complicated equations simpler and easier to understand. Although different systems use different function names, in general the following should be available on most FORTRAN systems:

Commonly Used Name	***Function Result***
sqrt(x)	square root
abs(x)	absolute value
int(x)	integer part of argument
alog(x)	natural logarithm
exp(x)	power function
float(x)	floating-point value of argument
dim(x,y)	difference x−y
sin(x)	sine
cos(x)	cosine
tan(x)	tangent in radians

These are just a few of the standard functions available. It is also possible for you to write functions of your own, called *user-defined functions.* Like subroutines, these are separate subprograms located between the declarations and the main program body. User-defined functions can be invoked only from inside an expression or equation, such as:

```
A = FUNCT(B,C)          --this line calls function FUNCT.
```

Function subprograms consist of two main parts—the invoking line and the function body itself. The function body consists of a heading, name, parameters, formula, and closing "RETURN" and "END."

```
Result = FUN (x,y)

FUNCTION FUN (a,b)
   FUN = a ** 4 + b.
RETURN
END
```

There are several important things to consider in writing functions. First, functions cannot be called outside of a numerical expression. Second, each function must have at least one dummy argument and parameter. These two variables are used to transfer the values from the main program to the function and then to return the calculated value back.

Each function that is written as a separate subprogram must be ended by a RETURN and END. Functions can be given special properties via the EXTERNAL, EQUIVALENCE, and COMMON specifiers. EXTERNAL is used to specify function names as parameters in subroutine calls, and EQUIVALENCE is used to give several variable names equivalence, that is, to have them refer to the same place in memory. COMMON, on the other hand, allows the sharing of certain variables among selected program units (such as the main program plus all the subroutines).

Input/Output

One of the distinguishing features of FORTRAN is its method of input and output. In its standard form, FORTRAN requires that each READ and WRITE statement have a corresponding line stating the FORMAT of the incoming or outgoing information.

The basic form of the READ and WRITE is as follows:

```
READ (U, F#), list of variables
WRITE (U, F#), list of variables
U=unit number                  F#=format line number
```

Let's discuss each aspect in detail. As you know already, READ is used for input (getting data from the terminal or disk file) and WRITE is used for printing to the screen or output file. The "unit" is the device specified for a particular operation, and, depending on the computer you use, a number is assigned to each main component of your system. For instance, when you are using Microsoft FORTRAN-80 on an Apple CP/M System, the following LUNs (logical unit or device numbers) are assigned:

Device	*LUN*
Terminal	1,3,4,5
Disk drive	6,7,8,9,10
Printer	2

After the proper device is indicated, a format line must be assigned. For every nonsimilar data line you use, you must specify a separate FORMAT statement. For example, let's suppose you wanted to read three integers from the terminal. The entire input code would look something like this:

```
        READ (1,30) L,M,N
30      FORMAT (I3, I2, I6)
```

In order to specify the type of each variable, you must use a format field specifier (or format code). In the above example, the I (integer) code was used to indicate that the three values to be read, L,M, and N, are all integers of field width 3, 2, and 6, respectively.

The most frequently used codes are I, F, E, A, and H. Here is a complete list of the format codes available. Some of these are not available on all FORTRAN compilers, however.

Format Code	*Data Type*
A	Alphanumeric characters
E	Exponentials
F	Fixed-point real
H	Hollerith literal strings
I	Integers
C	Characters—Burroughs systems
D	Double precision
G	Generalized format
J	Integers—Burroughs systems
L	Logicals
O	Octal numbers
P	Scaling factor
R	Right adjusted alphanumeric
T	Tabulation format
X	Blanks
Z	Hexadecimal

Following the format letter in each format code is a field specifier. For integers, a single number stating how many places the number may occupy should be indicated, but for real numbers it is best to indicate how many places you want on either side of the decimal point:

Integer	I3	XXX	
Real	F7.3	XXX.XXX	6 places 3 after decimal

On the WATFIV compiler and several others, you have the option of format-free output. When you use READ, PRINT, PUNCH, or WRITE, the compiler will arrange output according to a preset default setting, saving you the work of coding a FORMAT line. For instance, integers default to 12 digits, and exponents default to E16.7.

Conditional Statements

There are several flow-of-control structures available in FORTRAN, including the GOTO and several forms of IF.

First, we have the infamous unconditional GOTO, which will branch to any labeled line in the program. For example, GOTO 32 will make control jump to line 32, if such a line exists; otherwise, an error message will result. A variant of the GOTO is the computed GOTO. Here we can go to one of several branches, depending on the value of an integer control variable. Take the line GOTO (3,31,65,100),J. If J=1 then the branch would be to 3, and if J=2 then we would jump to line 31, and so on. The value of the integer control variable J controls the entire GOTO.

Another close relative of the computed GOTO is the assigned GOTO, where the control variable branches whenever its value equals that of the designated statement number. Here's a quick example:

```
GOTO K,(3,5,7,9)
```

When K=3, control will pass to line 3, and similarly when K=9, a branch will be made to 9. If K's value is 4, for example, nothing will happen.

There are two IF statements available, the arithmetic IF and logical IF. The first determines control branches based on the sign of a control variable (negative, zero, or positive.) If we were to consider

```
IF (A) 5,15,35
```

then on the basis of A's sign we could tell where to branch. If A is negative, we go to 5. If it's zero, then it's line 15. Finally, if A is positive, control will pass to line 35. The determining expression can be either a variable (like A) or an expression (like A+B).

The logical IF, on the other hand, is very similar to the IF..THEN in BASIC and other languages. However, you must remember that FORTRAN uses letter codes for each operator rather than symbols:

```
IF (A.EQ.C) THEN C=40
IF (B.EQ.D) THEN GOTO 20
```

In WATFIV-S, a structured form of WATFIV, the IF.. THEN..ELSE is supported, as well as a DO CASE case structure.

Subroutines

FORTRAN, like BASIC, has the subroutine as its major subprogram. Whereas BASIC offers only a very simple, in-program form, FORTRAN allows subroutines to be defined as separate modules which are not related to the main routine. Data must be passed in and returned through the use of dummy arguments and parameters. Also, instead of a GOSUB, FORTRAN subroutines are called by name, like procedures. The general structure is as follows:

```
CALL SUM(x)
SUBROUTINE SUM(j)
  {SUBROUTINE BODY}
RETURN
END
```

A CALL branches control to the beginning of a subroutine, and RETURN brings us back to the line following the calling statement. Commands are available that permit a RETURN to a different line or that cause a CALL to a line inside a subroutine body.

Loops

The primary loop available in all forms of FORTRAN is the DO loop. Although other types have been implemented (such as DO WHILE and REPEAT UNTIL), they usually aren't available on all forms of FORTRAN. The basic form of the DO loop is illustrated in the following example:

```
C    Do Loop
     DO 30 I = 1,4,2

     {LOOP BODY}

30   CONTINUE
```

In our example, we want to repeat two times, after which we exit the loop. All statements between the DO line and the specified end line (line 20) are repeated. "I = 1,4,2" means to loop from 1 to 4 in increments of 2; however if the third value is omitted, an increment of 1 will be assumed. The beginning and ending values (1,4) can be either integer constants or variables.

String Handling

FORTRAN is generally a "numbers language"; hence character string operations are rather limited. In general, characters are represented in FORMAT statements by the "A" code, and strings can be compared by means of the character's collating sequence (internal code like ASCII or EBCDIC).

On the WATFIV compiler, however, there exists a CHARACTER data type which is more versatile than standard FORTRAN character types.

Arrays

FORTRAN arrays can be either single- or multidimensional. In order to declare an array, you must use the dimension statement as follows:

```
DIMENSION B(40)          -- B now can hold 40 elements
```

To access a certain element of an array, simply indicate the array name with the proper subscript:

```
A(30) = 4

A(H) = 5                 --variables can also be subscripts.
```

Multidimensional arrays can be handled in the same way, but with more subscripts:

```
DIMENSION A(5,5)         -- 5 × 5 array, 25 elements

A(2,1) = 4               --assign 4 to element 2,1
```

Records and Files

FORTRAN allows you to store records on disk files and to retrieve, change, and delete them as necessary.

Like BASIC, FORTRAN does not have a record structure but simply stores little bundles of fields into the data files. In general, READ and WRITE are used, together with the proper logical unit numbers, field names, and any special disk commands as needed. Although the details are too complicated to discuss here, FORTRAN generally allows formation of sequential and direct (random) access files. Consult your system's FORTRAN reference manual for more information.

A CLOSING WORD

FORTRAN, despite its age and rumors of its imminent demise, is still an important language in our society. It is taught in a large number of universities as a beginning language, not only for computer science students, but for engineering, chemistry, and social science students as well.

Its ease of use when you are dealing with numbers and formulas make it both practical and popular for technical computing.

REFERENCES—FORTRAN

Books on FORTRAN are broken down into three categories: beginning/general, advanced, and microcomputer. Some may cover FORTRAN IV or FORTRAN 77, while some may cover both.

I. Beginning Books

ANSI FORTRAN IV with FORTRAN 77 Extensions, by J. Cole. A coverage of FORTRAN IV, with mention of the extensions available in Fortran 77. Includes log-on and log-off sequences for various Fortran timesharing computers, along with answers to review questions. (William C Brown)

FORTRAN IV, by Friedmann et al. A self-teaching guide presented in a programmed "frame" format. (John Wiley)

Problem Solving with Structured FORTRAN 77, by D. Etter. A book featuring both pseudo-code and FORTRAN listings, along with real-life examples in science and business. (Benjamin-Cummings)

ANSI FORTRAN IV and FORTRAN 77, by N. Wu. A book emphasizing business applications of FORTRAN programs. (William C Brown)

Introduction to Structured FORTRAN, by P. Chirlian. A standard textbook featuring numerous problems for solution. (Matrix)

FORTRAN 77, by M. Merchant. A textbook focusing on programming in the Fortran 77 dialect. (Wadsworth)

Structured FORTRAN with WATFIV, by Moore and Makela. Fortran using the WATFIV compiler. (Reston)

II. Advanced Books

The FORTRAN Cookbook, by T. Dence. A highly interesting book emphasizing mathematical applications for FORTRAN. Includes FORTRAN code. (TAB)

III. Microcomputer FORTRAN

Apple FORTRAN, by Blackwood & Blackwood. A complete guide to FORTRAN programming using the Apple FORTRAN system. (H.W. Sams)

Microsoft FORTRAN, by P. Chirlian. A beginning FORTRAN book, using examples from Microsoft FORTRAN-80 code. (Dilithium)

5 CHAPTER

PASCAL

Program Poetry;
uses Shakespeare;
Procedure Portia;
begin
if the quality of Mercy <> strained
Then it droppeth as The gentle
else
it is Twice bless'd;
end;
end (*Poetry*)

IF BASIC IS the most popular microcomputer language, then Pascal must run a close second. If you've advanced beyond the rather modest capabilities of BASIC and need more power and versatility, Pascal is the logical choice. In addition, Pascal is popular because it is a structured language, allowing descriptive variable names, powerful subprograms, and such advanced features as pointers and record structures.

Pascal features highly readable code. Unlike BASIC or FORTRAN, it has a highly structured format and syntax. Each program must declare data types and variables and code program statements in a certain format. Although there are variations among Pascal compilers, in general the language has a pretty standard form, so source text is portable between different computers. While BASIC is suitable mainly for short, quick programs, Pascal can be used to create much larger and complex ones without losing clarity or simplicity.

Niklaus Wirth invented Pascal in 1971, primarily as a teaching language. He felt that existing languages were much too complicated for the beginning computer science student and were not very effective for developing proper programming techniques. For instance, PL/1 and COBOL were both enormously complex, and the only "improvements" made to them over the years were the addition of more and more assorted features. Wirth wanted to develop a powerful, yet simple language that both encouraged structured programming and could be used for advanced projects.

Pascal's acceptance in the computer community has been phenomenal, especially among educational and personal computing users. By 1977, only six years later, over 400 colleges and universities were teaching Pascal, and a large number of compilers were available for both large and small systems.

The need to implement Pascal efficiently on a large number of microcomputer systems prompted Kenneth Bowles of the University of California–San Diego to invent the UCSD P-System. Instead of requiring the programmer to write a "true compiler" for each machine, which involved working with a specific microprocessor code each time, the P-System was based on a different concept. Every P-System compiler, regardless of the computer it was designed to be run on, would produce an intermediate-level *P-Code.* P-Code (pseudocode) would then be submitted to a special interpreter known as a *P-Machine*, which would in turn interpret and execute P-code for that machine. The only part of the compiler that needed to be written for each machine separately was the P-Machine, and therefore implementation was easy.

The main benefit of the P-System, as you may guess, is portability, meaning that generally you can run an Apple P-System program on an IBM P-System, although the disk formats required may need to be changed. The only drawback is execution time. Compared with a true compiler, a UCSD P-System Pascal program runs considerably slower, because of the extra interpretation done by the P-Machine. At the present time, there are both true compilers and P-System Pascal compilers available for microsystems. In general, P-System Pascal is more portable and generates smaller code.

The name "Pascal" isn't an acronym for anything. It's the name of a seventeenth-century mathematician, Blaise Pascal (1623–1662). The name is appropriate since he was honored for inventing the mechanical calculator, the forerunner of our modern computer systems.

If you're used to programming in BASIC, you'll quickly develop a "love and hate" relationship with Pascal. You will love the wide choice of data types and control structures, as well as its powerful procedures, functions, records, and pointers. The part you may hate is Pascal's structure. It is rather rigid in its syntax and you must use a specified format for declarations, subprograms, and executable statements. Rarely will you use the GOTO, one of BASIC's primary means of control flow.

Another difficulty for novice Pascal programmers concerns program development and compilation. The process of editing, compiling, and executing a program is a lot more tedious than turning on a machine, typing in some lines, and typing "RUN". Most major languages are used this way, however, and you'd be wise to get used to it!

In trying to assess Pascal's usefulness as a language, it is important to stress that the language is not well suited to short, quick programs as BASIC is. Instead, it can best be used to develop software of moderate length, especially if it contains advanced numeric and special data types (files, pointers, sets, user-defined types, etc.).

As a teaching language, it performs very well, because of its insistence on a clear definition of data types (a "strongly typed" language) and on a fixed format of declarations followed by subprograms and the main routine. As a result, developing a program can be approached as an orderly, planned activity rather than a haphazard one. The College Entrance Examination Board recently selected Pascal over BASIC as the language of choice for Advanced Placement in computer science.

Pascal is an excellent language to use in developing your programming skills. Although its use in industry is rather limited, in the academic and personal computing spheres it is highly regarded. Its popularity and easy availability will enable Pascal to remain an important language in the years to come.

Program Structure

You can always tell a Pascal program from other programs because it announces itself with the bold words "PROGRAM" followed by the program name and the files needed for execution. You can choose any name you like for the program name, but it is usually best to choose one describing the purpose for the program. The files INPUT and OUTPUT are usually required for proper execution of the program, since they define the console files needed for operation.

```
PROGRAM MULTIPLY (Input,Output);

VAR
  Table,Line: Integer;
BEGIN
  Writeln('Multiplication Table');
  Writeln('********************');
  For Table := 2 to 10 DO
  BEGIN
    Writeln(Table:2, 'Times-Table');
    For Line := 1 to 10 DO
        Writeln(Line:2,'X',Table:2,'=',Line*Table:3)
  END
END.
```

A Pascal multiplication table program

Following the program header line are the areas for declaring labels, constants, types, and variables. Pascal, being a "strongly typed" language, requires that all variables and non-standard types be declared and described before being used. Each set of declarations must include a heading followed by the statements themselves. The general structure of a complete PASCAL program is as follows:

```
PROGRAM NONAME (INPUT, OUTPUT);
LABEL

  // LABEL DECLARATIONS

CONST

  // CONSTANT DECLARATIONS

TYPE

  // TYPE DECLARATIONS

VAR

  // VARIABLE DECLARATIONS

{PROCEDURES}
```

```
{FUNCTIONS}

BEGIN

  {MAIN ROUTINE}

END.
```

Independent subprograms are located after the declaration sections, and each subprogram (whether it is a function or a procedure) must be described before being called. Finally, there is the main routine, from which the entire program is controlled and coordinated. Since Pascal has such a strict syntax and structure, a closer look at each of these parts is necessary.

Labels are needed to mark where to branch whenever you use the GOTO. Since most Pascal programs are rarely numbered by line, labels are used whenever you need to use the GOTO statement. In order to label a certain line as "30," you must not only insert the line number and colon in the text (30:   writeln...etc.) but also must declare line 30 up in the declaration section:

```
LABEL
      30;
```

Label declarations are not used frequently in Pascal since GOTO's tend to confuse the flow of control in a program and make debugging difficult. This is more of a programming philosophy than a rule, however. GOTO's, if used properly, are very useful.

Constants are declared for data items that don't change during the course of a program. Although constants can be of any acceptable standard Pascal data type, their values cannot be changed at any time. The equality symbol is used for constant declarations:

```
CONST
   A = 4;
   BET = 'YOU';
```

The type declaration area is designed to specify data that are nonstandard in Pascal. The standard types integer, real, Boolean, and character are predefined and can be used immediately in the variable (VAR) section. Examples of nonstandard types include arrays, records, sets, user-defined types, files, and pointers, and these must all be fully defined and described before a variable of that type can be created. The STRING type, an extension to Standard Pascal, is found in most microcomputer implementations instead of the usual string of characters.

For example, consider the case of a record containing a person's name and his favorite singer. You must first declare the record in the type section (MUSIC) before you can define the variable SING of type MUSIC:

```
TYPE
  MUSIC: RECORD
           NAME : STRING;
           FAVSNG : STRING;

         END;

VAR
  SING: MUSIC;
```

As in the record above, all nonstandard types must be declared in the type section, and will be covered in detail in following sections.

In the VARiable section you can create variables by indicating a name and a corresponding type. Any types not found in the type declaration area and not standard will cause an error message and stop compilation of your program.

Following the declarations, we come to the executable statements—procedures, functions, and the "main procedure." Procedures are separate entities, each with its own heading, BEGIN, and END. The main procedure is where the main logic of a program is contained and from where the procedures and functions are called. A Pascal program always ends with the word "END" followed by a period.

Pascal's source code is always in a free form, with no restrictions on columns or arrangement. However, it's always advantageous to indent and leave spaces between different sections, since debugging will be made much easier and your program will be less difficult to read. Semicolons (;) function as statement separators, not statement terminators; that's why there are semicolons on all lines except those that precede an END. Comments are highly desirable and are usually found in {BRACES} or between a (* STAR AND PARENTHESES *).

Data Types

Pascal is strong in the area of data types. Not only does it have the standard scalar types (integer, real, Boolean, character) but it also has user-defined types (sets, records, arrays, files, and pointers).

Of these, records, arrays, and files will be covered in later parts of this chapter.

Integers and reals are represented in the usual way, with scientific notation represented by the base value followed by E and the power:

250	Integer
4.28	Real fixed-point
3.5E6	Scientific notation

All character strings must be enclosed in single quotes and, in the case of the apostrophe, must include an extra quote ('ain''t').

Boolean operators consist of only two possible values, TRUE and FALSE. FALSE is less than TRUE, since it corresponds to 0 while the latter corresponds to 1. While some Pascal compilers will print the numbers, others will print the word TRUE or FALSE.

Enumerated types are a special type found in Pascal and are very useful for unusual sets of related data. In using this type, you can actually create a type of your own. Instead of designating integers for days of the week, wouldn't it be handy to use the names themselves:

Old Way

```
IF DAY = 1 THEN
   WD = 'monday'
IF DAY = 2 THEN
   WD = 'tuesday'
```

Enumerated Type

```
type
   wd = (monday,tuesday,wednesday,thursday,
   friday,saturday,sunday);
```

Functions such as PRED and SUCC return the preceding and following values in the data set, respectively. For instance:

```
PRED (TUESDAY) = MONDAY;
SUCC (WEDNESDAY) = THURSDAY;
```

The order in which the values are defined is very important. The entries coded at the beginning of your definition list are of a lower "value" than those later in the list. A more complete example, which compares a BASIC implementation and a Pascal enumerated type follows:

BASIC

```
 10 IF D=1 THEN D$="monday"
 20 IF D=2 THEN D$="tuesday"
 30 IF D=3 THEN D$="wednesday"
      .
      .
      .
 70 IF D=7 THEN D$="sunday"
 80 LET D=2
 90 PRINT D$
100 D=D+1
120 PRINT D$
200 END
```

Pascal

```
PROGRAM SCHEDULE (input, output);
TYPE
  WD = (monday, tuesday, wednesday, thursday, friday,
  saturday, sunday);
VAR
  DAYS : WD;
BEGIN
IF days = monday
  THEN
  writeln ("Go to work.");
IF ((days=saturday) OR (days=sunday))
  THEN
  writeln ("I don't work on ", days);
END.
```

Both of these code segments do the same thing, except that the Pascal enumerated type is neater and easier to use.

Pascal allows you to define specified portions of a certain data type, whether it be integer, character, or array. Looking back at the example on days of the week, suppose that you needed to deal only with the weekdays. In this case, you could work with part of wd by defining a new type, which would be a subrange type named workday (business days). This could be defined as follows:

```
type
   workday = monday..friday;
```

If you will recall from your basic math, a set is a group of related objects, such as a group of sports or computers or colors. Intersecting circle diagrams called Venn diagrams were used to show the relationship between different elements in the set, such as union, intersection, and equality. In Pascal you can work with sets with the restriction that every element must be of the same type and each set must be a self-contained unit. The set of days of the week is a good example of a set and is defined as follows:

```
type
   dayset = set of wd;
```

while operations are performed using familiar math symbols:

a + b	union of sets a and b
a = b	true if a and b are identical (equal)
a − b	difference in sets
a * b	intersection of two sets
a <= b	if every element of A is in B
'a' in b	if 'a' is contained in set B

As an example, consider the set of days in a week. For our purposes, two sets will be defined, one for all the days of the week and the other for workdays. First you must create a set of a certain type:

```
type
   days = (monday, tuesday, wednesday, thursday, friday
   saturday, sunday );

   week = set of days;
```

followed by the declaration and the initialization:

```
var
   time : week;
   work : week;
```

```
begin

    time := [sunday, monday, tuesday, wednesday, thursday];
    work := [monday, tuesday, wednesday, thursday, friday];
    union := time + work;
    intersection := time * work;
END.
```

In the example, the set "time" consists of five elements, sunday through thursday, while "work" contains the standard five weekdays. The union will return everything in the two sets together, not counting repetitions. The intersection will return only the values common to both sets.

Most of the commonly used methods of data storage are static in nature. In other words, they cannot be changed after being declared. A variable can hold only one value of a fixed type, while an array of 100 will be that length regardless of how many values are actually stored there. Pascal allows you also to create dynamic data structures which can be increased or decreased according to your needs. Linked lists and trees are examples of these dynamic data structures, which are created with pointers.

Pointers are memory locations that hold addresses of the next "link" in a chain of related data. Graphically, we can visualize a chain of records linked together with arrows, with the last pointer pointing to nowhere or "nil."

Pointers must be declared both in the TYPE and VAR sections of a Pascal program and are designated with a special symbol, usually an up-arrow or carat (^). To link together two records, each having an integer and a forward pointer, we would set up the following declarations:

```
type
   link = ^recd;

   digit = Record
              number = integer;
              next = link
              end;

VAR
   join : link;
   numb : digit;
```

The use of pointers is an advanced topic and beyond the scope of this book. An excellent book on the subject is *Data Structures Using Pascal* by Augenstein and Tananbaum (Prentice-Hall).

Variables and Assignment

Each Pascal variable must have a unique name and acceptable type. In terms of names, Pascal is very flexible. In Standard Pascal, up to the first eight letters are significant, and while the first character must be a letter, the following characters can be digits or special characters. Since most versions of Pascal offer several significant characters, you can form long descriptive variable names.

Pascal is a strongly typed language, meaning that every variable must have a clearly defined data type. Unlike some languages that base each variable's name on its context within a program, every variable you use in Pascal must have been declared earlier in the program, or else a nasty error message will appear during compilation. For instance, the compiler would be unhappy to see A:=4.9 when you originally declared A as an integer.

You can give values to variables using the assignment operator (:=), which is a combination of the colon and the equal sign. This is different from the most common assignment symbol, the equal sign, and helps to remind users of the differences between assignment and equality. As was mentioned before, you must make sure that the value you assign agrees with your declared type!

Operators

Pascal uses the standard operators for addition, subtraction, multiplication, and division (+,−,*,/). The language offers a special feature for division in the form of DIV and MOD functions. DIV returns the quotient from a division between two integers, and MOD returns the integer remainder. For example, examine the following:

```
A := 11
B := 4;
C := a div b          (answer is 2)
D := a mod b          (answer is 3)
```

Comparisons and Boolean Data

Pascal offers the usual comparison operators (< > <= >= <>) as well as the Boolean operators AND, OR and NOT. The only thing that you must be careful of is not to mix data types such as real and integer. Aside from the solitary case of integers and reals where reals were expected, all other cases would cause a fatal error.

Input and Output

On many larger computer systems such as minis and mainframes, program data are put right after the source program itself. Commonly known as a *batch run*, and often done through punched cards, this was an earlier method of submitting programs to a computer.

With the advent of the microcomputer and interactive processing, data could now be entered through the keyboard or through a disk data file. We will cover interactive input and output in this section and will discuss files later on.

The two basic input statements are the READ and the READLN. Although they both read data from the terminal keyboard, READLN includes a carriage return while READ does not. For instance, consider the following examples:

```
WRITELN("ENTER CHARACTER")
READ (A);
WRITELN(A);

?XX
```

```
WRITELN ("ENTER CHARACTER");
READLN(A);
WRITELN(A);

?X
X
```

In both cases, A is defined to be a character. If you enter the wrong kind of information, it may cause the program to function abnormally or to terminate. In addition, the same data item will have different meanings depending on the receiving variable's type. The character "1" is different from the integer number "1".

For getting data out of a program, we have the counterparts WRITE and WRITELN. As with the READ statements, WRITELN outputs a carriage return after each printed line, and WRITE doesn't. As an illustration of the differences, examine this:

```
WRITE ('a');                    WRITELN('a');
WRITE ('x');                    WRITELN('x');
WRITE ('e');                    WRITELN('e');

axe                             a
                                x
                                e
```

In any output command (WRITE,WRITELN), the operands can be of any standard type, and several can be included in each output line:

```
a := 5;
writeln ('his age is',a);

his age is 5
```

Pascal also has ways of formatting data for printing. Although each data type has a preset default setting, you can set field widths and decimal points using formatting commands such as:

```
WRITELN (R:6:2,S);
```

If R=4.23, the default value is 4.23000E+01. When you use your format, the result is 4.23.

Conditionals and Branches

Pascal has available one unconditional branching statement, the GOTO, and two conditional structures, the IF..THEN and the CASE.

In order to use the GOTO, you must first select a specific line to branch to and must give that line a number. After labeling that, you can write GOTOs directing control there. Examine the following illustration:

```
LABEL 100,110;

BEGIN
   100:  A := A + 4;

     .
     .
     .
   IF X < 10 THEN GOTO 100;
```

Many Pascal compilers limit the GOTO statement jumps to within a single procedure or function.

The IF..THEN, a common form of conditional, takes the form:

```
IF (condition) THEN

   {imperative statements}

ELSE {STATEMENTS};
```

The ELSE is optional and may be used or left out at your discretion. For an IF..THEN with multiple imperative statements, a BEGIN..END must be inserted between them:

```
IF (condition) THEN
BEGIN

   {imperative statements}

END;
```

Another useful conditional construct is the CASE structure. Using CASE, you can easily provide multiple results for multiple conditions. Let's suppose you're writing a Horoscope program and must provide different results for each sign. Instead of using an inelegant chain of IF..THENs, the CASE could be used:

```
CASE sign OF

      'aries' : WRITELN ('very lucky today');
      'virgo' : WRITELN ('don't take risks');
        .
        .
        .
      'leo' : WRITELN ('powerful forces abound')
      END;
```

If the value of SIGN was "aries", then the program would print out "very lucky".

Procedures

One of the most important building blocks of a Pascal program is the procedure. Rarely does a programmer code entirely in the main procedure; rather, the problem is broken into manageable minitasks and coded into procedures. The main procedure would be used primarily to coordinate these procedures into a complete program.

Procedures are individual subprograms, located between the declarations and the functions in the program setup. In coded form, they closely resemble functions. However, they can do a lot more than just calculate a value. The general form is as follows:

```
PROCEDURE name (PARAMETERS);

VAR
    {LOCAL VARIABLES}

 BEGIN

    {PROCEDURE STATEMENTS}

END;
```

The word PROCEDURE is followed by a procedure name and any applicable parameters. After this, the VAR area can be used to declare any local variables. As you will recall, local variables are those used only within a specified procedure and cannot be used anywhere else. The executable code follows, located between the BEGIN and END.

An example will best illustrate the concept of procedures in Pascal. Let's suppose that we want to derive some statistics from a set of five test scores—MEAN, DEV (standard deviation), TOTPT (total points), and PCTPASS (percentage passing). Our program, in skeleton form, would look like this:

```
        .
        .
        .
        .
PROCEDURE mean (x:int,y:int,z:int,j:int,k:int,var meanres:int);
BEGIN

END;

PROCEDURE totpt (x:int,y:int,z:int,j:int,k:int,var totpcres:int);
BEGIN
```

```
END;
PROCEDURE pctpass(x:int,y:int,z:int,j:int,k:int,var pctres:int);
BEGIN

END;

BEGIN (* main procedure *)

READLN (a,b,c,d,e,f);
MEAN (a,b,c,d,e,f);
TOTPT (a,b,c,d,e,f)
END.
```

We have here three subprograms that are called in the main program procedure. As was said earlier, calling a procedure involves just typing the procedure name followed by the appropriate arguments in parentheses. The computer will branch off to that procedure and perform all the commands you coded, then control returns to the line immediately following your calling statement. Each of the procedures in the example above performs some operation and prints out a result of some kind; then the procedure terminates and returns a value to the main procedure.

Notice carefully the one-to-one correspondence between the calling line's arguments and the procedure's parameters. Each corresponding variable must match the other in type, and there must be an equal number of each. The value of each argument will be passed up to the procedure and may be brought back with a new value, depending on whether it is a value parameter or variable parameter. In our example, the last variable in each parameter variable string is passed to the main procedure.

Value parameters retain the same value before and after being passed into a procedure while variable parameters can change their value at any time inside the procedure body. When coding parameters, a variable parameter has a VAR preceding each name. A general rule to follow in using Pascal parameters is to use value parameters when passing data in, and then use variable parameters for returning the new values. In the example above, the last parameter in each procedure's parameter list was a variable parameter.

Pascal allows a procedure to call other procedures, other functions, and even itself. A recursive procedure, which calls itself, is very useful for sorting and data structure algorithms.

Loops

In Pascal you can be very versatile when it comes time to repeat yourself. The language features three loop structures, the WHILE..DO, the REPEAT..UNTIL, and the FOR..DO.

The WHILE..DO tests for a certain condition at the beginning of the loop structure, after which it will repeat the statements again if the condition is true. The REPEAT..UNTIL does almost the same, but here the testing is done after each loop is completed. It will repeat until the certain condition becomes true. The FOR..DO loop will repeat a set number of times, then quit.

```
WHILE (a < 10 ) DO
BEGIN

      {LOOP BODY}
END;

REPEAT

      {LOOP BODY}

UNTIL (a > = 10);

FOR I := 1 to 10 DO
BEGIN

      {LOOP BODY}

END;
```

Built-In and User Functions

Written into the Pascal language are a number of useful functions. Some of the most commonly used ones are absolute value (ABS), Cosine (COS), Natural Logarithm (LN), Sine (SIN), and Square Root (SQRT). These are executed simply by the function name followed by a designated operand. For example:

```
WRITELN (SQRT (144));                    --answer is 12
```

If you need to use a more unusual function, your best course of action would be to define it yourself. In general, these are coded as individual modules separate from the main procedure and declarations and must take the following form:

```
FUNCTION name (parameters): type of function;
BEGIN
  {FUNCTION BODY}
END;
```

The word FUNCTION must be followed by its name, parameters, and the data type of the value to be returned. A function differs from a subroutine in that its main purpose is to define the value of the function name. Somewhere within the program body a value must be given to the function name:

```
FUNCTION G (a: real) : real;
BEGIN
     G := (a + 4) * 0.9
END;
```

A final distinction between functions and procedures lies in the area of the call or invocation. Whereas procedures actually require a separate statement to be called, functions need only be used in a formula to be invoked, as in this example:

```
IF (f(x) > f(y)) THEN .....             ---will call function F for x and y
```

The execution of the function is transparent, returning only the final value.

String Handling

After examining so many of Pascal's strong points, we come to one of its weaker sides. In Standard Pascal, the version first created by Niklaus Wirth, strings are represented as a PACKED ARRAY of single characters, each array element containing exactly one character. Character strings can have from 0 to 255 characters.

Fortunately, on many of the microcomputer implementations available now, a STRING type has been added that greatly simplifies working with character strings. For instance, in Apple Pascal, a UCSD system, there is a string type that can be used instead of the packed array. It includes functions such as CONCAT, POS, COPY, and DELETE, which are used to manipulate data of type STRING. The format of these functions is shown below:

CONCAT (a,b,c)	will put together strings a, b, and c into a new string
POS (pattern,string)	will return the position of the first character of the substring indicated
COPY (string, position, length)	will extract a part of the string starting with the position and continuing for the specified length of characters
DELETE (string, position, length)	will remove part of a string starting at the specified position and continuing for the specified length of characters

Arrays

Pascal's arrays are very versatile, since you can create arrays out of almost anything—records, sets, and other arrays. In addition, you can declare integers, ranges, subranges, and even user-defined types to be subscripts.

In general, an array is defined with the keyword ARRAY followed by an array index (subscript) and the type. This array must be declared in the TYPE section and assigned a type name. Some examples of array declarations follow.

```
type
    DIGITS = array [1..100] of integer;
    MARKS = array [5..25] of real;
    PASSING = array [-2..45] of 65..100;

    GALAXIES = (milkyway,andromeda);
    UNIVERSE = array [GALAXIES] of 1..9;
```

Multidimensional arrays can be defined just as easily, except that now you must set up an array (first dimension) of another array (second dimension). A two-dimensional array would be declared in a way similar to the following:

```
GRADES = array [1..5,1..5] of integer;
```

or as

```
STATS = array [1..10] OF array [1..10] of 1..100;
```

Although the figures are different, either of the above methods can be used to define a multidimensional array.

Records and Files

Records and files are special data types in Pascal and must be declared before use in the TYPE declaration area. For creating records, there is a special structure available. Let's look at an example. Suppose you want to create a transaction record of the following information:

```
Customer Name (20 characters)
Account Number (5 integers)
Order Item (30 characters)
Catalog Number (3 integers)
Price (real);
```

To declare this record in Pascal, you could code the following:

```
type
    purchase = record;
                    custnam : string ;
                    acct : integer ;
                    item : string ;
                    catalog : integer ;
                    price : real
                    end;
```

The name "purchase" is given to the entire record, and suitable field names are assigned for subrecord variables. In order to work with this record structure, you need to define a variable in the VAR section of type "purchase." To access individual fields within a record, you need to indicate the proper record and field using dot notation. Let's assign the value "21453" to catalog:

```
var
   sale : purchase;           --creates variable

begin
   sale.catalog := 21453;     --record variable is sale.
                                field name is catalog
                                value assigned is 21453
```

Referencing a record variable by using the record name followed by a dot and a field name is called *dot notation.*

Record fields can contain not only single values, but arrays, case structures, and even hierarchical (nested) records. In the latter case, you are creating records containing subrecords.

Using sequential files, you can store information for your use permanently, usually on disk or tape. In Pascal, files are declared in the TYPE section, in the following manner:

```
type
    store = FILE OF purchase        --"purchase" being your
                                    previously defined type.
```

In using files, you again must use dot notation, this time using a special "window" variable that tells the current "window" location of where you are in the file. The file name, followed by the carat or up arrow (not to be confused with a pointer), a dot, and the field name, is all that is needed to access a file record:

```
store^.acct := 33453;        --assigns 33453 to account
                             in STORE file.
```

In the above example, you access the store file and the account field within it. The value 33453 is written into the file at the current record count.

Five special functions are available for working with file structures. In general, use REWRITE to prepare for writing into a data file, and RESET to prepare the computer for reading in information from an existing file. The actual writing and reading are accomplished with the PUT and GET commands, respectively. Finally, you can use EOF to determine if you have reached the end of a file and must stop the file operation currently in progress. As a final note, files can be made up not only of records, but of integers, user-defined data, characters, and real numbers. An example of a file in Pascal is given below. Here data are stored in a Pascal file record.

Other Features

Microcomputer versions of Pascal often include useful extensions to the Standard. Some of these are string data types, random access files, and the ability to create and interface machine language (UCSD Pascal, for example). The Apple

```
PROGRAM FILER(Input,Output);
TYPE
    Recotype= RECORD
      Name: STRING;
      Account : INTEGER
      END;
VAR
    Recfile : FILE OF Recotype;
    SpecRec: Recotype;
    Index: Integer;
BEGIN
    Rewrite(Recfile);
    For Index := 1 to 10 DO
      BEGIN
        WITH Specrec DO
            Readln (Recfile,Specrec.name,Specrec.Account)
END.
```

Pascal files example: Storing data in a Pascal file record

Pascal system even includes the famous TURTLEGRAPHICS drawing system, which is a very popular feature of the Logo language.

REFERENCES—PASCAL

Because of the great popularity of Pascal, both for micro users and academic use, a great number of Pascal books have been written. The books will be divided into the following categories: beginning books, advanced books, specialized applications, and microcomputer.

I. Beginning Pascal Books

Oh! Pascal! by Cooper & Clancy. A comprehensive textbook on the language, written in a nonmathematical style. Includes advanced techniques such as files, records, and pointers. (Norton)

Pascal Programming: A Spiral Approach, by Brainerd et al. A standard textbook on Pascal. (Boyd & Fraser)

Writing Pascal Programs, by Rohl. A textbook featuring extensive examples from real-life problems. (Cambridge)

Pascal, by G. Ledlin, Jr. An introductory book designed for beginners, with many examples and listings. (Mayfield)

Introduction to Structured Programming with Pascal, by Underkoffer. This book, although set in typewriter print, includes many listings and flowcharts. Recursion, trees, and lists are included, along with useful appendices. (PWS Publishers)

Pascal, by Dale & Orshalick. This book includes information on data structures and includes answers to exercises as well as extensive appendices. (Heath)

Introduction to Pascal, by R. Zaks. This book includes UCSD Pascal and has the feature of complete solved program problems. (Sybex)

Practical Programming in Pascal, by K. Porter. A popular-level book on Pascal. (NAL)

Speaking Pascal, by K. Bowen. A friendly, conversational introduction to the Pascal language. (Hayden)

Pascal, by Paul M. Chirlian. A beginning text on the language. (Matrix)

II. Advanced Books on Pascal

Software Development in Pascal, by S. Sahni. Advanced techniques of developing software and using data structures in Pascal. (Camelot/MN)

The Pascal Handbook, by J. Tiberghien. A reference handbook to the language. (Sybex)

Advanced Pascal Programming Techniques, by P. Sand. For advanced programmers wishing to develop more sophisticated and elegant programs. (Osborne/MGH)

III. Specialized Applications

Recursion Via Pascal, by Rohl. Recursive techniques for advanced programs. (Cambridge)

Fundamentals of Data Structures in Pascal, by Horowitz & Sahni. Covers arrays, trees, lists, and sorting in Pascal, with a heavy mathematical emphasis. (Computer Science Press)

Data Structures with Abstract Data Types and Pascal, by Stubbs & Webre. Covers data structures using the Pascal language. Includes many descriptive charts and applications. (Brooks/Cole)

Scientific Pascal, by H. Flanders. Describes and solves scientific-level problems using PASCAL. (Reston)

Pascal Programming Structures for Motorola Microprocessors, by G. Cherry. Programming data structures on M6809 or M68000 Pascal system. (Reston)

Paradigms and Programming in Pascal, by D. Wood. Advanced program development techniques and patterns. (Computer Science Press)

Standard Pascal Reference Manual, by D. Cooper. A reference manual for programmers. Includes syntax chart pullout. (Norton)

Pascal Plus Data Structures, by Dale & Lilly. A comprehensive textbook on Pascal data structures. Includes many illustrations, diagrams, listings, solutions, and glossary. (Heath)

Program Your Own Adventure Games in Pascal, by R. Vile. Teaches how to create adventure games in UCSD Pascal. (TAB)

IV. Microcomputer Pascal

Apple Pascal, by Luerrman/Peckman. Guide to the Apple UCSD Pascal system. (McGraw-Hill)

Macintosh Pascal, by Carmony/Holliday. Programming in Pascal on the Apple Macintosh computer, using its special functions. (Computer Science Press)

Introduction to the UCSD P-System, by Grant & Butah. Explains the workings of the UCSD P-System in relation to Pascal programming. (Sybex)

Apple Pascal Games, by Hergert & Kalash. Includes a description and complete listings for interactive Pascal games. (Sybex)

Problem Solving in Apple Pascal, by Carmony et al. Programming with emphasis and examples from Apple Pascal system. (Computer Science Press)

UCSD Pascal, by Haigh/Radford. Specifically for the Apple UCSD system. (PWS Publishers)

Microcomputer Problem Solving Using Pascal, by K. Bowles. Programming in UCSD Pascal. (Springer-Verlag)

I Speak Pascal to My Apple, by Jones and Jones. A course on Pascal for class instruction. Presumes no background in computers or Pascal. Includes extensive teacher support materials. (Hayden)

Part III

SPECIALIZED LANGUAGES

Ada
APL
Assembly and Machine Language
C
Forth
Lisp
Logo
Modula-2
PILOT
PL/1
Prolog

CHAPTER 6

ADA

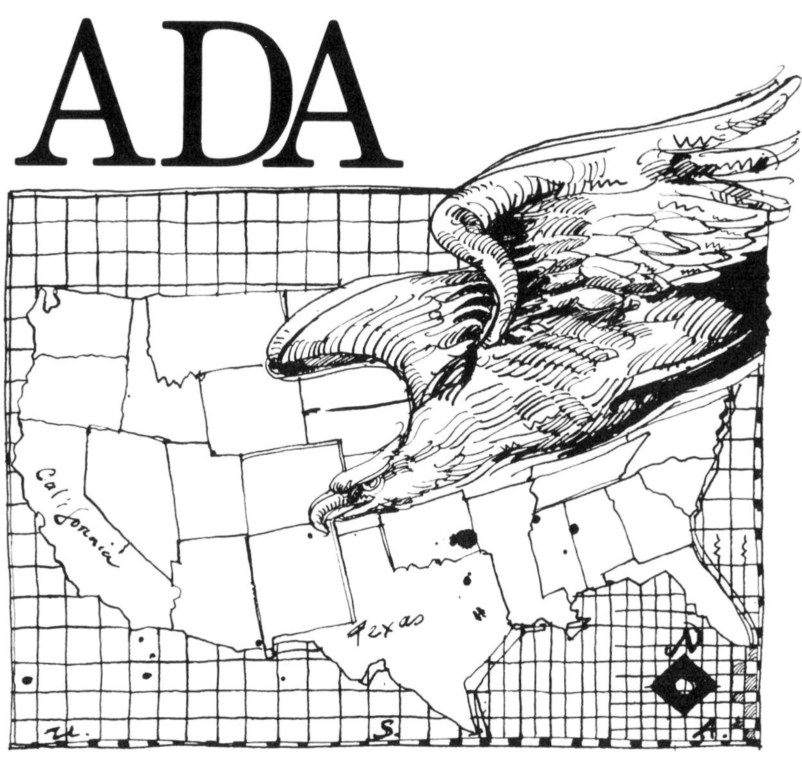

ONE OF THE newest languages available, Ada has attracted a great deal of attention because of its background and its powerful software development features. Developed by the U.S. DOD (Department of Defense) in 1975 for use on its military computer systems, Ada is well suited for the production of large software systems.

The Department of Defense, faced with a serious problem some years back due to the increasing costs of software development, decided to investigate the matter. Their findings showed that one main cause of the problem was the vast number of programming languages available. Different languages were selected for different types of applications, and in the case of a specialized need, a custom language had to be designed.

A committee, the HOLWG (High Order Language Working Group) was assigned the task of finding the right language for the DOD's needs. After careful study, it was agreed that no current language was entirely suitable, so a new language

(Ada) had to be developed. It was named for Ada Lovelace, a woman who worked on Charles Babbage's primitive computer and who is considered the world's first programmer.

At first glance, Ada code appears very much like that of Pascal. However, Ada includes a number of features that distinguishes it as a true "software development language." It can be used to create large numerical and statistical programs as well as compilers and operating systems. The language allows you to break enormous problems into manageable parts, each of which can be compiled and tested separately, making large programs much easier to create, debug, and maintain.

It also includes such advanced capabilities as overloading, generics, tasks, exception handling, attributes, and pointers. These will be discussed in the sections to follow.

As you might expect, there is always something "secret" when it comes to the military, and Ada is no exception. In Ada programs, or "packages," not only can you keep your program code private, but you can even declare "private" data types, which only you will know!

Ada's strengths are in the area of structured software engineering. Following in the footsteps of Pascal, which it resembles closely, Ada is highly structured and follows a relatively organized format. Its code is easily readable and not difficult to follow.

When it comes time to write a million-line systems program, Ada is superior to other languages. While Pascal requires that an entire program be compiled at one time, Ada allows different segments to be compiled, such as subprograms, library units, or tasks. These can be tied together to form a complete unit. Real-time operations can also be implemented with Ada's multitasking facilities.

Unfortunately, because of its relatively young age, Ada is not yet available for many systems, whether mainframes or micros. Those available on mainframes are usually full implementations, but on micros you may have to settle for a stripped-down subset. In the future, a much wider range of compilers should be available for different systems.

Although Ada has a simple structure, using it to its fullest capabilities would require a considerable amount of experience. It is a language designed for serious software designers in a technical capacity, not for beginners. However, its power and versatility may make it a widely used programming language in the future.

Program Structure

In most languages that we will deal with, the idea of a program is a very simple one. Anything that you write in Pascal starts with the program header and ends with the "END." statement. In APL and Logo you define procedures, and in Forth you define new "words" or "screens." In all these cases, there is usually one structure or format that could be generally described as a "program." In Ada, the idea of a "program" is much more complicated.

On the highest level, a "package," consisting of many procedures and functions, could be called a complete "program," while each individual procedure could be given the same name. In this section we will describe the general structure of each as though they were separate; however, usually a procedure or function is contained inside a package structure.

An Ada procedure is quite simple in appearance, with the first line listing any predefined library units that will be needed in the particular procedure. One commonly used unit is text_io, which performs input/output operations. Then comes the keyword PROCEDURE followed by the declaration of any variables that are needed. The executable statements are listed between the words BEGIN and END, and these few parts make up an entire Ada procedure. Let's look at an example that prints some message at the terminal:

```
WITH TEXT_IO; USE TEXT_IO;
PROCEDURE INPUT_OUTPUT IS
   A,B: INTEGER;

BEGIN
   A := 3;
   B := 4;
   PUT_LINE("the two numbers are");
   PUT_LINE(A);
   PUT_LINE(B);
END;
```

This short Ada procedure prints two numbers to the screen. The first line allows you to make available and visible the library unit named TEXT_IO, which contains packages that are used for input and output. Access to the unit is accomplished through the use of WITH, and direct visibility is gained with the USE clause. The PROCEDURE clause announces the start of the procedure, which is followed by declarations of the variables A and B. The BEGIN and END signal the start and end of the executable statements, which consist of two assignment and the output (PUT LINE) statements.

From procedures we come to the new concept of *packages.* Packages consist of two basic parts, specification and implementation. The *specification* part contains necessary data type declarations, headings for subprograms, and other specifications. The *implementation* part, or "package body," contains the declarations, subprograms, and executable statements that make up the software package. An example of a package shell is as follows:

```
WITH { LIBRARY UNITS }; USE { LIBRARY UNITS };
PACKAGE { NAME } IS

   we define different types and
   function headers here

END { NAME };

PACKAGE BODY { NAME } IS
   {DECLARE ANY LOCAL VARIABLES}
   {FUNCTIONS AND PROCEDURES}
   {OTHER EXECUTABLE STATEMENTS}
END {NAME}
```

The program shown on the opposite page is an example of a longer Ada program.

BASIC FEATURES OF ADA

Data Types

In Ada there are quite a number of data types to choose from. Predefined in the language are INTEGER, FLOAT, and BOOLEAN numbers as well as the types CHARACTER, STRING, and POINTER. The INTEGER type refers to whole numbers without decimal points, while FLOAT refers to real numbers and those represented by scientific notation. BOOLEAN numbers have only two values, "true" and "false." All of these should be familiar, since they are standard in many languages. CHARACTER refers to a single character, and STRING refers to a string of alphanumeric characters. These are all

```
    with TEXT_IO; use TEXT_IO;
    procedure prime_number is
        element : INTEGER := 3;
        divisor : INTEGER;
        prime : BOOLEAN;

    begin
      put_line (" Prime numbers up to 1999 ");
      put_line (" ");
      put_line ("2");
      put_line (" ");
      put_line ("3");   --start with 2 & 3; done separately

    loop
      divisor := 1;
      element := element +2;
      prime := true;
      while divisor*divisor <= element loop
          divisor := divisor +2;
          if element mod divisor = 0 then
          prime := false;
          exit;

      end if;
    end loop;
    if prime then
        put (element );
        put_line(" ");
    end if;
    exit when element = 1999;
  end loop;
end prime_number;
```

This Ada program finds all the prime numbers less than 2000

declared between the procedure header line and the BEGIN keyword, in the following form:

```
A,B:INTEGER;
C : FLOAT;
D,E: BOOLEAN;
F,G,H: CHARACTER;
I: STRING;
J: POINTER;
```

The variable names are written first, followed by a colon and the proper type. All of the types listed above are known as predefined types and need not be declared elsewhere in the program. You can create more complicated data types and structures, such as arrays, records, private types, and subtypes. These will be covered in detail in the sections to follow.

Variables and Assignment

Like other modern structured languages, Ada lets you create long variable names. This feature is important in recalling the purpose of a certain name months after it is created. Especially in the case of Ada, whose strength is in developing large projects, it is important to choose meaningful identifiers (names) not only for variables but for names of procedures, functions, tasks, and packages. The only requirement is that the first character be a letter; after that any combination of letters or numbers can follow. The underscore character (_) is also used frequently in Ada identifiers. Examples of valid identifiers are START_VALUE and SEQUENCE_TIME; however, the identifiers 75_PERCENT or BOB/GRADE would be invalid since the first starts with a number and the second includes a slash (/).

Ada clarifies the difference between assignment and equality by having a different symbol for each. Taken from Pascal, the symbol of assignment is represented by the := symbol, while equality uses the equal sign (=). So, using these, we could indicate A:=5 as "assign 5 to A" and use A=5 in a statement where the number 5 and the value in A were to be compared.

Math Operators

Ada has a number of predefined operators, the majority of which are common to several languages. The usual mathematical operations exponentiation (**), multiplication (*), division (/), addition (+), and subtraction (−) are available. There are distinctions when it comes to division, however. The standard operator (/) returns the quotient, while MOD and REM return the remainder. The REM returns an integer remainder, taking the sign from the left-hand-side dividend, while MOD does the same but takes the sign of the divisor (right-hand side). If the signs are the same, there is no difference between MOD and REM:

Dividend	*Divisor*	*MOD*	*REM*
12	7	5	5
−12	−7	−5	−5
−12	5	3	−2
12	5	−3	3

The operator NOT is used to negate a Boolean value (change T to F or F to T), and ABS returns the absolute value of a given number. Arithmetic expressions are formed pretty much as in languages such as BASIC or FORTRAN:

```
A := 4 ** 2;        -- A is assigned the value of 4 squared
B := 6 + 4;         -- B is assigned the value of 6 + 4
C := F * G          -- C is assigned the value of F times G
```

Comparisons

With the exception of NOT (represented by a /) the comparison symbols are familiar. Equality is represented by the equals sign (=), larger than by >, smaller than by <, and combinations by putting these symbols together:

```
A = 5     B /= 5     B <= 7     C >= 16
```

Boolean data are compared using AND, OR, NOT, NOT IN, IN, and XOR. The first three are the usual logical operators (AND means both must be true, OR means one must be true, and NOT represents the negation); IN and NOT IN are used to ascertain whether the value in question is or is not part of a type or range. XOR is the exclusive OR of the expression, which simply means that whenever the two values are different (one is true, the other false), the value of the XOR is true; otherwise, they are false. These comparisons are often represented in truth tables, such as the two presented here for OR and XOR:

A	*B*	*A OR B*
T	T	T
T	F	T
F	T	T
F	F	F

A	*B*	*A XOR B*
T	T	F
T	F	T
F	T	T
F	F	F

User Functions

Functions, as you will recall, are used to calculate some formula and then return a value back to the main program. In general, functions are written much like procedures with parameters. A function always has a type and yields a value after execution. Function subprograms can be either compiled separately or inserted as part of another subprogram, and almost always must have parameters in order to operate.

The general form of the two types (separate and internal) are represented below by program shells:

```
FUNCTION < function name > (parameters) RETURN < type name >
BEGIN
   {MAIN FUNCTION BODY}
END < function name >;      --internal function

FUNCTION < function name > (parameters) RETURN <type>IS SEPARATE;
BEGIN
      {MAIN FUNCTION BODY}
END < function name >;      --separately compiled function
```

One very important and interesting aspect of using function subprograms in Ada concerns overloaded operators. By "overloading" an operator, you can give it powers unheard of in other languages. Suppose that you wanted to add two matrices. Your first thought might be to define a function named "ADD_MAT". But in Ada you can define the operator "+" in a function subprogram as an algorithm to add two matrices (by adding corresponding elements). In your main program, all you need do is input two matrices, A and B, and specify C := A + B, and you will be returned the sum. Most of the operators for arithmetic calculations, as well as ABS, AND, OR, XOR, NOT, and MOD, can be overloaded.

Input/Output

Ada has both general input/output statements and special formatting commands for making printed output come out as you desire. The two most commonly used basic commands available are PUT, for terminal output, and GET, for terminal input. If PUT_LINE or GET_LINE are used, a carriage return is inserted after each line for formatting purposes. With these forms, there isn't much control over how the data are to be read in or printed out to the output device.

By using specifier parameters for each of these functions (which are part of the library text_io package), you can specify exactly what format you want to use in your input/output.

For the GET command, the general format is as follows:

```
GET (name, field length)
```

which specifies for name the variable name or constant value. The field length is the number of columns the data will occupy from the current column position. The statement

```
GET (A, 5)
```

will take the data for A from the first five columns of your data file or card.

When you are using the PUT statement, the format is:

```
PUT (data, number of columns)          (for integer)
PUT (data, number of columns, cols after decimal)
                                       (for real/floating point)
```

The PUT statement for the integer functions much like the GET command, specifying the number of columns in which the data are to be printed. For floating-point numbers, you need to specify the number of columns on both sides of the decimal point. Some examples of the PUT command usage are:

```
PUT_LINE ("GRADE IS ");PUT (GRADE);
PUT (FIGURE,5);
PUT (PRICE,5,2);
```

Other formatting commands available include NEW_LINE for skipping lines, SET_COLUMN for tabbing over to a certain column, SET_LINE for soaring down to a certain line, and NEW_PAGE for moving to the top of a new page.

Conditions can be set for printed output by the following:

```
SET_LINE_LENGTH
SET_PAGE_LENGTH
```

Using these formatting commands, you can specify data to be printed out in the exact format you require.

Conditional Statements

Ada has several conditional structures to choose from. Not only are the IF..THEN and the GOTO available, but also the CASE, IF..THEN..ELSE, and the IF..THEN..ELSEIF..ELSE.

For all the IF conditionals, there is a corresponding END statement, so an unlimited number of statements can be indicated for each condition. The IF..THEN..ELSE, as you may know already, specifies the ELSE for the case where the IF condition is not true. The ELSEIF structure is used where you want several different results if the original IF is not satisfied. Let's consider a case where you want to assign letter grades:

```
if avg > 90 then
   grade = 'A';
elseif (avg > 80) and (avg <= 90) then
   grade = 'B';
elseif (avg > 70) and (avg <= 80) then
   grade = 'C';
elseif (avg > 60) and (avg <= 70) then
   grade = 'D';
else
   grade = 'F';
end if;
```

In this example, we use the IF for the highest grade condition, ELSEIF for the next three conditions (since a specific range must be specified), and a plain ELSE for the failure condition. Doing this eliminates the problem of too many IF..THEN statements. Control will proceed sequentially down this structure, testing for >90 first. If the value fulfills the condition, "A" will be assigned as the grade. The next three ELSEIF statements test (if the above tests fail) whether the value is between a specified range. The final ELSE is the default or failure condition and is executed only if all other condition tests fail.

Although the use of the GOTO is not generally regarded as desirable in structured programming, in a few instances it can be useful. When you use the GOTO, the place to be jumped to must be marked by means of a label name in double-angle brackets:

```
<<here>>      statement;
              (other statements)
              goto here;
```

The CASE is an important structure when there is a large number of possible results for a certain condition. Let's suppose that for a grade example, you, taking grades seriously, decide to make judgmental comments about a student's progress based on the grade received. With the CASE, it would be very simple to do:

```
case GRADE is
   when 'A' => put ("good work—wonderful");
   when 'B' => put ("you did okay");
   when 'C' => put ("you did not study well");
   when 'D' => put ("what a lousy student");
   when 'F' => put ("time to drop out????");
   when others => put ("your grade was recorded in error");
end case;
```

For each case, a corresponding message would be printed. Any values not included in the listed values would be taken care of by the "when others". The CASE is a neat and organized way to handle multiple conditions.

Procedures

Procedure subprograms are very important in the development of large programs. Not only do they make the program more understandable, but they also make program development easier, since a large project can be written by a team of programmers and put together to form a significant piece of software.

At first glance, the word procedure may seem to be plastered all over the code. However, there is a carefully designed structure to all these procedures. The entire "program" consists of a main procedure, within which are smaller subprocedures. These subprocedures can be either written in to the main procedure or developed and compiled separately.

Procedures need parameters in order to communicate with the rest of the main program. In Ada there are two types of parameters—one for information entering the procedure and one for procedure output. The name, type, and direction specifier "IN" or "OUT" must be specified in the parameter list.

Here is a sample procedure "program" using both an external procedure and an internal procedure. The details of each procedure section have been omitted for the sake of clarity:

```
procedure POPULATION is
   procedure get_data(A: out INTEGER) is
   begin
      (procedure body)
   end get_data;

   procedure print_table is separate;
   procedure print_graph is separate;

begin
   get_data(N);
   print_table;
   print_graph;
end POPULATION;
```

In this example there is the main procedure, POPULATION, which calls three procedures, one internal and the others separate. The get_data procedure is part of POPULATION and has one parameter, which will return a value back to the main procedure. The other two, print_table and print_graph, are compiled separately and are not part of POPULATION's body; however, they will be called when the program is executed. When the procedure POPULATION is executed, control will drop down to the statements between the begin and end, and each procedure will be called in turn. The flexible features of Ada's procedures make them very powerful and useful.

Loops

Ada's looping structures include a simple LOOP loop, a FOR loop, and a WHILE loop. There are variations in the ways to exit from each of these loop types.

The simple LOOP loop is an eternal loop; it never ends. An exit statement must be coded inside the loop to finally terminate it (we will cover this shortly). The structure of the LOOP loop is as follows:

```
loop
   (statements)
end loop;
```

The FOR loop should be familiar to those who know BASIC or another widely used language. It is a counted loop which executes a given number of times, then stops. The format of this loop is as follows:

```
for (counting variable name) in (range) loop
   (statements)
end loop;

an example of which is:

for I in 1..50 loop
   put("A");
end loop;
```

This example consists of a simple PUT statement inside a FOR loop structure. The I loop counter variable will increment from 1 to 50, each time printing out a single "A" character. The END statement ends the loop.

The WHILE loop, which is also available in a number of other languages, bases the next looping on a Boolean condition, such as (IF A = 0). The format for such a loop is as follows:

```
while (Boolean expression) loop
   (statements)
end loop;
```

Note that the term "Boolean expression" for the WHILE loop means that the result of the expression will be either true or false.

Now that we've covered loops and how they work, we will discuss ways to escape from a loop. Ada's exit statements allow you to specify exactly when and where to exit from a given loop structure. If you wish to exit from a loop before it is finished, you can use either the simple EXIT, EXIT WHEN, or EXIT (loop) WHEN.

The simple EXIT is usually used together with an IF..THEN within a loop to effect an escape from going around once more. For instance, in a simple LOOP loop, the use of the IF..THEN will allow us to exit the eternal loop:

```
loop
A := A + 1;
if A = 50 then
exit;
end if;
end loop;
```

This example uses an eternal LOOP loop, which will proceed to loop continuously, each time incrementing the A variable by 1. When A reaches 50, the EXIT statement will effect an exit from the eternal loop.

Another way to exit a loop would be to use the EXIT WHEN. This functions much like the simple EXIT, except that the IF..THEN is no longer necessary. This statement will exit whenever the corresponding condition is satisfied. For example:

```
for I in 1..100 loop
   A := A + 1;
   exit when A = 60;
exit loop;
```

In this example, a counted FOR loop is used, which will, in its approach to 100 repetitions, increment A. When A is equal to 60, the EXIT WHEN will effect an escape from the FOR loop.

The final EXIT variant works just like EXIT WHEN, but you give a label name to a loop and use EXIT (loop name) WHEN. If your loop is named ADD, you would code EXIT ADD WHEN followed by the condition.

With these three loops and the EXIT variants, you can use the right loop for any application. In most cases, EXIT is used when unusual conditions or errors occur. It is an unstructured method for handling special cases.

Arrays

Arrays of single or multiple dimensions can be created in Ada. Before they can be used, they must both be declared as a type and then set to a variable name. In addition, the elements of such an array must have a type, such as INTEGER or BOOLEAN.

Arrays are usually declared in a main procedure before the executable statements. An array named SCORES of dimension 100 and set to variable FINAL would be coded as follows:

```
type SCORES is array (INTEGER range 1..100) of INTEGER;
FINAL : SCORES;
```

Array elements would be accessed by the array variable name followed by the subscript in parentheses, as shown below:

```
FINAL(1):=165;
```

Arrays of more than one dimension are available, and all that is required is to define additional subscripts and ranges. Any programming done using a multidimensional array requires that the correct number of subscripts be used and operated on.

One type of array is better known under another subheading. Strings in Ada are in actuality arrays of characters put together to form some meaningful word or name. The definition of strings requires both the subtype POSITIVE and an array definition for STRING. They would be defined as follows:

```
subtype POSITIVE is INTEGER range 1..INTEGER‘LAST;
type STRING is array (POSITIVE range <>) of character;
name : string (1..15);

name := “William Rodgers”;
```

With arrays, strings of bits can also be created, which are known as BIT STRINGS. In general, Ada has powerful array capabilities.

Records and Files

Arrays are limited in that they can hold information of only one data type. For programming, however, we often need to store together related pieces of information, such as a friend’s name, address, and phone number. The record structure answers this need. Consider the following example, where a record structure is declared with the name FRIEND:

```
type FRIEND is
     record
          name : string (1..30);
          address : string ( 1..40);
          cszip: string (1..40);
          phone_number : string (1..10);
          end record;
PAL : FRIEND;
```

In the record above, you have four fields, for name, address, city/state/zip, and phone number. You then set the type to the variable PAL. In order to access these fields, you use "dot notation," which is the variable name followed by the field name:

```
pal.name     pal.address     pal.cszip     pal.phone_number
```

You must use these dot-notated variables when you deal with records, since different records may have identical field names but different record names. Records are useful, but without the use of files none of this organized information could be stored away on a permanent memory device. However, if files are used, all this data can be stored away for future retrieval on a disk, tape, or other memory device.

Ada allows the formation of two types of files, sequential and random. *Sequential files*, as you may recall, must be processed from start to finish. These are useful when a whole stream of data must be read and manipulated. *Random files*, on the other hand, can access any record in a file without reading through all preceding ones. This type is useful in a situation such as a bank, where the teller can pull up your account information by typing in your account number.

Ada's compiler comes with packages designed to be used in working with files. Appropriately, they are named SEQUENTIAL-IO (for sequential) and DIRECT-IO (for random) files. When you use these packages, you can use special commands for creating and working with files.

In order for you to use a file, it first must be CREATEd or OPENed. Depending on whether the file already exists, you use CREATE for new files and OPEN for files that already exist. Examples of creating and opening a file are given below:

```
OPEN (old_file, out_file, "pdata1.txt");
CREATE (my_new_file, out_file, "score.data");
```

For sequential files, SEQUENTIAL_IO is a generic package that must be instantiated; that is, the SEQUENTIAL_IO package must be told what record type you are working with for this program. Two lines must be coded, one to instantiate (tell what record type) and one to access the package itself. In simple terms, a *generic* is a package that can work with different types of information. When you instantiate a generic package, you tell it what kind of information you want it to accept. Here is an example of some code that uses the SEQUENTIAL_IO package. The first line instantiates the package, while the second line allows you to access the package itself:

```
package our_sequential_io is new sequential_io (info_rec);
use our_sequential_io;
```

The commands for different file operations are listed below:

CLOSE (file name)	closes a file from processing
WRITE (file name, record variable)	writes a record to the disk
READ (file name, record variable)	reads a record from the disk

It was mentioned before that we opened an "out_file". This is used for writing data into a file. If the designation in the OPEN or CREATE statement was an "in_file", then we would be preparing for reading in information from an existing file.

Random access files work much the same way as sequential files, with one significant difference. Using the DIRECT_IO, you can indicate what specific record you want to access using an INDEX, which corresponds to the record number. If the record number is known or can be correlated in some way with the data, data from a certain record can be obtained directly and quickly. The corresponding READ and WRITE statements must all include this index. Random access and sequential files make the storage and retrieval of data fast and efficient.

ADVANCED FEATURES OF ADA

Much of Ada's strength lies in its special features, which are covered in the following sections.

Packages

One of the most important features of Ada is the ability to group subprograms, data, and data types into a special structure known as a *package.* A package is a descriptive name for this structure, since we tie together a number of related items into one big bundle.

There are two parts to any Ada package—the package specification and the package body. The *specification* part is visible to everyone and includes general information about the function of the package, such as type declarations, variable declarations, and procedure/function names. Although this section gives the reader a good sense of the program's structure, none of the executable statements or other details is included in this section.

The details of the package's programming are contained in the package *body,* which is hidden from the user. Since the package body is secure from the view of anyone who did not develop the program, it prevents the theft of your program code. In addition, the two parts can be developed and compiled separately. This technique also contributes to program reliability, since a procedure can affect only those variables specified in the header section. Thus the risk of side effects is reduced, especially when a large number of people work together on a large software project.

There are several types of packages. The first, the *data package,* holds only data and data types. Since there are no executable statements, this type consists only of a specification section. Data packages are not executed like programs, but rather are put into a program library. As in the example of the library packages we called previously, we then use it in applicable programs, using the WITH and USE statements.

Program packages consist of a number of procedures and functions that are stored for later use. In the package specification section are coded the different declarations and types necessary, as well as procedure and function calls. The package body holds the executable code and the actual details of the procedures and functions defined earlier.

Packages are very useful for the development of large software projects. Shown below is a program shell for a program package named "accounting," which consists of related procedures that are useful for accounting applications. The package specification section holds all the background information and procedure names, while the package body contains the executable code for each of the procedures. The general structure of the package is as follows:

```
package accounting is
   (types, constants, etc.)
   procedure input_sales;
   procedure print_report;
   procedure figure_commission;
   (other declarations, etc.)

end accounting;        (package specification)


package body accounting is

   procedure input_sales;
   begin
      (statements)
   end;

   procedure print_report;
   begin
      (statements)
   end;

   procedure figure_commissions;
   begin
      (statements)
   end;

begin
   (statements)
end accounting;
```

Generics

The word *generic* may make you think of drugs that lack a brand name. In Ada, a *generic* refers to a package or subprogram that isn't "branded" with any particular type on which to operate. In other words, it is a "blank procedure" that can work on a number of data types, depending on what you specify.

In order to use a generic package or subprogram, you must instantiate (give a type to) the generic, as in the previous section on files, where we instantiated the package's SEQUENTIAL_IO and DIRECT_IO with the type of data record.

A generic procedure takes the following form:

```
generic

   type FIG is private;
   procedure SWAP(A,B : in out FIG);

   procedure SWAP(A,B : in out FIG) is
   begin
      (statements)
   end SWAP;
```

The first three lines are known as a *generic declaration.* Here, we define the procedure SWAP as a generic procedure, with the parameter FIG, which is of type private. The procedure body is the same as any other. Generics cannot be called but must be "instantiated," which is to "create an instance" of the procedure with a certain type. This can be done as follows:

```
procedure CHANGE is new SWAP(INTEGER);
```

This will execute a procedure named CHANGE, using the generic procedure SWAP, but instantiated with the type INTEGER. The procedure will function like a standard one after installation.

Private Types

Like the package structure, data types and structures can be broken down into visible and hidden parts. In the type section, a type is declared as:

```
type (data name) is private;
```

and later in the program, in a private section, hidden from the user's view, are the exact details of the data type's makeup:

```
private
type (data name) is
   (description of data type).
```

Private types are useful for keeping the structure of your software secure from public view. A developer of a certain software package or segment can control the visibility of his ideas by using private types.

Exceptions

Many times in the execution of a program abnormal conditions and errors put a halt to everything happening. In Ada, special commands are available that will take action whenever this problem, known as an *exception,* occurs. Some of the options available are abandoning execution, retrying a subprogram, and programming in response to different problems. See an Ada textbook for more details on exceptions.

Tasks

Tasking, a powerful feature available in Ada, means that more than one program can be executing in the computer at one time. This feature is used for such applications as operating systems and real-time systems. Tasks are used in Ada much like procedures, with the keyword TASK, a task name, and an executable task body. The task body may contain both executable statements and procedure calls. All tasks that are defined in a main procedure will execute in parallel with each other. There are two different types of tasks: independent and synchronized. While *independent tasks* execute independent of each other, *synchronized tasks* can relay information between themselves. Tasks are important in programming software for real-time control systems. See Ada textbooks for more information on taskings, since it is an advanced topic and requires some knowledge of computer operations.

Other Features

Ada is a very sophisticated language that also includes such features as real-time interfaces, list processing, and discriminant pointers, which are used in creating advanced software projects. Books on Ada programming should be consulted for more information on these and other features available.

CONCLUSION

Ada is a language for advanced programmers and is especially suited for large projects, real-time systems, and systems programming. Although it is not very difficult to learn on the basic level, using it to its fullest capacity requires programming knowledge and experience. Ada is at the moment in its infancy, and in the years to come it should become influential in the computer world.

REFERENCES—ADA

With the current interest in the new language Ada, a number of books have been released on this subject. Since there are a limited number compared with the more established languages, all books here are listed in one main section.

Programming in Ada, by Wiener & Sincovec. For computer scientists and students, this book features extensive examples (program listings) for each concept presented. (John Wiley)

Understanding Ada, by K. Shumate. Covers the basic concepts of Ada in an easy-to-understand format, citing various examples. (Harper & Row)

Ada: An Introduction, by S. Saib. A clearly written book covering all major beginning concepts and featuring summary boxes and problem exercises. (Holt Rinehart Winston)

Ada: An Introduction, by H. Ledgard. A short and basic guide to ADA, featuring practical examples. (Springer-Verlag)

Invitation to Ada and Ada Reference Manual, by H. Katzan, Jr. Half this book is a tutorial textbook, and the second half is a reprint of the 1980 DOD Standard reference manual. (Petrocelli)

An Introduction to Ada, by S. Young. Although written on more of a detailed level than some of the other books listed, Young's text is comprehensive and thorough. (Ellis-Horwood)

Software Engineering with Ada, by G. Booch. Designed for advanced software designers, this book covers the creation of large software projects using Ada. (Benjamin Cummings)

Ada for Programmers, by Olsen & Whitehill. For those already familiar with programming, this book provides a good reference to the language. (Reston)

Program Verification Using Ada, by A. McGettrick. A specialized text relating Ada to the topic of program verification (or proving). An advanced book. (Cambridge)

An Introduction to Ada: A Topdown Approach, by Caverly & Goldstein. A beginning textbook on Ada programming. (Brooks and Cole)

CHAPTER 7

APL

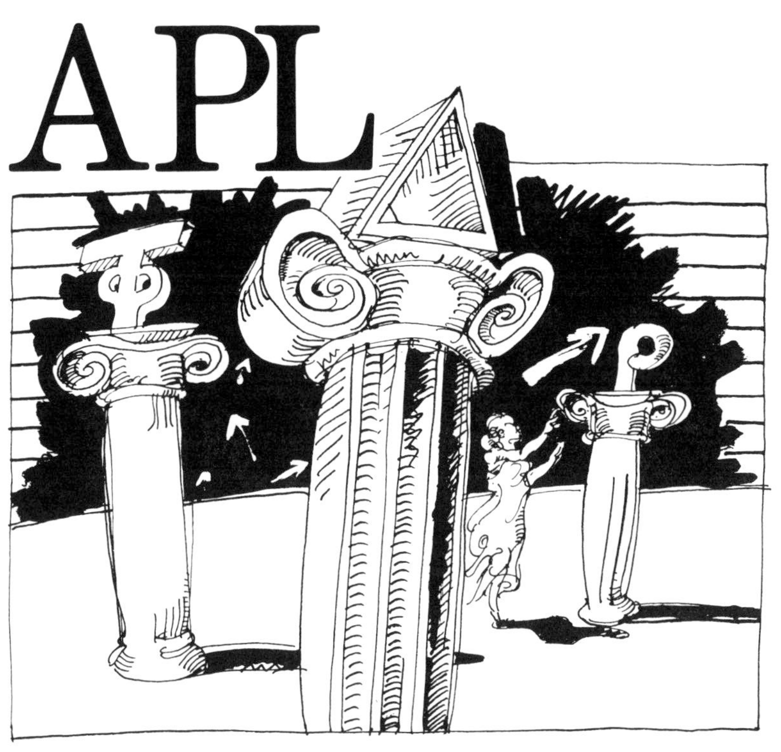

MANY PEOPLE, ESPECIALLY those who are not computer-literate, may look at a computer program, throw up their arms in despair, and cry, "It's Greek to me!" I'm sure computer scientists would agree with them, if the language happens to be APL.

APL, an acronym for A Programming Language, is one of the most unusual languages you'll come across. Not only does it contain Greek characters and special symbols (requiring a special keyboard and character ROM), but it is terribly concise and powerful. APL is "terribly" concise, meaning that a program requiring ten lines in a BASIC or Pascal may require only one if written in APL. Although this is very convenient, understanding a small segment of code may take hours. On the other hand, its computing power is very great, allowing manipulations of large arrays and other structures in just a few keystrokes.

Developed by Kenneth E. Iverson in 1962, APL was originally designed as a way of notating mathematical formulas on the computer. It developed over time into a programming language and now is used widely for business and scientific applications. It is an interpreted language, allowing the convenience of immediate response to problems submitted. APL does not function as a separate program like a Lisp interpreter or COBOL compiler but is used only as a part of an APL system. An APL system is a complete program development environment, including an editor, workspace manager, and interpreter, which is devoted exclusively to APL. Several major companies, such as I.P. Sharp and STSC, offer both worldwide timesharing APL networks and microcomputer implementations. In addition, Portable Software puts out PortaAPL for the IBM PC microcomputer and Apple Macintosh.

APL is different from most programming languages in that it can deal with arrays of numbers (typically of one dimension, known as *vectors*) as single entities and can perform large tasks with an amazing conciseness. For instance, transferring the information from one vector to another may require several lines in BASIC or a similar language, but in APL only three characters are required!

Reflecting its mathematical background, APL is very strong in the area of mathematical functions and statistics. The "strange, funny-looking symbols" commonly associated with APL are actually very powerful "primitive" (built-in) functions that can accomplish such tasks as factorial, combinations, and matrix math with just a single function symbol.

When one considers the advantages of using APL, its superiority in handling matrices, arrays, statistics, and extensive mathematical calculations is clear. In addition, APL is suited for working with characters, data files, multidimensional arrays, and user-defined functions. It also includes a report formatter and editor. Since it is an interactive and interpreted language, its programs are easy to create and use.

From a more negative viewpoint, however, APL is quite difficult to learn and understand. When you look at the APL code in this chapter, you will notice how concise and difficult APL is to understand. A small segment of code may take a substantial amount of time to understand, even for an experienced APL programmer. Also, the method of thinking used in developing a program is so different from that in most other languages that it can take a while to adapt to this new way. Finally, the characters used in APL are not part of the ASCII code, so implementation is difficult on small computers. There are versions available for some microcomputers, however.

In general, APL is best used by mathematicians and engineers for scientific and technical applications. However, it is also used extensively to develop business programs. For the general user, it would be a difficult and unusual "adventure," but one filled with surprises and pleasures along the way.

The APL System

An APL system is a complete "operating system" which is used solely for the creation, execution, and storage of APL programs (or functions). Besides the language interpreter, there is a function editor and manager for each user's workspaces and "library."

As an introduction to a representative APL system implemented on a timesharing system, we will cover some of the basic commands. To start off you will need to log on, using a username and password:

```
)35461:SECRET
   WELCOME TO APL SYSTEM 4 !
```

A successful log-on using the username 35461 and password SECRET is the first step to getting onto an APL system. The main functions and editing procedures will be covered in detail later, so we will proceed to saving a program and retrieving it from memory. Just like a work file found in other language systems, an APL workspace holds the text of a program (otherwise known as a user-defined function) while you are editing and working with it. However, as soon as you log off, everything in the workspace will be gone, so the system provides a way of saving your function for future use. The APL system will, upon execution of your command:

```
)SAVE PROG1
```

save a copy of your workspace PROG1 into your private "library" (storage area). Execution of the command

```
)LIB
PROG1
```

will list all workspaces in your private library. It is also possible to get your program back by executing:

```
)LOAD PROG1
```

which will bring the function back to your active workspace. Several other commands available are)VARS,)FNS,)CLEAR, and)DROP.)VARS and)FNS will return the names of the variables and functions, respectively, that are stored in the active workspace, and)CLEAR is used to clear out the active workspace for new data.)DROP is used to drop workspaces from a library. To leave the APL system, type:

```
)OFF
LOGGED OFF APL SYSTEM 4
LINE 35 4/18/85 35461 JHSU
CONNECTED  0.15.15   TO DATE   2.21.13
CPU TIME   0.01.20   TO DATE   0.06.30
```

which will disconnect you and display some vital usage statistics. Since various APL systems differ from each other, the commands used may vary, so it's wise to consult your reference manual.

Some of the details about using a large-scale APL system are provided here for the benefit of those who will be using APL on a timesharing or university mainframe system. For microcomputer implementations, the details such as log-on procedures and system commands may be different, so it's wise to consult your software manual.

APL Programs (Functions)

The word *function* is commonly used when one is dealing with APL, and to beginners it may seem a bit confusing. Not only are the Greek and special symbols functions, but so are the source texts that you would create and edit. The symbols are primitive functions that are part of the APL language, much like SIN or SQRT in BASIC or Pascal. With these primitive functions, which are usually divided into two classes, *dyadic* (requiring two arguments or operands) and *monadic* (only one needed), complex program functions can be created.

A program function is created by a "definition command," which takes the format:

```
∇Z←NAME ARGUMENTS
```

The little upside-down triangle will tell the system that you want to define a function, and the arrow will make the function execute like any APL primitive. The system will respond with line numbers and a cursor (⍂) to tell where you can begin to define your function:

```
[1] ⍂
[2]
[3]
```

Then, using the function name, you can tap the power of your newly defined "program" by typing in the function name and any necessary parameters.

This is the way most APL programs are created, although there may be variations depending on the type of function you wish to create. A somewhat larger APL program is shown on page 132.

Basic Primitive Functions

Primitive (built-in) functions in APL form the heart of the APL language. With simple one-character function operators, complex formulas and program functions can be created and used.

The first group of function operators are familiar, as they are found in most languages. We have the + for addition, the − for subtraction, the × for multiplication, and the ÷ for division. APL returns us to the days of childhood arithmetic, since the × and ÷ are used instead of the more common "computer operators" * and /. These operations can be either executed directly or put into a program function. Typing in the following would give immediate results, much as in BASIC:

```
      5+6
11

      2×5
10

      36−6
30

      36÷6
6
```

```
∇GPA;GR;CR;M
M←5  25 ρ(25 ρ 4),(25 ρ 3),(25 ρ 2),(25 ρ 1),(25 ρ 0)
GR←MxCr  (3×GR3)+(2×GR2)+GR1
'PUPIL GRADE POINT AVERAGE IS ',⍕(+⊤GR)÷+⊤CR
'THE FULL CLASS AVERAGE IS ',⍕(+/+⊤GR)  +/+  CR
```

A grade-point average program

APL may not seem very unusual when doing the above calculations, but let's try a *vector* (one-dimensional array) and you'll begin to see how powerful APL can be.

```
    5 5 5+3 4 5
8 9 10
```

Here we are adding two separate lists of numbers—one containing the numbers 5 5 5 and the other 3 4 5. Corresponding elements will be added together, revealing the result.

The examples shown above have all been operations on constants, making the operations very limited in use. In APL, variables can be created of numbers, arrays, vectors, and character data. You can assign values to a new variable by using the assignment operator ← as in:

```
A←3
```

which assigns the value of 3 to A. You can use these values just like constants to do math calculations or any operation you desire. If your variable happens to be a vector, any operation you apply will apply equally to each element in the vector. In this case we create a vector of length three which contains three elements, 3, 4, and 5. To make sure that you have entered the data correctly, typing A will reveal the contents of A. Finally, applying the A + 3 operation will cause APL to add 3 to every element in the vector:

```
    A←3 4 5

    A
3 4 5

    A←A+3
6 7 8
```

So far we have looked at vectors, or one-dimensional arrays. For arrays of two dimensions, or *matrices*, you can use one of the special symbols. Suppose that you have two matrices, both of dimension 3×3:

```
A          B

123        461
456        172
789        391
```

You can represent each of these in one line and by one variable name using the special symbol (ρ) which is called a *reshape function.* It takes the horizontal row of numbers and reshapes it into a multidimensional matrix. With ρ, the matrices above are rewritten as:

```
A←3 3ρ1 2 3 4 5 6 7 8 9

B←3 3ρ4 6 1 1 7 2 3 9 1
```

and are assigned to their respective names. Using the mathematical symbols mentioned before, you can use APL to add, divide, subtract, and even multiply matrices instantly.

APL has many more interesting functions, including the outer product, power function, exponentials, logarithms, and maximum/minimum.

Let's suppose that you needed to find out all the results from multiplying two vectors. There is a handy function in APL called an *outer product,* which can be used to find all possible combinations of an operation between two arrays. In other words, you have a certain function, and two vector operands. All the possible values (as in a times table) are given when you execute the following:

```
A°.×B
```

The little circle is called a *jot,* and the line is read as "A jot dot times B." For instance, the following two vectors could be multiplied to reveal the outer product:

```
A 1 2 3 4 5

B 1 2 3

A°.×B

1        2        3
2        4        6
3        6        9
4        8       12
5       10       15
```

There is also a function operator for powers, as in 10 raised to the third power. The asterisk (∗) is used to raise a number to a certain power:

```
    10∗3
1000
```

The power function can also be used for vectors and matrices. An extension of the power function is *exponential* or *scaled notation.* The figure 1+.30E3 represents a value used in APL for exponentials. Logarithms are represented by an unusual symbol, a combination of two separate characters, the circle (○) and the power symbol (∗). They are put together as the operator for logarithms:

```
    10⍟100
 2
```

Although this example uses a base of 10 to operate on 100, any base and number can be used. The syntax of this statement is as follows: base, logarithm symbol, and number to be processed.

One function that you often need to perform is to find out the smallest and largest number in a group. APL provides two symbols for explicitly determining these values. The special APL symbol ⌈ is used to determine the maximum number and ⌊ indicates the lowest number. These symbols are very easy to remember since ⌈ is called *ceiling* (highest) while ⌊ is called *floor* (lowest). A couple of examples follow:

```
      5⌈10
10

      3⌊−1
−1
```

There are even more interesting and useful functions available. Besides our old friends the relational functions <, <, =, >, >, and =, we have two sophisticated functions known as the combination and residue. If you will recall your statistics course, a *combination* is a number stating the number of ways a number of objects can be grouped differently. For instance, the number of ways to group four objects in groups of 2 is 6. This is represented by the formula

$$\frac{n!}{g!\,(n-g)\,!} \qquad \frac{4!}{2!\,(4-2)\,!}$$

with the exclamation points representing factorial. In APL, the function can be implemented with just one special symbol between the two operands. The n represents the number of total objects, and g represents the number selected. The examples illustrate the use of this function:

```
g! n      or      2! 4
```

The symbol ! is not represented by an exclamation point, but rather by a combination of the period, backspace, and quote character. You must type the period, backspace, then type a quote character to complete the special symbol. The function will return the value 6.

When doing calculations, often you need to know the remainder of a division rather than the quotient. APL supports a special function, *residue*, which resembles modulus functions in that it returns the value left over from a division. When you use the residue function, represented by a vertical bar, you are returned the "residue" from whole-number division, as in this example:

```
     4|0 1 2 3 4 5 6 7 8
0 1 2 3 0 1 2 3
```

Here you use residue on a whole vector of numbers, revealing the results of division by the number that appears before the function operator, in this case 4. Division by zero will not cause a problem in APL.

By now you should already have some idea of the great power of APL in dealing with numbers. Operations can be performed on vectors and arrays of data very easily. But what about operations across an array, such as the sum of all elements or the product of all elements in an array? In BASIC, a FOR loop must be set up in order to add or multiply across the elements of an array, but in APL three characters will do it:

```
      A←1 2 3
      +/A

  6

      B←1 2 3

      x/B
  6
```

What you just saw is an example of reduction, whereby a vector can be operated on as though it were a single element, although in reality it is a complete list of numbers. Reduction can be done on matrices and vectors with operations of maximum (⌈), minimum (⌊), subtraction (−), or even scan (where partial reduction is performed). An example of scanning is as follows:

```
      +/50 −5 −5 10
  50 45 40 50
```

Here you keep adding different values to the base value (50), producing a new result each time. As a result of the three "transactions," the value of 50 goes down to 45, then 40, then back up to 50.

There are still more primitive functions in APL. These include negation, factorial, absolute value, and reciprocal. These four are familiar and can be illustrated by some examples:

Negation

```
      −3 7
  3 −7
```

Factorial

```
         5!
   120
```

Absolute Value

```
       | 3 5 ¯2 ¯15
3 5 2 15
```

Reciprocal

```
        ÷1 2 4
  1 .5 .25
```

Factorial is useful in mathematical calculations, especially in statistics for figuring combinations and permutations. The symbol operators for factorial are a combination of the period, backspace, and quote, as described under combination. APL will calculate the factorial of 5 (5 × 4 × 3 × 2 ×1) instantly.

The last four functions that we will discuss here are ceiling/floor, roll, direction, and Pi times. These and the preceding ones are all *scalar functions* that return results of the same type as the inputs. In other words, if a vector goes in, a vector comes out.

For some applications, a whole number rather than a real is preferred. Many times, you would want to round off a real to get an integer. Ceiling/floor are used to give the integer closest to the real value. In effect, they round the value given up or down to the nearest whole number. The ceiling function (⌈) rounds numbers up, and floor (⌊) rounds numbers to the lower value.

```
      ⌈3.30  2.01  4.6
4 3 7

      ⌊2.1   3.9   1.99
2 3 1
```

As always, *ceiling* and *floor* can be used with vectors and variables as well as numeric constants.

For some uses, such as for writing a game of chance or simulating an event, you need to generate random numbers. APL has the *roll* function, symbolized by an italic question mark, which generates random integer numbers. It returns a random integer from 1 up to the operand. To simulate a pair of dice, try:

```
      ?6 6
 5 2                          --lucky seven !!
```

The last two functions, *direction* and *Pi times*, return the sign and the value of Pi, respectively. In the latter function, the operand must reflect an integer value to be multiplied by the value of Pi (3.141592654...).

```
      x−1 4 0
 −1 1 0                       --direction

      o1 0 2
 3.141592654  0              6.283185307        --Pi times
```

This ends our coverage of primitive functions. Additional functions will be discussed in the context of their applications.

User-Defined Functions

In order to create more complex functions or "programs," you must take these primitive functions and put them together in an organized way. APL systems have a built-in editor from which you can create and edit your own APL programs. It is very easy to define a function, since all that's required is a definition command, the program statements, and the closing symbol.

To start, you must define the function name, the arguments, and its state as follows:

```
   ∇S← A FC B
```

which means that we will define the function name FC, with the arguments A and B, and that S FC will make the function act like a primitive after definition. The system will respond by:

```
   [1]⍔
```

which means it is ready to accept function statements. When you are done adding statement lines, simply type a △ and the system will exit edit mode. From that point on, the function can be used like any primitive function.

Mixed Functions

The preceding sections dealt with primitive functions that had the same data type for both arguments and results. In addition, the shape (such as vector or scalar) has also been the same. However, with mixed functions, the data type may be the same but the shape may vary. The functions we will cover are all useful in solving a certain type of numeric problem.

The first function we will look at is the interval. From early math, you know that an interval is a sequence of numbers, like (1, 2, 3, 4, 5) or (−1, 0, 1, 2, 3). Normally, an interval must be defined by means of several commands, such as:

```
+\ 5 ρ 1     for   1 2 3 4 5
```

but with our new function, the iota (ι), a sequence can be generated with great ease. Both simple intervals such as:

```
    ι10
1 2 3 4 5 6 7 8 9 10
```

and more complex ones such as:

```
    ι3636+ 5
3637 3638 3639 3640 3641
```

can be formed. For applications requiring a sequence of numbers, the interval function is very handy. A related function to the interval, the *squad* ([]) returns all the permutations of the arguments given. For example:

```
    R [] 3
1 2 3
```

and for two arguments:

```
    R [] 1 3
1 1
1 2
1 3
```

will perform the same function. You should keep in mind that for interval vectors, the result of [ ] 1 is always 1 and for [ ] 0 is an empty space. Although these functions may not seem very useful by themselves, when combined with others in a user-defined function, they will make dealing with a sequence of numbers much easier to implement. There is no longer any need to specify a sequence of numbers by listing all its elements.

Character Data

For almost all the functions we have looked at so far, we have dealt with numbers. This is not surprising, since APL is best suited to working with numerical data. However, since the language is also used for business programs, interactive games, and electronic mail, it also has the ability to work with character data.

Characters can be used as character strings, as character variables, and also in vectors and arrays. Character strings are almost always enclosed in single quotes, and they may be assigned to a variable name just like any numeric variable. Character strings can be manipulated like both vectors and single characters. They can be put into matrix format as in:

```
A←'ABCDEFGHIJKLMNOPQRSTUVWXYZ'

6 4ρA

ABCD
EFGH
IJKL
MNOP
QRST
UVWX
```

or compared via the rank function. In the string above, each individual character has a rank according to its position in the string array:

```
    A←'ABCDEFGHIJKLMNOPQRSTUVWXYZ'

    A← 'BAD'
2 1 4
```

The 2, 1, and 4 represent the position of each character of 'BAD' in the array A. In summing up our coverage of character data in APL, character strings are treated both as a complete entity and as a vector or array of individual characters.

Other Features of APL

APL is a complex and sophisticated language and includes a wide range of other features and functions: branches, extensive report formatting features, multidimensional arrays, files, and various other specialized functions. Just to describe briefly the details of all these would take many pages, so consult one of the textbooks located at the end of this chapter for sources of information on these more advanced features.

CONCLUSION

APL is a very unusual and powerful language which can be used to solve various problems both concisely and elegantly. Although it is a difficult language to learn and use, it is a major language in use today. With a character ROM chip and the interpreter software on your micro, you can program in this unusual language and really claim that it's Greek to you.

REFERENCES—APL

The book that I recommend highly for learning APL is the text by Gilman and Rose. This book is listed along with a few others for your reference.

APL: An Interactive Approach 3/E, by Gilman & Rose. A complete guide to both APL and using the interactive APL system. Includes exercises and complete solutions, as well as information on the APL2 and micro APL systems. (John Wiley)

Learning APL: An Array Processing Language, by James A. Mason. A beginning APL text for readers with a basic programming background. Offers countless examples and exercises. (Harper & Row)

Computing in Statistical Science Through APL, by F. Anscombe. This book concentrates on statistical applications using the APL language. Includes many cases and examples. (Springer-Verlag)

8 CHAPTER

ASSEMBLY AND MACHINE LANGUAGES

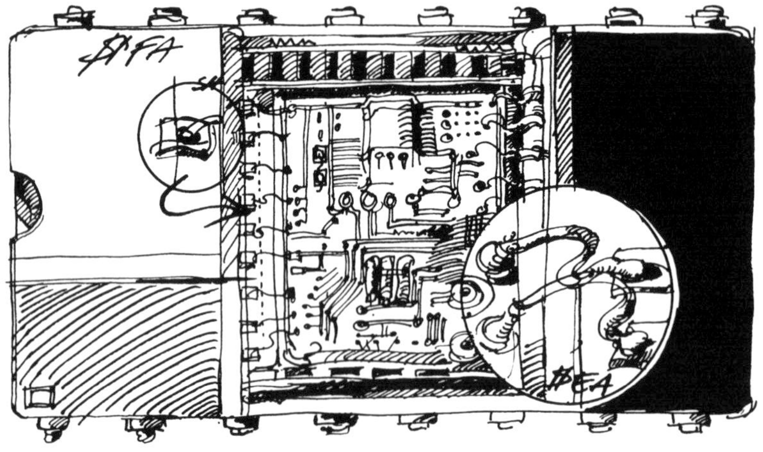

MOST OF THE languages that are covered in this book could be considered "high-level languages" in that they are designed to remove the user from the workings of the computer hardware itself. For instance, in BASIC you could write a program to play blackjack or figure out interest on a principal without ever knowing anything about the internal workings of the hardware.

Assembly and machine language are at the opposite ends of the spectrum from high-level languages; they are very "low-level languages" that allow the programmer to program in the computer's native language, eliminating the need for translation through compilers and interpreters. A machine language programmer must be concerned with registers, memory locations, hexadecimal or binary numbering systems, and the internal structure of the computer system.

Before we proceed further, we need to clarify the difference between "assembly" and "machine" language. Although they are often used interchangeably, there is a distinction between the two terms. Machine language refers to programming done in raw machine code (hexadecimal or binary numbers) and consists entirely of long sequences of these numerical instructions. This is what the computer actually works with whenever you execute any program. Machine language is tedious, difficult to read, and extremely error-prone and hard to debug. To remedy this problem, a program known as an *assembler* was invented. An assembler is a relatively simple program that will translate a symbolic form of machine language (known as *assembly language*) into its equivalent numeric codes.

So, instead of representing the instruction "transfer data from accumulator to register Y" by the hexadecimal code A8, we can use the mnemonic (memory jogger) instruction TAY, which is much simpler to remember. A simple program that computes the larger of two numbers would look like the following in assembly and machine language:

6502 Assembly Language	***Machine Language***

`        LDA $10`
`        CMP $11`
`        BCS SES`
`        LDA $11`
`SES     STA $12`
`        BRK`
	A5 10 C5 11 B0 02 A5 11 85
	12 00

Since the advent of assemblers, the machine code used for programming has been virtually replaced by assembly language, so that is what we will cover from here on.

Assembly could be described as a very primitive language, in that there are very few powerful commands as in other languages. Compared with a high-level language such as COBOL, which with one command will execute dozens of machine-level operations, in assembly only one machine operation will correspond to each assembly command (or *op-code*). Therefore, each assembly language program must consist of hundreds of these very primitive "tiny" instructions, which in turn must be tied together to do a useful task.

Because of the number of instructions needed, the hardware knowledge needed (such as the registers, memory locations, storage location, and execution locations) makes assembly for many people quite difficult to learn. In addition, complex structures such as records, arrays, pointers, and procedures must all be created—assembly provides only such operations as addition, subtraction, branches, logicals, transfers, comparisons, and loads/ stores.

Another problem with assembly is that it's not portable. Every microprocessor or computer system has a different instruction set (list of assembly/machine commands), so a program written for a 6502 cannot be run on an 8080. Similarly, a program written for the IBM 370 cannot be used on a PDP-11.

If assembly is so difficult to use and filled with problems, why use it? Why are so many professional programmers taught to use assembly language and why do they use it so frequently? The reason is that assembly offers many benefits not available in high-level languages. First of all, it is very fast, since no translation or interpretation is needed. Let's suppose that you decided to sit down and write the world's next best-selling arcade-type graphics game. Only a few of the high-level languages include graphics capabilities, and these (such as BASIC or Logo) are much too slow to provide the speed required for very fast continuous action. Only assembly language is appropriate for your game program.

Next, let's consider machine-specific operations. Locked away among your computer's chips are capabilities for interfacing, special input/output, graphics, and various operations. While most languages prevent you from accessing these functions, assembly allows you to have full control of your computer. For example, consider the Apple II computer's sound. From Applesoft BASIC, you can click the speaker. Using 6502 Assembly, you can create everything from "Mary had a little lamb" to complex electronic masterpieces!

In addition, assembly language object files (assembled machine codes) are very compact and will save a considerable amount of memory space compared with other languages. Assembly is also needed for programming real-time devices, since these devices require more complex control and fast computer execution speed.

In our coverage of assembly language, we will discuss the instruction set for the 6502, an 8-bit microprocessor used on a number of popular microcomputers. In addition to describing the instruction set itself, we will cover both applications and the use of assemblers.

Assembly/machine language, then, is programming on the machine level. Although it is useful for applications where speed, system operations, and memory space are important, its structure requires users to be familiar not only with computer architecture but also with the fitting together of many simple instructions into a useful piece of software.

THE 6502 INSTRUCTION SET

The 6502 microprocessor uses a set of close to 60 instructions to perform all its tasks. Everything that you can do with a 6502 computer comes down to these basic instructions, regardless of whether you use assembly or a high-level language; remember that compilers/interpreters in other languages simply translate your source code into machine language.

In other languages, we deal mainly with variables and other data, manipulating them to accomplish some task. We could call them "application-oriented languages." In assembly, we work almost entirely with certain parts of the computer itself, namely registers and memory.

Registers are storage areas in the microprocessor itself that are of primary importance in writing assembly language programs. In the 6502 there are six main registers, each with a name and function. These are the accumulator (A), the X index register (X), the Y index register (Y), the program counter (PC), the stack pointer (SP), and the status register (P). The *accumulator* is typically used for calculations and temporary data storage; you will understand its importance as we review the instruction set in detail. The *X and Y index registers* are used mainly to hold indexes for a certain type of addressing, and also counters and offsets. These three registers will be used quite frequently in your programming, and each is 8 bits long. A commonly used name for the A, X, and Y registers is *general-purpose registers.*

The other three registers serve very important purposes and are known as *special-purpose registers*. The *program counter*, or PC register, tells the computer how to proceed in executing a program. In other words, it holds the address of the next instruction to be executed, so when the current instruction is completed, the computer will execute the next one specified in the PC register. The assembly language programmer can specify instructions to change the address put into the PC register, thereby changing the flow of control. This is an extra-large 16-bit register.

The *stack pointer* (SP) indicates the address of the top of the data stack in memory. Stacks are special structures which can be visualized as a pile of plates in a push-down holder. You can take plates only from the top, and the last one you put in is the first one to be taken out. The use of stacks will be discussed later, but take note that the SP register holds the address of the top "plate" in the stack, and since it is only 8 bits long, the leftmost byte is assumed to be of value 01. (For example, SP = 3C means that the stack address is 013C.)

The *status register* (P) is very interesting in that each bit of the 8 available is used separately to indicate the state of some condition. Currently, seven of the eight bits are used in the following pattern:

P bit number:	7	6	5	4	3	2	1	0
status flags:	S	V		B	D	I	Z	C

Each bit is known as a *status flag* and it indicates some condition by the values "set" (1) or "cleared" (0). The values may be changed after a series of calculations such as additions/subtractions, or register manipulations.

At the leftmost bit above is the sign bit. This tells you whether the value present is positive or negative. Then comes the overflow flag (V), which is also used when you are dealing with signed numbers. The next bit is blank. Then come the B and D flags, which concern breaks (interrupts) and the arithmetic code in force (decimal or binary), respectively. The final three, I, Z, and C, are also important. The first deals with interrupts, the Z indicates zero values, and C indicates the carry needed for addition and subtraction. The meanings of these will become clearer as we present some examples a bit later.

Addressing Modes

As was mentioned before, assembly language works with registers and memory. One difficulty in doing assembly language is that each basic instruction may have a number of operating formats, more commonly known as *addressing modes.* Addressing modes are crucial to the proper use of the instruction set and simply are the ways in which you want to use or obtain data. The main addressing modes available are immediate, direct, zero-page, indexed, indirect, pre-indexed, post-indexed, and relative.

Immediate addressing is very simple in that the data needed to complete the operation is contained right in the operand itself. For instance, if you wanted to load the accumulator (A) register with the hexadecimal value $45 and then store it to memory location $31C2, you would use the # sign to indicate that you were using the immediate mode:

```
LDA   #$45
STA   $31C2
```

The second mode, the *direct* addressing mode, always specifies the memory address of the data to be gotten or where data is to be stored. The value, usually indicated by a $ sign, indicating hexadecimal, is an address and not an actual piece of data. The instruction given above, STA $31C2, is an example of direct addressing.

When dealing with memory addresses, it is common to divide the total area into "pages" of 256 bytes each. With *zero-page* addressing, in order to save memory you can designate memory addresses of the first page ($0000 to $00FF) by only one byte, the second one; the first byte is always zero, so that is assumed when you are coding. For example, $30 would be the same as $0030 when you use zero-page addressing.

So far, we have immediate, direct, zero-page direct, and now we come to *indexed direct* and *zero-page indexed direct* addressing.

Sometimes we need to access a whole group of consecutive memory locations instead of just one. Since it would be tedious to list a whole group of addresses, there is a way to set up a type of "base address" and then move to different locations using an index variable, such as the X or Y registers. If we set up the following:

```
LDA $04CA,X
```

we have specified the base address as $04CA and the index variable as X. The address value would be added to the X register's value to form the actual address. If X = 0001, then the address would be $04CB. The zero-page form of this mode would function in the same way, except that only the rightmost byte would be specified; the left would be assumed to be zero.

In direct addressing, the address of the data we are concerned with is given as the operand. In a sense, you are "directly" given the value of the data by just looking into the said location. However, in cases where that is not convenient or possible, you can use "indirect" addressing, which indicates as an operand the address of the data you are looking for. In other words, you look to an address to find the address where the data are contained. For instance:

```
JMP   ($15A5)
JMP   $15A5              value stored in $15A5 = $2011
```

The first line has $15A5 in parentheses, indicating indirect addressing. Here you will JMP (jump to the address, like BASIC'S GOTO) to the address located in the operand, which is NOT $15A5, but $2011. The computer will automatically take the value from $2011 and $2012, since all addresses must have two bytes. The second line is in direct addressing mode and will effect a jump to location $15A5.

There are also two variations of the indirect addressing mode which include indexes. These are known as pre-indexed and post-indexed indirect addressing. *Pre-indexed* addressing functions much like an indirect address, since everything enclosed in the parentheses refers to a memory location where the address of the operand can be found. The main difference occurs in that it is also indexed, with the value of the X register added to the address on the left, and this address must be zero-page.

```
($05,X)            is an example of this : value $0005 + X
                      if X = $0001 then addr = $0006
```

Post-indexed addressing is a bit different. Here, we take the value stored in the left entry, which is the base address, and add the value contained in the Y register to it, yielding the correct proper address for our data. An example of this could be:

```
($15),Y            which is the required zero-page address
                      followed by the Y index
```

The final major addressing mode, *relative* addressing, is used in branches, where you want to tell the computer how far forward or backward you want to branch. When programming in machine language, you must manually count the offsets for every branch. With assemblers, however, you can use a label for lines where you would need to jump back and forth between them. The assembler program would take care of figuring out what all the actual numerical forward or backward branch addresses are. Examples of these will be given in our coverage of branches.

Now that we have covered the major background areas needed in assembly language, we will proceed to examine each instruction of the 6502 instruction set in detail.

Loads and Stores

Loads and stores are very important in assembly language, and are found in almost all programs.

LDA Load accumulator from memory. This will take data from a memory location and put it into the accumulator. It can be used in immediate, direct, direct indexed, zero page, and both pre- and post-indexed addressing modes.

LDX Load X index register from memory. Takes memory and puts it into CPU X register. It can be used in immediate, direct, zero page, and indexed modes.

LDY Load Y register from memory. Works in much the same fashion as LDX and uses similar addressing modes.

STA Store the contents of the accumulator into a memory location. It can be used in direct, zero page, indirect, and the indexed addressing modes.

STX Store the contents of the X register into a memory location. Used only in direct, zero page, and Y indexed modes.

STY Store the contents of the Y register into a memory location. Functions much like the STX.

Transfers/Increments/Decrements

TAX Transfer the contents of the accumulator to the X index register.

TAY Transfer the contents of the accumulator to the Y index register.

TSX Transfer the contents of the stack pointer to the X index register.

TXA Transfer the contents of the X register to the accumulator.

TXS Transfer the contents of the X register to the stack pointer.

TYA Transfer the contents of the index register Y to the accumulator.

INC Increment a selected memory location by 1. Uses zero page, absolute, and corresponding indexed forms of addressing.

INX Increment index register X by 1 (adds 1).
INY Increment index register Y by 1 (adds 1).
DEC Decrement a selected memory location's value by 1. Uses zero page, direct, and indexed forms of addressing.
DEX Decrement index register X by 1.
DEY Decrement index register Y by 1.

Control Branches

BCC Branch if carry clear. Branches only if C flag = 0.
BCS Branch if carry set. Branches only if C flag = 1.
BEQ Branch only if zero flag = 1.
BMI Branch only if a result is negative, in other words the sign flag = 1.
BNE Branch only if a result is not equal to zero, which is indicated by the zero flag value's being 0.
BPL Branch only if the result is positive, that is, the sign flag = 0.
BVC Branch only if the overflow status is clear, i.e., V flag = 0.
BVS Branch only if the overflow status is set, i.e., V flag = 1.
JSR Branch to the subroutine at the operand address.
JMP Jump to the memory location specified. Uses direct and indirect addressing.
RTS Return from a subroutine.

Arithmetic Operations

ADC Add the value in a memory location to the accumulator's value. Used in all major addressing modes.
CLC Used to clear the carry flag before additions.
SBC Subtract the value in a memory location from the accumulator, with a borrow. All major addressing modes available.
SEC Set carry before a subtraction.
CLD Clear (discontinue) BCD (binary-coded decimal) and return to binary.
SED Set the binary-coded decimal mode.

Comparisons

CMP Compare the value in a certain memory location with that in the accumulator. All major addressing modes are available.
CPX Compare the value stored in the X register with memory. Uses the immediate and direct addressing modes.
CPY Compare the value stored in the Y register with that in memory. Uses the same modes as CPY.

Stack Operations

PHA Push the value in the accumulator onto the system stack.
PHP Push the value of the status register onto the stack.
PLA Load the accumulator with the value at the top of the stack.
PLP Load the status register with the value at the top of the stack.

Logical Operations (all major addressing modes)

AND AND a memory location with the value in the accumulator.
EOR Exclusive-Or the value in a memory location with the accumulator.
ORA Logically OR a memory location's value with the value in the accumulator.

Miscellaneous Instructions

ASL Shift the bits in the accumulator or memory, increasing the value.
BIT AND a memory location with the accumulator, but set only condition flags. Known as BIT TEST.
BRK Break in execution.
CLI Enables interrupts in the 6502.
CLV Clear the status register overflow bit to 0.
LSR Shift the bits in accumulator or memory 1 bit right, decreasing the value of the entire number.

NOP No operation—only increments the program counter by 1.
ROL Rotate the value in accumulator or memory through a carry to the left.
ROR Rotate the value of accumulator or memory right, through carry.
RTI Return from an interrupt.
SEI Disable interrupts.

THE ASSEMBLER PROGRAM

As was discussed before, hand assembly, or writing programs using machine codes, is an extremely tedious and exacting task. It is a very error-prone and unreliable way to write programs. Since the computer is adept at doing detailed tasks repetitively without errors, computer scientists devised a program known as an *assembler* that would take a type of symbolic code (assembly language) and turn it into machine object code for a specific microprocessor or CPU.

Although all assemblers generally perform the same tasks, there are several specific types of assembler programs. The most commonly used type of assembler both runs and produces code for the same microprocessor and hardware system. A cross-assembler, on the other hand, will run on one computer and produce object code for another system. Typically an assembler of this type would run on a large mainframe (IBM 370, for example) and produce code for a microprocessor like an 8080 or 6502. The need sometimes arises to repeat a certain sequence of instructions many times. For this need, a macroassembler is available, which will allow you to define predefined sets of instructions as "macros" to be called much like a procedure. A meta-assembler is very powerful in that it can handle several instruction sets, so it can produce code for a number of computers.

Assembly language programs are formatted into three or four columns, depending on whether comments are allowed. These columns, or *fields*, contain labels, op-codes, operands, and comments. The fields may be divided either by a fixed field length (labels 1–5, op-code 6–8, for example) or by a delimiter, such as a space. The labels field holds special names used to mark important parts in a program for branching or documentation. The op-code field holds the mnemonic code for a machine instruction, and the operand field is for the data required by the particular instruction. Finally, for documentation purposes, a comment field is available. Comments are generally advisable, since even assembler codes are very cryptic.

A typical assembly language source code would look like this:

```
      LDX   #0
      LDY   #0
SRN   LDA   $42,X
      BPL   CHT
      INY
CHT   INX
      CPX   $41
      BNE   SRN
      STY   $40
      BRK
```

whereas the comparable assembler listing would look like this:

```
0000  A2 00         LDX  #0
0002  A0 00         LDY  #0
0004  B5 42   SRN   LDA  $42,X
0006  10 01         BPL  CHT
0008  C8            INY
0009  E8      CHT   INX
000A  E4 41         CPX  $41
000C  D0 F6         BNE  SRN
000E  84 40         STY  $40
0010  00            BRK
```

In our assembler listing, we have both the memory locations represented (starting with $0000), then the produced object code, followed by the assembly language code we saw above. The assembler did all the work of assembling the text into numerical machine codes.

Aside from the assembly instructions themselves, you also have certain commands that are useful in giving instructions to the compiler regarding your source and object codes. Known as *pseudo-ops* or *pseudo-operations,* they are important to the proper creation of assembly language programs.

Although each assembler has its own set of pseudo-ops, most of them have the following, which are necessary for program development. The first, DATA, is used to insert fixed data into a program. It can be used whenever you want to specify some constant value into an assembly program. Usually you would specify a label, the op-code DATA, and an appropriate operand, such as:

```
MESS    DATA   'STOP'
VALUE   DATA   15
```

The DATA pseudo-op actually puts the value of the operand into a place in memory, and you access it by using the label value. This differs from EQUate, which associates a value with a certain name. The name (or label name) is stored in the assembler's symbol table, but no value is stored in memory. One important reason is for clarity in reading assembly programs. If you wanted to call a subroutine that clicks the speaker or clears the screen, using a label name would be easier to understand than constantly trying to recall what an address stands for:

```
SPEAK        EQU    $FB15
SCREEN       EQU    $FBDD

             JSR    SPEAK
             JSR    SCREEN
```

The final pseudo-op we will mention here, ORiGin, is used to locate data or programs in memory. This is most commonly used to tell the assembler where to put an assembler language program in memory. Careful placement of assembly programs is important to avoid destroying important memory locations, especially in limited memory microsystems. To place a certain program at $300, the ORG pseudo-op is put before the rest of the program.

```
ORG     $300        --starts program at $300 hex.
```

Macros, Linkers, and Conditional Assembly

As was mentioned before in the discussion of macroassemblers, some assemblers allow the formation of sequences of code, each referenced by one name. Once a macro has been defined and stored, you can call it by inserting the macro name in an assembly program. The assembler will automatically generate all the macro's instructions and insert them into the calling program. Macros are useful for instances where certain instructions need to be repeated several times.

Linkers perform the function of taking the assembler-produced object code and putting it into memory for execution. Linkers can be simple or complex; some require a separate editing and linking, whereas others will combine them into one step.

At times it may be necessary to perform parts of an assembly program only if they are based on a certain condition. In other words, depending on a condition determined at assembly time, a certain segment will or will not be executed. Conditional assembly is available only in certain assemblers and requires the coding of a special type of IF statement.

Using Assembly Language Instructions

In most languages we have been discussing, a wide range of structures and commands have been programmed into the respective compiler or interpreter. Mathematical operations, comparisons, functions, input/output, and conditionals, among other things, have all been provided for your use. In assembly, which is the lowest level language available, none of these is provided except the basic instruction set. Even simple addition and subtraction require the addition of carry instructions in order to function.

In order to proceed in assembly at a beginning level, it would be better to cover how to program several high-level type commands in assembly language, namely arithmetic operations, conditionals, logicals, and subroutines.

The two main arithmetic operations available in assembly are addition and subtraction, indicated by the ADC and SBC instructions. These are very simple to implement, compared with multiplication and division. Here we have typical addition and subtraction programs:

```
CLC
LDA  $30
ADC  $31
STA  $32              --addition

SEC
LDA  $30
SBC  $31
STA  $32              --subtraction
```

The above programs add and subtract values stored in memory, but do little else. Nothing is printed to the screen, but the new value is stored in the indicated memory location. The CLC (clear carry instruction) must be used before each addition so as to maintain the proper result during the addition process. The LDA $30 instruction loads the accumulator (A register) with the value contained in memory location $30. This is direct addressing, as you will recall from a previous section. The ADC instruction takes the value in the operand's address and adds it to the value in the accumulator. The total of the addition is put into the location $32. The same procedure is in effect in the subtraction example, except that we must first SEC (set carry) instead of CLC and this time the result is a subtraction. The same procedure with the load into the accumulator is used. In both cases, 8-bit numbers are being operated on, each of which is stored in one byte of memory. For addition and subtraction of larger numbers (since there is a maximum range for 8-bit numbers) a more complicated approach is necessary, since there are two bytes each to work with.

Now that you know how to add and subtract, you might like to make some decision. After all, a computer is useless without provisions for making decisions of some kind.

Conditional statements are usually related to a form of the branch instruction, since all conditions are determined on a basis of the value of a certain bit in the status register. In this register, we are concerned mainly with the Zero, Carry, Sign, and Overflow bits.

We will present three examples here that will show how conditional instructions work, each of which will include other instructions that we will discuss shortly. The first will obtain a value (symbolized by the subroutine GET), subtract $10, then compare it with zero. If it equals zero, $5 will be added to the total; otherwise the BEQ will bring it up back up to loop again:

```
START  JSR   GET
       SEC
       SBC   #$10
       BEQ   START
       CLC
       ADC   #1
       BRK
```

The START label indicates the start of the loop. The JSR calls the subroutine to get a value, the details of which are not indicated here. The next two are the two needed to perform a subtraction, which lead to the BEQ statement. If the value remaining after the subtraction is equal to zero, control proceeds on to the CLC and ADC; otherwise a branch will be made back to the line labeled START.

Although the above example made a comparison between two values in the BEQ, there is also a way to compare two separate values not as a result of an addition or subtraction. Here you use both the BCS (branch if carry set) along with the CMP (compare memory with accumulator) to find the larger of two numbers in memory:

```
        LDA   $50
        CMP   $51
        BCS   WHE
        LDA   $51
WHE     STA   $52
        BRK
```

In this example, first you load the accumulator with the value stored in $50. You then compare the value in the accumulator with the value stored in $51. The CMP comparison makes the determination whether to branch based on the value of the carry flag in the status register. If the value in the accumulator is larger, then the carry flag will be set, and the branch will be made. Otherwise, C = 0 (the carry flag is clear) and control will drop down to the line LDA $51. This program will store the larger value in memory location $52 and then terminate at the BRK.

For our final example, we will find the sum of the data stored in a sequence of memory locations. In this example, we will use indexed addressing, which will use the X register as a "counter" as we proceed through a number of memory locations:

```
        LDA   #0
        TAX
SUMD    CLC
        ADC   $45,X
        INX
        CPX   $42          ; # of locations stored here
        BNE   SUMD
        STA   $41
```

This is probably the most complicated example that has been presented so far. In the first line, set the accumulator (where the sum is to be put) to zero, and then in the following line set the X register to the same value by transferring the value of A to X. The data locations start at $45, and in the CLC and ADC add the values to the accumulator's value. The INX serves to increment the value of the X index counter by 1. The CPX compares the value stored in X with the maximum stored in $42. If they are equal, control proceeds on, but otherwise a branch will be made back up to SUMD. The sum will be stored using STA from the accumulator to location $41.

In assembly language, there are facilities for working with machine-level data such as strings of bits. 6502 Assembly provides the instructions AND, ORA, EOR, BIT, ASL, LSR, ROL, and ROR for working with binary information.

AND, ORA, and EOR are familiar, as they are very basic logical instructions. AND will take the bits in a memory location and that in the accumulator and logically AND them; this means that if any two corresponding bits are 1, the ANDed result will be 1; otherwise it will be zero. For ORA, the bits in the accumulator will be ORed with a memory location, based on the pattern that if one bit is 1 of the two being ORed, then the result will be a 1. The EOR (exclusive OR) works similarly to the standard OR with the exception that if both compared bits are 1, then the result of that bit's EOR will be zero instead of 1.

The BIT operation works exactly like the AND, except that neither the accumulator nor the memory location is changed in any way, but the condition flags in the status register are affected and changed accordingly. The last four instructions are used to "rotate" the bits in a register, affecting its value. The rotation is done only one bit at a time, with the bits wrapping around the ends of the register. The ASL and LSR can be used only on the accumulator, whereas ROL and ROR can be used with any register. Shifting a string of bits to the left increases its value, and shifting it to the right decreases the value. For example:

```
$30 = 01111010

LDA     $30
ASL     A
STA     $41
BRK

$41= 11110101
```

Here we have shifted the value stored in $30 01111010 and shifted the bits left by 1, increasing the value to 11110101.

An important aspect of any language is the subprogram. In BASIC and FORTRAN, there are subroutines, and in Pascal and PL/1 we have procedures. In assembly language, there are subroutines, which are necessary to break large tasks into smaller, more manageable parts. The basic parts of subroutines are the label name, JSR (jump to subroutine) command, and RTS (return from subroutine) command. For simplicity's sake, we will present here only a program shell illustrating how subroutines are implemented:

```
        JSR  FIRST
        JSR  SECOND
        JSR  THIRD
FIRST   EQU  *

        {BODY OF FIRST}

        RTS                   ; RETURN FROM SUBROUTINE
SECOND  EQU  *

        {BODY OF SECOND}

        RTS
THIRD   EQU  *

        {BODY OF THIRD}
        RTS
        BRK
```

The simple program shell illustrated above shows the basic structure of coding subroutines. Each subroutine is called by a JSR instruction. The body of a subroutine consists of a label and EQU statement, followed by the main instructions, and terminated by a RTS return instruction. The entire program is terminated by a BRK (break) command.

Although assembly language appears to be simple and straightforward, long programs containing hundreds of statements are needed for programs performing any significant task. As was mentioned before, assembly and machine language require you to think and implement problems from the machine point of view, and require detailed and exacting work. For instance, the program for a Forth language interpreter, written in 6502 assembly language, requires 115 pages of code, close to 6000 lines of instructions, and it produces almost 10,000 bytes of machine code. For projects like the Forth compiler, fast arcade games, and anything requiring machine-specific features, assembly language is the logical choice.

REFERENCES—ASSEMBLY/MACHINE

Since there are no general instructions for assembly languages for different computers, each system must use the instruction set (or language) designed for its CPU. The books available for microprocessors are listed first, followed by those for mainframe or minicomputer systems.

Microprocessors

OSBORNE SERIES ON ASSEMBLY LANGUAGE. This series of reference-type books on specific microprocessors features a listing and description of each instruction, followed by relevant application examples. Each is a complete reference handbook to that specific assembly language. If the author is not specified, assume it is Lance Leventhal. The subroutine series offers prewritten subroutines for that instruction set, ready to be used in your programs, written by Leventhal & Saville. (Osborne MGH)

Reference Handbooks

6502 Assembly Language.
6809 Assembly Language.
6800 Assembly Language.
68000 Assembly Language, by Kane, Hawkins, & Leventhal.
Z80 Assembly Language.
8080A/8085 Assembly Language.
Z8000 Assembly Language.
The 8086 Book.

Subroutines

6502 Assembly Language Subroutines.
Z80 Assembly Language Subroutines.
8080/8085 Assembly Language Subroutines.

Apple (6502) Assembly Language

Apple Assembly Language, by W.D. Maurer. A clear and complete college-level textbook on 6502 Assembly programming, specifically on the Lisa 2.5 assembler. (Computer Science Press)

Apple II Assembly Language Programming, by M. De Jong. A hardware and interface-oriented book on Apple 6502 Assembly programming. (H.W. Sams)

Apple II Assembly Language Exercises, by L. Scanlon. Develops advanced programming techniques through a workbook-styled text. (John Wiley)

Apple Graphics and Arcade Game Design, by J. Stanton. Unlocks the secret of writing fast arcade games on the Apple in 6502 Assembly. (The Book Company)

Apple Machine Language, by Inman & Inman. Covers machine language using raw machine code. (Reston)

Apple Assembly Language Programming, by Whapshott. Complete with book and assembler software, this is an interactive course in assembly for the Apple. (Hayden)

6502 Assembly

6502 Assembly Language Programming, by Fernandez et al. A programmed self-teaching guide on 6502 Assembly. Designed for beginners. (John Wiley)

6502 Systems Programming, by Windeknecht. Programming the 6502 using the Brevity assembly language. (Little, Brown)

Z80/8080 Assembly

Programming the Z80, by R. Zaks. A combination of a reference guide and tutorial. Very complete. (Sybex)

Z80 and 8080 Assembly Language Programming, by K. Spracklen. An introductory book on Z80/8080 Assembly language programming. (Hayden)

Z80 Instruction Handbook, by Wadsworth. A reference guide to the Z80 instruction set. (Hayden)

CP/M Assembly Language (Z80/8080/8088/8086)

Introduction to CP/M Assembly Language, by J. Lindsay. A guide to using the CP/M assembler. (Hayden)

System Programming Under CP/M-80, by L. Hughes. Shows how to program under CP/M-80 and use the operating system on the basic level. (Reston)

TRS-80 Assembly Language (Z-80)

Machine and Assembly Language Programming, by D. Alexander. Beginner's guide to TRS-80 Assembly language. (TAB)

Mini and Mainframe Assembly

370/360 Assembler Language Programming, by Stern et al. A college-level text on IBM 370 assembler programming. (John Wiley)

Assembler Language with Assist, by Overbeek et al. A text on using the Assist student assembler for IBM 370 Assembly. (SRA)

Structured Assembly Language for IBM Computers, by Johnson. A college-level IBM assembler text, stressing business applications. (Mayfield)

Introduction to Assembler Language Programming, by C. Feingold. A comprehensive guide to IBM Assembly. (W.C. Brown)

CHAPTER 9

C

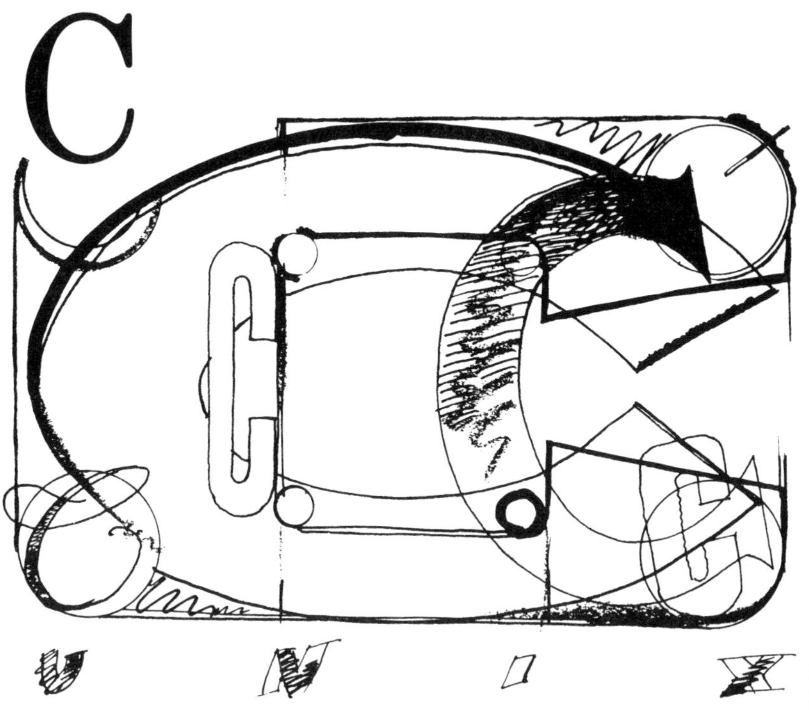

ONE OF THE "hottest" languages in recent years, C has enjoyed a lot of success in the last few years. It is a compact, fast, and transportable language that allows programmers to reach down and program at the machine-language level. Although it is considered a high-level language, actually it could be considered a middle-level language, somewhere between Pascal and BASIC and straight assembly language.

C was used to create the special effects and graphics for popular films such as *Star Trek II* and *Return of the Jedi*, and it was the language of choice for program development at Digital Research and Microsoft. Although the language was invented in the early 1970s, it is only in the mid-1980s that it began to experience widespread acceptance and success.

The language was invented by Dennis Ritchie at Bell Laboratories in 1972 on a DEC PDP-11 Unix minicomputer, and this original version is considered the standard. For many years it was used mainly in academic environments, but eventually it was adopted by computer professionals who realized the value of C in software development. Because of its flexibility in dealing with different types of problems and its association with the popular Unix operating system, C has influenced the microcomputer community. There are many C compilers available, many of which are full implementations, as well as a large number of C books and manuals.

C's success is probably due to its many desirable qualities. First, it is fast and has a rich set of commands and operators. Its low- and high-level qualities make it equally well suited for writing both operating systems/compilers and business packages. In addition, C is portable, and therefore easily transportable between different computer systems. The portability is due in part to its small core size. The central part of the language consists of only about 30 keywords (commands), with external functions taking care of many of the other needs (such as input/output). The language executes very quickly, thus being comparable to assembly languages, while being relatively simple to learn and use. Finally, C is a structured language, requiring the user to think of a particular program in "blocks," a collection of which would comprise a complete program.

On the negative side, C is not a beginner's language. A C program is generally rather cryptic, without the neat "sentences" of COBOL and Pascal, and may bewilder the novice. Another aspect of C is that its compiler is relaxed and unrestrictive, allowing the programmer a lot of liberty in writing a program. Although this characteristic is helpful at times, it may also leave undiscovered obscure, hidden errors that would be difficult to find and debug. Finally, C uses lower-case and unusual symbols, such as the brace ({}), the OR (¦¦), and the one's complement (~), all of which would be difficult to use on computer systems with limited keyboards and character sets.

All in all, C is an up and coming language that is well suited to the needs of professional programmers, and it is becoming available for a substantial number of microcomputers.

Program Structure

All C programs can be thought of as a group of functions. In simple programs, the terms *program* and *function* may refer to the same thing, but for larger ones much of the code would be contained in separate function subprograms. For a properly documented program, comments should precede the executa-

```
/* bubble sort program */
#include "stdio.h"
#define ARRY_SZ 8150
main ()
{
     int array [ARRY_SZ];
     int index,element;
while (!kbhit())
  ;
bsort(array,index);
printf(BELL);
printf("the array is sorted/n");
}
/* sort function */
bsort(a,n)
     int a[];
     int n;
{
int i,j,temp;
for (i=0;i<n-1;++i)
  for (j=i+1;j<n;++j)
  if (a[i]>a[j])
{
  temp = a[i];
  a[i]  = a[j];
  a[j]  = temp;
  }
}
```

A C program bubble sorts an array

ble code. As in many other languages, comments are specified between the /* */ symbols, as in:

```
/* this is a comment */
```

After the comment lines is the main procedure header, written as MAIN followed by a pair of parentheses () which indicates the start of a function. Although usually MAIN() (the main procedure) is specified with no parameters, sometimes parameters are needed, such as in the case of files. Following this header are the braces and program statements. C is one of only a few languages using braces, and here it indicates the beginning and end of the main function.

The main () function is very important, as it tells the C compiler where the program starts, and it must be included in each program. A C program to print a line of text looks something like this:

```
/*  sample C program */
/*  prints a message to the screen */
main()
{

   printf( "Hello. Do you like C ?\n");
}
```

We see here the comment statements, followed by the main program header, followed by the left brace, program statement, and closing brace. The command printf will output the line in quotes, followed by a carriage return (\ n or "newline"). Printf is actually a separate function, stored in an external C library. Using printf with the argument (Hello, etc.) will call the external function and execute it, so that the above program will print:

```
Hello. Do you like C ?
```

You may have noticed that lower case is used frequently in the sample program. While many languages do not differentiate between cases and may default everything to upper, C is case-sensitive and differentiates between the two. Hence, "Sum" is not the same as "sum". In addition, C is a free-form language and will accept your text in any format. The program above could have been squashed into much less space; however, readability would be greatly affected. For writing in C, it is always best to follow the suggested format detailed in most C books. One final syntactic note concerns semicolons—each C statement line must be followed by a semicolon, which acts as a statement terminator.

Data Types

There are three basic data types in C (int, float, and char) along with four qualifiers (long, short, double, and unsigned). Int, as you may guess, stands for integers, the positive and negative whole numbers. Numbers such as −45, 32, and 0 are all examples of integers. Standard integers are notated just like the numbers we use every day. There are special forms of integers that you can use, and these are numbers in base 16 (hexadecimal) and base 8 (octal). If the number is preceded by a zero (0) and an x, then the number we are dealing with is a hexadecimal number; use the digits 1..9 and the values 10–15 (decimal 1–15) represented by the letters A..F. If a number is preceded by only a zero, then you can assume that it is an octal number. A hexadecimal number would be represented like 0x4A, and an octal number looks like 03415.

Floating point numbers, indicated by the type specifier 'float', are used to denote both real numbers and those with exponents. Real numbers are those with decimal points, such as 0.02 or 112.4. For very large or small numbers, you can use scientific notation. For an example, let's consider the number 240000, which is represented in C by 2.4E5. The left part, 2.4, called the *mantissa*, gives the base number, while E5, the exponent, tells us the raised power.

The char designation is used to indicate single characters, such as "w" or "$" or even "\n". The first is a lowercase w, the second a dollar sign, and the third (even though it has two symbols) is the "newline" character, which functions much like a character return.

The qualifiers long, short, double, and unsigned are used to modify the precision of integer variables. Take as an example the DEC PDP-11 minicomputer, whose C int variable can handle numbers up to 32,767. By prefixing the qualifier "long" to "int", you can extend the numerical range up to 2,147,483,647. Now you can work with much larger numbers before you reach the limit. Now consider the opposite. Perhaps you need to use only small numbers up to 127 and would like to save some memory space. If you use the qualifier "short", the computer will expect smaller numbers and will not allocate the full amount of memory space as it would for an int designation.

Double, or double-precision, numbers are used to hold floating point numbers that have more significant digits than the standard float type. Although it depends on the particular machine, usually a number designated as "double" can hold twice as many digits as the float specifier. Use of the word "unsigned" before an integer specification would limit your numbers to positive values only; however, the range for positive numbers would be increased significantly. The various combinations of these available are:

```
int   long int   short int   unsigned long int   unsigned short int
```

Variables and Assignment

C variable names can begin with either a letter or underscore character (_) and then can be followed by any combination of alphanumeric characters. You may not use any of C's keywords as variable names, nor can you use special characters (! $). One important thing to remember is that in C there is a distinction between upper and lower cases; therefore, you must be careful about using your names exactly as you defined them. Underlines are typically used in system calls and compiler routine names.

Variables are defined inside a function, usually before the executable statements. The type (int, char, real) is written first, followed by the variable names, finally terminated by a semicolon. Assignments are done with the equal sign (=), the same symbol often used for equality in other languages. Below is an example of variable assignments and declarations:

```
/* example of variables & assignment */
main ()

  {

    int  numb1, numb2;

    numb1=5;
    numb2=2;
    printf("the numbers are %d and %d \n",numb1,numb2);
  }
```

The printf statements will be covered in detail in the section on input/output.

Math Operators

For simple math, C allows you to add, subtract, multiply, and divide. The standard symbols (+, − ,* ,/) are used. A simple expression could be formed as such:

```
third = first + second;
```

or

```
product = left * right;
```

Another operator, the modulus (%), will return the remainder of the two numbers you are dividing. The remainder will be given in integer values.

Comparison Operators

Values can be compared in C much as in other languages, the only difference being that C uses a slightly different set of operators. For equality, you use two equal signs (==) to differentiate between equality and assignment. Less than and greater than are represented by the common symbols (<) and (>), respectively. The operator NOT as in "not equal to" is represented by the exclamation point (!), so the expression "J not equal to K" would look like:

```
J != K .
```

For Boolean operations, C uses a specialized set of operators. Instead of using words for these, special symbols are used. AND is represented by &&, OR by ||, and NOT by !.

Being an intermediate-level language, C also offers low-level assembly language type operations. Since the assembly/machine language chapter gives a good coverage of these operations, we will merely mention them here. They are the one's complement (~), an AND for bit data (&), an OR for bits (|), an exclusive OR for bit data (^), and arithmetic shifts left (<<) and right (>>).

Built-in and User Functions

The C language is in actuality very small. Many of the features that you would commonly expect to be included in all languages (such as input/output) are missing from C. But what about the fact that we used printf to print out a line to the screen? Isn't that input/output?

Printf, like many other independent functions, is not a part of C itself but instead is stored in a "library" ready for use when necessary. A C program merely calls the function, which is then taken and used to execute your commands. The ability to use functions from a library is one reason why C is such a portable language. Some of the function types available in a standard Unix C library include string manipulation, character functions, input/output, memory data conversion, and memory allocation. Here are some examples from these categories:

```
char*strcat(str1,str2)                 (concatenates str1 & str2)

isalnum(c)                             is c an alphabetic character?
                                         ( tests T/F)

FILE*fopen(file name, access mode)     (opens a file for use)
```

You can also define your own functions. User-defined functions are subprograms that you write for your own use in solving some formula or problem. Once you have defined a certain function, it becomes part of your personal "library" of functions, which is in addition to the standard C library. A user-defined function has the following form:

```
type specifier          function name (arguments);
                        argument type declaration;
                        {
                           Declarations;
                           function statements;
                        }
```

The first order of business in writing a function is to define a type. Function values can have a type of char, int (long and short), double, and float. If you leave out the type specifier, the compiler will default the type to integer. Function names should be created according to the rules for variable names, and ideally should reflect something of its nature (such as cube for cubing a variable). The list of arguments is necessary if variable values from outside the function are needed. In other words, if you need the values of A and B to calculate C in function PRODUCT, then you would need the following arguments:

```
integer   PRODUCT(A,B);
```

Following this header line, you declare the types of all your arguments. Although the compiler will assume all undeclared arguments to be type integers, it is always best to declare all arguments. The information contained inside the braces is the body of your function. We have here the declarations (for all variables or previously undeclared arguments) and the main function statements. Since there is no separate procedure and function subprogram in C, you can either calculate formulas or create an executable "procedure-type" function; either way it is called a function. A closing brace ends the function.

As you may recall from BASIC, the keyword RETURN in a subroutine returns control to the line following the calling line. In C, the same word is used to do the same thing. However, the closing brace of a C function will do the same thing, so in many cases the RETURN is not necessary. If you need to return some value back to the main program (such as the result of a calculation), the same keyword can be used but with a slight variation. RETURN(B) will return the value of the B variable back to the main program.

C's variables are not just of one general type. Actually, there are four distinct "storage classes" of variables, the main differences being in how they are stored and used. The first, *external variables*, are used for both variables and functions. This kind of variable is declared outside of the function body and can be used by all functions within a complete program (main function) body. It could be termed a *global variable. Automatic variables*, on the other hand, can be used only by the declaring function. For instance, in your main function, you have a subfunction B. If you declare a variable within B, it can be used only within that function, and after the function is done executing, the values will be gone forever. You could say they come and go automatically. The third type, *static variables*, are much like automatic variables except that the values of each stay in memory permanently and at the next invocation will again be there for use. The final type, *register*, is used when speed is needed. Here, a CPU register is reserved for the variable, making execution time a lot shorter.

In short, user-defined functions are an important part of C programming and should be used frequently in C programs.

Input/Output

As was mentioned before, C does not have any input/output facilities. Instead, it provides these capabilities through library functions. One example that you've encountered is the printf function, whereby data can be printed to the screen or printer. Depending on the type of computer and the C compiler/utilities, you will have a number of functions to use.

Input/output functions cannot just be called without previous preparation. First, you must tell the compiler to read the contents of a library file into memory, such as the "stdio.h" file (standard input/output header). To do this, you must use the preprocessor directive #include. Whenever you use this command, or a similar one (noted by the pound sign), you are telling the computer something before actual compilation. Thus, preprocessor directives are often coded before the beginning of the main() function. However, they can be coded throughout the body of a C program header, wherever needed.

You use the #include whenever you need to use certain function libraries. Another command of this kind, #define, is used to define global constants. You can #define a variable name to be a constant of a specified type, whose value will not change throughout the duration of a program.

The general input function in C is SCANF(). It works much like an INPUT statement in other languages. Unlike low-level functions such as getchar(), the SCANF can be used to input different kinds of data. The general format of the scanf is as follows:

```
scanf("control string",argument1,argument2....);
```

The control string can contain not only the message printed to the screen (such as "enter a number:") but also the format of the data being received. Let's look at an example before we proceed further:

```
scanf("enter number: %d",nbr);
```

Here we see the control string, with the message "enter number" followed by the format specifier. The % means "convert to" and the d stands for decimal integer. The actual variable name follows, nbr. The data type intended to be input can be changed at will by your simply replacing the format letter (d in the previous case) to one of the following:

o	octal integer
h	short integer
x	hexadecimal integer
f	floating point number
c	single character
s	character string

The printf() function, which should be a bit familiar by now, is the most commonly used output function. This is a very flexible function, unlike putchar(), which only outputs a single character, and puts(), which displays only character strings. Below is the general format for printf():

```
printf("control string",arg1,arg2...);
```

This is very similar to the scanf function above. However, it has a greater number of choices, since output can be done in a myriad of ways. The control strings can contain a regular string of characters, or indicate the format for variables using the conversion character (%) followed by a specifier:

d	decimal
o	octal
x	hexadecimal
u	unsigned decimal
e	decimal floating point with exponents
f	floating point
c	character
s	character string
long	long integer
double	double-length real number

Character or control strings can have escape sequences added for the sake of output formatting. We already demonstrated the \n (newline), which outputs a character return. Other escape sequences are listed below:

\t	tab
\b	backspace
\f	form feed
\0	null
\'	single quote
\\	backslash

The arguments following the control string are names of the variables to be printed. Check your compiler's reference manual for other functions available for input/output.

Conditional Statements

Conditional statements are used to make decisions and direct program control to different places. Usually these statements are decided upon according to the value of a certain condition, hence the name, *conditionals.*

The first, familiar to many programmers, is the IF..ELSE, known in some other languages as the "IF..THEN..ELSE." Here we can decide what to do on the basis of the truth or falsity of a condition. Suppose you have a survey, and you code the numbers 1 for "man" and 0 for "woman." In printing out a report, you would like to have the English equivalents:

```
if (x == 1) then
        printf("man");
else
        printf("woman");
```

For more than one statement per condition you must use braces to indicate what goes with what:

```
if (x == 1) {
        printf("man");
        ++man;
        }
else    {
        printf ("woman");
        ++woman;
        {
```

As you see, there is one group of braces for each group of statements. You may have noticed the strange pair of pluses before the variables "man" and "woman." These are increment operators and work much like the machine-level instructions of the same name. It adds one to each of the variables. Decrementing is just as simple. Just use two minuses:

```
--a
--value
```

One final note about the use of IF. If you want to work with only one condition at a time, the IF can be used without the else, such as:

```
IF (b==0)
      number = number / 2;
```

The need also arises for compound conditions to be tested. You might want to know if the value of grade is between 80 and 89. Using C, you can combine two expressions into one:

```
if (( grade >= 80 && grade <=89 )) then
        printf("your grade is B");
```

More complicated IF structures can be created, such as the need for two choices after the first is rejected. To illustrate, consider the prizes for a certain game:

```
if (score > 8)
     printf ("you win a teddy bear !\n");
else
  if (score <=8 && score >=4)
     printf("you win a quarter !\n");
  else
     printf("sorry—you lose.\n");
```

The above program is a "carnival game" application. If the score you received is larger than 8, you win a big stuffed teddy bear. If the score is between 4 and 8, then you win a quarter (25 cents). Otherwise, don't win anything.

The final conditional structure, the SWITCH, is known as a CASE structure in other languages. Here we can specify a different set of commands for each outcome, based on the value of the SWITCH expression:

```
  .
  .
scanf("enter the grade: %c",grade);

switch (grade)
  {
     case 'A':
       printf("excellent work !");
       break;
     case 'B':
       printf("good job.");
       break;
     case 'C':
       printf("not bad.");
       break;
     case 'D':
       printf("could do better.");
       break;
     case 'F':
       printf("you failed your exam.");
       break;
     default:
       printf("grade entered in error.");
     }
```

In this example, we test the value of grade (which we just typed in) against our CASE groups. If one matches, execution proceeds to the CASE group, continues through until the BREAK, then exits the entire structure. This structure is very handy for cases where there are many choices and using IFs would be too tedious. The default case group would be executed only if all preceding match tests had failed (meaning that he didn't get an A, B, C, D, or F). The BREAK command is used to cause an exit from the SWITCH structure if one of the top five cases were true.

Loops

C has a counted loop, the FOR, along with WHILE and DO loops. The structure of these in C is somewhat different from that in BASIC or PASCAL, so we will look at them in detail.

The FOR loop works much like others of its kind, looping a set number of repetitions, with the general format:

```
for ( x = 1; x <= 100; ++x )
   {
      printf("%d\n" ,x);
   }
```

The first expression in this FOR loop is the initial start value. The program loop count starts at 1. The second expression is the test value. While this condition is true, it loops again. The third is the loop increment control, like the STEP in BASIC. In this example, everything within the braces will be repeated the set number of times specified. In the case of only one statement inside the loop, the braces can be omitted, but they are included here to show the full format. Multiple statements must be enclosed within braces. Notice that the increment operator is used in the increment figure, ++x. This is the same as "x=x+1".

The WHILE loop is used where you want to test a condition at the beginning of a loop. It has a much simpler form than the FOR, as it continues to loop as long as your stated condition is true. Consider an example where you want to sum the integers from 1 to 10:

```
/* sum the integers from 1 to 10 */

main ( )

   {
   int numb = 1;
   int sum = 0;

   while ( numb <= 10 )
       {
       sum = sum + numb;
       ++numb;
     }

   printf("the sum is %d\n",sum);
   }
```

The statements in the WHILE loop (between the braces) will be repeated a total of ten times, each time adding the current number to sum and incrementing the variable numb. At the end, the sum will be printed.

The exact opposite of the WHILE, the DO loop will test the condition specified at the completion of each repetition. The general format of this structure is:

```
do
{
     [program statements here]
}
while (condition);
```

The three loops available in C are useful when you need to perform some action repeatedly.

String Handling

In previous sections it was mentioned that C can handle character data using the char data type. Although this is adequate for strings one character long, for character strings an "array of characters" must be formed. Thus, to store the word "hello", an array of length five must be created of type char. A string char array would be defined as follows:

```
static char (name of string) [ ] = {CHARACTERS IN ARRAY}
```

an example of which could be:

```
static char greeting [ ] = { 'H', 'i', '!'};
```

The string character array "greeting" would be assigned a size of 4 for three characters (C arrays start at 0). Character functions can be written to concatenate, take substrings, and make comparisons. There is a shorthand way to initialize character arrays, which is equivalent to the full declaration given above. "Greeting" could be declared as follows:

```
static char greeting [ ] = { "Hi!"};
```

As was explained in the input/output section, you use versions of printf and scanf when dealing with character strings. You would use these commands in the same way as numbers, with the exception of the data format conversion character, which must be "s" for string. You could print and read character string arrays as follows:

```
printf ("%s\n",<var name>);

scanf("%s",<var name >);
```

For dealing with single characters, there is a separate GETCHAR function. This can be used instead of the scanf function and is easier to use since no arguments or parameters are needed.

In the character strings you may have noticed the presence of the "\n", or the newline character. This is one of a group of special "functions" known as *escape characters*, or sometimes *backslash characters*. Each of these is preceded by a backslash followed by a letter or symbol. These were listed earlier under input and output.

Arrays

Arrays are available in C, in both single and multidimensions. In order to set up and use an array, you must first declare it. You do this in the declaration section by simply adding a range dimension to each variable you wish to make into an array:

```
main ( )
  {
    int  value[20];
  }
```

You will note that the dimension is enclosed in brackets, not parentheses or braces. Declaring and filling arrays with values must be done manually, since there is no shortcut method. In order to fill an array, you may specify values either in the declaration statement or in the main body:

```
main ( )
    {
     static int scores[10] = {4,3,5,1,2};

     scores[5] = 0;
     scores[6] = 9;
    }
```

In the declaration line, the first five elements of the array are set to 4, 3, 5, 1, and 2. In the following assignment statements, the next two values are assigned to 0 and 9. In three lines, the first seven elements of the array SCORES have been initialized. All arrays in C start with element 0.

Multidimensional arrays (or tables) represent data in a two or more dimensional arrangement. Therefore, each array element must have two subscripts. In the following example, an array of dimension 4 by 5 is declared, after which values are assigned to all spaces in the array:

```
main ( )

  {
   static int NUM[4][5] =  {  4,  -2,   4,   6,  19
                           {  2,  -1,  39,   0,  99
                           {  3,   8,  11,  -4,   1
                           { 21,   0,   1,   2,   3
                        }
  }
```

From the declaration, NUM[0] [0] would be 4, while the value of NUM[3] [4] would be 3. Arrays are very useful for dealing with large numbers of similarly typed information; in the next section, however, we will examine the *structure*, which can hold information of varying types.

Structures

The structure is a very important part of C because it allows related information to be dealt with together in an organized unit. For instance, consider the date, which consists of month, day, and year. Taken separately, they are just random pieces of information, but together they represent a significant indicator of chronological time—June 20, 1984, for example. You could define the date as follows as a structure:

```
main ( )

     {
      struct    calendar
        {
           int     month;
           int     day;
           int     year;
        }
}
```

The structure illustrated above, CALENDAR, consists of three parts, MONTH, DAY, and YEAR, all of which are of type integer. Another set of braces surrounds the structure body, to differentiate between structure variables and others.

The structure name CALENDAR identifies the structure you just saw, but it cannot be used as a variable. You must declare a new variable name that would be of type CALENDAR, and this new variable would actually be used and manipulated in a program.

```
struct calendar date;
```

The declaration sets up a variable of type CALENDAR called DATE. From then on, you could access individual fields in a structure by simply using the variable name, a period, and the field names as follows:

```
date.month = 10;
date.day = 15;
date.year = 61;
```

Structures can be initialized either by assigning a value to each field or by using a shortcut method:

```
static struct date = {10,15,61};
```

As you can see, value was assigned to all three fields in one command, instead of the three in the previous case. For more advanced applications, it is possible to define structures containing arrays, arrays containing structures, and structures within structures! Consult a textbook on C for details on how these can be written and implemented.

Unions

A *union* is a special data type available in C that can hold different data types. When you declare a union, you give a name to a memory space and specify which types of data it may hold. The compiler will in turn allocate the maximum amount of space necessary for the largest type. Union variables can be accessed with the union name, then a period, and then the data type field name. Although a union can hold different types of data, you must be careful to take out the same type that you originally put in; otherwise some troublesome problems may result. An example of a union declaration is as follows:

```
union fourtype {
        int number;
        double int bigger;
        float    expo;
        char     lettr;
};
```

Here the union name is "fourtype" and it features four possible types—int, double, float, and char. In order to put a number in "fourtype" of type float, you must assign a value to fourtype.expo. Below is an example of unions:

```
union geom_fig {
float radius;
float t [2];
int s [3];
};
```

which can take on different values when used for various geometric figures. Radius is used fcr circles, t for rectangles, and s for triangles. You can use the union geom_fig by assigning a value to one of the variables. For example:

```
geom_fig.radius = 4.35.
```

Pointers

Pointers are an important part of the C language. Not only are they useful for the creation of linked data structures (such as linked lists), but they allow you to alter variables outside a certain function without any undesirable problems or side effects.

A C pointer declaration consists of a data type, an asterisk (*), and the pointer variable. The asterisk is very important, as it indicates the declaration of a data type:

```
int *point;
```

You would now know that there exists a pointer variable of type integer called "point", which holds the address of the integer value. However, you don't yet know where your pointer is pointing, so you must initialize it to something. In this example, suppose you point our pointer "point" to the location of "num":

```
point = &num
```

Stored in the pointer variable now is the location (address) where the value of "num" is stored. Keep in mind that point will contain an address value, not the value of num. Consult C programming texts for various techniques of using pointers in C.

Additional C Topics

As was mentioned under operators, it is possible to work on bit data using the bit operators for AND, OR, Exclusive OR, One's Complement, SHIFT LEFT, and SHIFT RIGHT. The first two are familiar; the remaining ones have special functions. The Exclusive OR returns true if one of the two operands is a 1 (true) but not both. In other words, if you want to EXCLUSIVE OR two Boolean numbers, they must have values of either 1 0 or 0 1 to return a value of 1. Otherwise, it is zero. The One's Complement simply changes each bit to its opposite. For instance, 1001 would be changed to 0110 using the One's complement. The Left and Right Shifts move the bits in a binary string either leftward or rightward. They have the effect of increasing or decreasing the value of the binary number.

In a previous section the term *preprocessor* was mentioned. You would use preprocessor statements to "customize" a program by defining certain conditions to the compiler before analyzing and compiling the main program. Preprocessor statements are usually distinguished by the presence of a pound sign and its location outside the main function.

The major preprocessor statements available are the #define, #include, #ifdef..#else..#endif, #if, and #undef. The first is used to define constants and other relevant values (such as bit sizes and expressions). The #include is coded to allow certain library files or macros to be used in your program, such as in the input/output library programs. The #ifdef..#else..#endif looks a bit like our familiar IF..THEN..ELSE, and, in fact, it is a conditional compilation structure. You can set up different conditions (integer size, for example) based on the type of system and even branch using the #else. Finally, the #if is another form of conditional, and the #undef is used to "undefine" a certain name. For instance, if you wanted to compile a different segment of code depending on the microprocessor of your system, you could code preprocessor if..then statements as follows:

```
#define Z80 1
#define 65C02 2
#define 8080
#define computer Z80
#if computer == Z80
      < code >
#else
#if computer == 6502
      < code >
          .
          .
      etc.
```

which would direct the compiler to use different segments of the code based on the microprocessor type.

There are also provisions in C to create enumerated (user-defined) data types and convert between types. Files, in cooperation with the UNIX or CP/M operating systems, are also available.

CONCLUSION

As you can see, C is a language with many strengths, and it is both efficient and easy to use. Its low-level capabilities and high-level structure make it useful for writing a variety of applications and systems programs.

REFERENCES—C

The popularity of C in recent years has spawned a great number of new C books. These will be grouped into beginning and advanced levels.

I. Beginning books

Programming in C, by S. Kochan. Covers the basic concepts of C. Designed for beginners, it describes all topics in great detail and provides examples. (Hayden)

C Primer Plus, by Waite et al. Another suitable book for beginners, it features a conversational style, charts and cartoons, and even a C reference card. (H. W. Sams)

Introduction to C, by P. Chirlian. A basic guide to the C language. (Matrix)

Learning to Program in C, by T. Plum. A workbook-style guide to beginning C. (Plum Hall)

Understanding C, by B. Hunter. A beginner's book to C. (Sybex)

II. Advanced books

The C Programmer's Handbook, by T. Hogan. An easy-to-use handbook reference guide to language statements. (Brady)

C Language for Programmers, by K. Pugh. A concise reference guide to programmers wishing to explore C. (Scott Foresman)

C Programming Guide, by J. Purdum. A readable guide to the C language, although not for beginners to programming. (Que)

Applied Programming Techniques in C, by T. Ward. Advanced concepts and applications in C, along with useful appendices. (Scott Foresman)

C Programming Guidelines, by T. Plum. A style standard manual for C programmers. (Plum Hall)

C: An Advanced Introduction, by N. Gehani. An advanced introduction, designed for readers with programming background. (Computer Science Press)

C Programmer's Library, by Purdum et al. A complete coverage of library functions, with both examples and guidelines. (Que)

The Small C Handbook, by J. Hendrix. User's guide to the Small-C microcomputer compiler. (Reston)

The C Puzzle Book, by A. Feuer. Contains problems to be solved using C. (Prentice-Hall)

Advanced C: Food for the Educated Palate, by N. Gehani. Designed for more advanced readers, this book covers the language, including advanced features. Includes information on exceptions, preprocessor statements, and library functions. (Computer Science Press)

CHAPTER 10

FORTH

FORTH IS ONE of the most unusual languages that you will encounter. It represents a completely new way of thinking regarding programming, and while it is tremendously popular in certain circles, in others it may be virtually unknown.

Forth "fanatics" love it for its very fast program execution, compact object code (saving memory), interactive nature, systems capabilities, and structured building-block approach to programming. Forth programs can be visualized as a pyramid of "words," with the basic "language core" words at the bottom and additional words defined on each successive level with "higher" words. In other words, executing one word may put into action countless numbers of subwords, which call other words, until execution proceeds to the lowest level, which consists entirely of core nucleus commands. This type of program structure is known as *threaded code* and results in very fast and efficient execution.

Charles Moore started developing Forth in the early 1960s, but it was not until the early 1970s that it received its name and was actually released as a programming language. Moore invented the language basically to help him become a better programmer, and during those ten years he experimented with such techniques as stacks and reverse Polish notation. Using his new language, he could increase productivity several times over FORTRAN and other languages he had been working with. He first implemented his language on an IBM 1130, which was classified as a third-generation computer. Moore felt that his new programming language was such an improvement as to be termed a fourth-generation language, but because of the computer's five-letter identifier length, "fourth" became "Forth."

Although Forth did not gain any widespread support or popularity throughout the 1970s, Moore did make his creation known. He not only started Forth Inc., which marketed Forth systems for solving scientific and industrial problems and needs, but also used Forth to control the radio telescope at the Kitt Peak National Observatory in Arizona. He also put his language in the public domain, making it available to interested users at little or no cost.

The language did take root, and before long Forth user groups had been formed, with one major group, the FIG (Forth Interest Group) growing to become an important part of the Forth world. The group also formed the Forth Implementation Team to produce FIG-Forth, a microcomputer version of Forth that could be run on many different micros. Since then several other implementations have become available for microcomputers, including PolyForth (by Forth Inc.), MMS Forth (by Miller Microcomputer Services), and MVP Forth, which is the product name for FIG-Forth and is marketed by Mountain View Press. These are just a few of the Forth implementations available.

Forth is very powerful, fast, and compact. It increases productivity, it runs as fast as assembly language, and its system takes up only a very small amount of memory space. Its speed makes it useful for real-time application, as in the example of observatory control. Finally, many large companies, including IBM, use Forth for software development.

On the negative side, Forth programs are concise and difficult to understand. In contrast to a language like COBOL or Pascal, which has English-like readable source code, Forth's short commands and symbols make it confusing to everyone except a Forth programmer. In addition, the unconventional uses of the stack and reverse Polish notation call for a complete change in programming thought and process.

Words and the Dictionary

In starting out with Forth we deal with two simple concepts, the idea of a word and that of a dictionary. From your childhood, you'll remember that words are the means of producing meaningful sentences and communication, while dictionaries serve to list all words in their correct form for referral.

In Forth the dictionary serves as both a translation and "lookup" area for your "words." "Words" could be compared to functions or procedures in other languages: they perform some function based on predefined instructions. The concepts of a word and the dictionary are best illustrated by an example:

```
:ASTERISK  42 EMIT;
```

which is a user-defined Forth word which will print an asterisk (*) to the screen. When you use the colon (:) definition, that indicates to the dictionary to store that word away for future use. In the example, 42 is the character for the asterisk character, and EMIT is another Forth word, which has already been defined in the dictionary. So, in the larger perspective, Forth programs or "words" are built up of other words of a lower level:

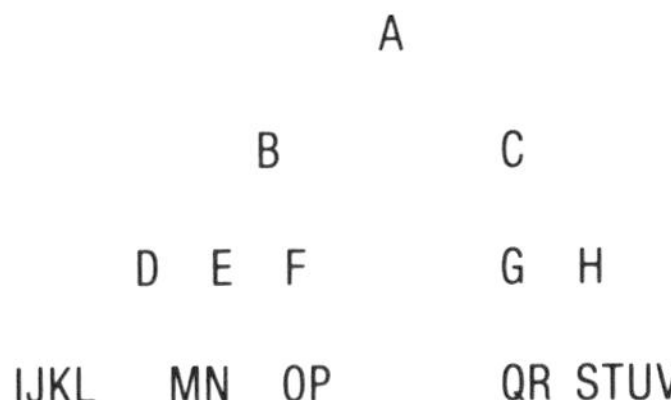

By executing the word "A" you are actually calling a number of other words, each of which is defined by means of other lower-level words. So, in essence, the word "A" is calling all the lower-level words down to the most basic I, J, K, L, M, N, O, P, Q, R, S, T, U, V words, which are predefined in the Forth language dictionary. Thus, Forth programs have a pyramid-type structure, with more powerful words being built from more basic ones.

When you use the colon definition as in the above example, you are in compilation mode, where your new definition is put into the dictionary. When you wish to execute one of your Forth words, you must enter execution mode.

In execution mode, the text interpreter (a Forth word called INTERPRET) is invoked. This word takes your definition string, separates it into substrings, and attempts to locate the word in the dictionary. If the word is found, control will pass to another Forth word called EXECUTE. The commands will then be executed as you specified. Otherwise, the interpreter will call NUMBER and attempt to use it as a number. If this last case fails, the text interpreter will return the string to your screen with a question mark. This procedure holds true for all Forth words, regardless of their level or complexity.

From the dictionary concept you will see that Forth is quite a different language from most. Not only does it handle its programs using the "word" concept, but also it does its calculations using the less familiar postfix stack notation. In the next section the concept of stacks will be covered.

Stacks in Forth

For many programmers, the concept of a stack may be a foreign concept. However, those who are familiar with data structures and computer organization will know that stacks are available in many computer languages but are normally hidden from the user. In Forth the programmer is given direct access to the power and unique operations of a stack structure.

The usual analogy for stacks is that of a pile of plates. Plates can be stacked or removed only from the top, so the entire structure can be categorized as a LIFO (last-in, first-out) data structure. In Forth, there are two stacks, the parameter stack and return stack. The parameter stack is the one usually referred to when you are programming in Forth, and the return stack is used mainly by the Forth system itself.

The two most basic operations on the stack are the *push* and the *pop*. Pushing a number onto a stack makes it the uppermost value, whereas a pop removes the top item and makes the one below the new stack the top. To push some values onto a stack, you just have to type in a sequence of numbers:

```
−35 42 37 45 6 <cr>
```

which in the stack would be arranged as follows:

```
top--  6
      45
      37
      42
     -35
```

To print the top value of the stack, all you have to do is type a dot followed by a carriage return:

```
. <cr> 6 OK
```

After you type in the dot command (period), the top value of the stack is removed and its value printed to the screen. The response "OK" is output by the Forth system and tells you that it has completed your command and all is well.

There are special commands available in Forth that affect values stores in a stack. These are DUP, DROP, SWAP, ROT, and OVER.

DUP will remove the top value from a stack, then replace the top with two copies of this element. Executing the word DUP will cause a change as follows:

```
top -->  45  16  33  14  12
top -->  45  45  16  33  14  12
```

The word "DROP" will remove the top value of the stack but not replace it with anything. The stack diagram shows this straightforward change:

```
top -->  45  16  33  14  12
top -->      16  33  14  12
```

SWAP will switch the top two elements of the stack so they are in reverse order, leaving the other elements intact:

```
top -->  45  16  33  14  12
top -->  16  45  33  14  12
```

ROT will make a more drastic change in the stack, moving the top three values. The lowest (in position) of the three will be moved to the top, while the other two will each be moved down one space:

```
top --> 45  16  33  14  12
top --> 33  45  16  14  12
```

The word OVER creates a copy of the element that is second closest to the top, then puts this value at the top of the stack:

```
top --> 45  16  33  14  12
top --> 16  45  16  33  14  12
```

These are the basic stack-manipulation commands available in Forth.

Postfix Notation

Most calculations that you would do in other languages are known as *infix operations*, in that the operator is placed between the two operands. For example:

```
5 + 5
```

In Forth stack operations, expressions must be written in postfix form, with the operator following the operands. This type is also known as *Reverse Polish Notation*, named after its Polish inventor, Jan Lukasiewicz. Some examples of postfix notation are:

Infix	*Postfix*
5 + 5	5 5 +
A * (B + C)	A B C + *
(A + B) * (C − D)	A B + C D − *

The use of postfix notation is important in Forth programming, as well as in advanced computing. Because the stack is used frequently in Forth programming, mastery of this new format is necessary. This is just one of the reasons why Forth does not adapt to the conventions of other languages.

A New Forth Word

New "words" can be defined in Forth. They are defined as a result of the programmer's using previously defined words in order to create more complex words. Therefore, Forth words could be called Forth "programs." Words are like program segments, which can be created either in an immediate (interactive) mode or through an editor. In the latter case, memory areas of 16 lines of 64 characters each (1024 bytes), called *screens*, are used for storing your edited Forth program code.

To define a new program, or Forth word, you use the colon definition character. Everything between this colon (start symbol) and the concluding semicolon (termination symbol) is part of this newly declared Forth word. To call this word, you need only type in the word name followed by any necessary operands. For example:

```
: ADDTWO 2 2 + .<cr> OK
```

will return the following:

```
ADDTWO <cr> 4 OK
```

You will notice the postfix notation for the addition, as well as the syntax for defining Forth words. This example featured both operands in the definition itself. An operand can also be input into the word:

```
:  ADDFOUR 4 + ;<cr> OK

4 ADDFOUR .<cr> 8 OK
```

Numeric Operations

Forth has several commands that are designed to handle numeric operations. These include both operator symbols and words, and they can operate on both single- and double-precision numbers. The operators available for single and double precision are listed below. Single-precision numbers are 16-bit numbers in the range of − 32768 to +32767. Double-precision numbers are twice as large (32 bit), with a range of −2147483648 to +2147483647.

Operation	*Single*	*Double*
addition	+	D+
subtraction	–	D–
multiplication	*	M*
division	/	M/
modulus	MOD	
divide modulus	/MOD	
absolute value	ABS	DABS
maximum	MAX	
minimum	MIN	

The standard arithmetic operations +,–,*, and / are familiar and need no further explanation. The MOD, or modulus function, returns the remainder after division, and the /MOD returns both the quotient and the remainder. The ABS computes the absolute value, and the MAX and MIN return the maximum and minimum values, respectively, of the top two values on the stack. With all the commands described, the result is placed at the top of the stack after completion.

Forth usually works with only single- and double-precision integer numbers using the operators defined above.

Constants and Variables

As in other languages, data can be represented as either constants or variables. *Constants* are assigned a fixed value which cannot be changed during the course of the program, whereas *variables* can be changed at will.

The declaration of constants and variables is straightforward, with the names and values of each compiled into the dictionary.

```
10 CONST HUND <cr> OK

90 VARIABLE DIG <cr> OK
```

The designation CONST or VARIABLE takes the preceding values and inserts them into an appropriate memory space instead of just putting them onto the parameter stack. You can use the values of these constants and variables very easily by simply typing the desired name. These names can also be used in expressions and Forth words.

Two other words commonly used in relation to constants and variables are FETCH and STORE. FETCH takes the top value from the stack and interprets it as an address where your data is stored. The command leaves the data at the top of the stack. The STORE word, on the other hand, places a value in memory at a specified address.

Conditionals and Loops

As in any language, the ability to make decisions in computer programs rests in a number of conditional statements. In Forth there are available the conditional structures listed below:

IF..ELSE..ENDIF	Fig-FORTH
IF..THEN or	
IF..ELSE..THEN	FORTH-79

The following comparison operators are available for making comparisons:

<	less than
>	greater than
=	equal to
0=	equal to zero
0>	greater than zero
0<	less than zero
U<	unsigned less than

Conditional statements are programmed into Forth programs much as in other languages, although, because of Forth coding structure, they may seem to be somewhat more difficult to read. A simple use of the IF..ELSE..ENDIF could be programmed as follows:

```
: .>50
 DUP
 50 >
 IF .
 ELSE DROP
 ENDIF
```

This little segment of code will test whether the top value of the stack is more than 50 by first duplicating the value, then testing it for the condition. If "true," then the value will be printed (.). Otherwise, the top value will be dropped from the stack. The other conditional variations work in much the same way.

In Forth there are two kinds of loops—DO loops and BEGIN loops. DO loops are indexed loops, which repeat a certain number of times, whereas BEGIN loops are indefinite loops which will stop only after a certain condition is satisfied. An example of a DO loop is as follows:

```
: FIVER
  5 0
  DO
   CR I .
  LOOP
;
```

In this little program, called FIVER, we want to print the numbers from 0 to 4. The second line outlines the start value (0) and the termination value (5). The computer will perform the statements between the DO and the word LOOP the number of times specified to reach 5, after which control will exit the loop. The indefinite loop structure, on the other hand, is similar to DO WHILE and DO UNTIL structures in other languages. The structure is illustrated in the following example:

```
:USEINDEF
 1
 BEGIN
    DUP 40 >
 WHILE
    CR DUP . . DUP .
    2 +
```

```
REPEAT
DROP
;
```

This example, called USEINDEF, will set the counter to 1, then set up a loop structure. The conditional test is contained between the BEGIN and WHILE, with the executable statements located between the WHILE and the REPEAT. As is clearly shown, the first loop section is the test condition (where a TRUE condition allows another looping) while the latter section is the actual loop body.

The program above will continue to loop while the counter which was initialized to 1) is smaller than 40. The action performed is a carriage return, a DUP, 2 dot commands, another DUP, and a dot command. Try this on a Forth system to see what it does!

Other looping structures include the BEGIN..UNTIL and the BEGIN..END, both of which function in a related fashion.

Input/Output

Forth, being an interactive language, has provisions for various types of input and output. There are several "words" that are specifically used for handling these kinds of operations. The three main operations are KEY, EMIT, and CR.

KEY and EMIT work with single characters, the first used for input, the second used for output. The operands used for these commands must be the ASCII code for the character desired. The CR command sends a carriage return to an output device for spacing purposes.

For working with text strings, several new commands are available. To output text to an output device such as the string, the TYPE string will print a designated string of n characters starting at a certain address. The EXPECT and QUERY commands are available for input. EXPECT will accept a designated string of characters and store them into memory, whereas QUERY will store them in an input buffer, awaiting further processing. Although these are quite easy to use, they are more complicated than the PRINT, WRITE, or PUT statements in other languages. An example of these input/output commands is shown below:

```
action: prints ASCII code of next character pressed

KEY CR DUP EMIT SPACE . ok
87        --for letter "W"
```

Other Aspects of Forth

Forth is a complex language to understand since, unlike the case with BASIC or COBOL, a knowledge of stack operations, memory, and other system details must be mastered before Forth can be used effectively.

More in-depth words and operations on the dictionary and memory are available for your use, as well as provisions for mass storage, buffers, editing, and even multitasking. Textbooks on the Forth language are now available for exploring the details and workings of this unusual, yet valuable programming language.

Forth is an important language because it has many very desirable features. It is a personalized language, since you create your own version of Forth by writing new "words." It is well suited for use on microcomputers, because of its small memory requirement, and, unlike a language like BASIC, it allows the programming of real-time and machine-level operations.

Forth does have weaknesses when it comes to data types. It doesn't support very sophisticated string or floating-point data, and it isn't suitable for use in developing very large programming projects, as is Ada or Modula-2.

CONCLUSION

Forth is a language designed for users who have progressed beyond their first steps. For a skilled programmer, it is a very effective tool, but it may be rough going for the novice. It is an important language and one that will reap rewards for users for years to come.

REFERENCES—FORTH

Invitation to Forth, by H. Katzan Jr. Although reproduced from a dot-matrix printout, this book is easy to read and a good introduction. (Petrocelli)

Starting Forth, by Leo Brodie. A delightful intro to Forth, especially with relevant cartoons, examples, and a witty style. (Prentice-Hall)

Forth Fundamentals, Volumes 1 and 2, by C. K. McCabe. The first volume is a clearly written guide to the language for beginners. Volume 2 is a handbook-reference manual. (Dilithium)

Discover Forth, by T. Hogan. A basic introduction for novices. (Osborne MGH)

11 CHAPTER

LISP

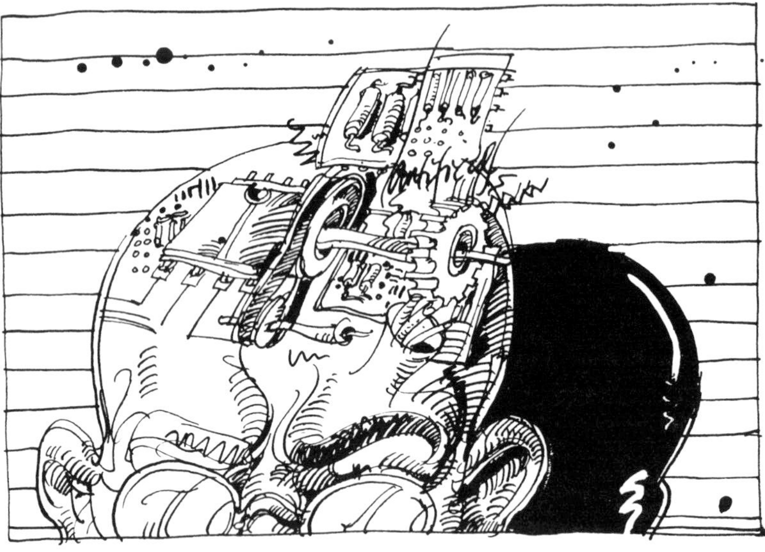

THE LANGUAGE LISP is synonymous with the field of artificial intelligence. *Artificial intelligence* is the branch of computer science in which attempts are made to design computer systems that can "think," or in other words, simulate the thought and reasoning powers of humans. Some of the fields of artificial intelligence, or "AI," as it is called, include expert systems and robotics. Lisp is useful for artificial intelligence because of its special list manipulation structure. Even with the development of new languages such as Prolog, Lisp still remains the "king" of AI languages.

Lisp, which is best known for its strings of parentheses, may at first glance seem difficult and forbidding, but to acquainted users it is both simplistic and expressive for defining data structures and recursive algorithms. Instead of dealing with data items as numbers or characters, Lisp concerns itself mainly with lists of items, such as words and numbers.

John McCarthy invented Lisp in the late 1950s, so it was one of the first computer languages. Although many of the other programming languages developed during that period are now obsolete, Lisp is still going strong. The first complete implementation of the language was created in the very early 1950s (1950–1952). McCarthy's work at MIT was in lambda calculus and the list form, and these two areas heavily influenced the development of the Lisp language.

An early version of the language, Lisp 1.5, was a greatly enhanced version of McCarthy's original Pure Lisp dialect. Over the years, quite a number of dialects of Lisp interpreters were developed, including MACLISP, FRANZ LISP, UCI LISP, TLC LISP, INTERLISP, COMMON LISP, and P-LISP. Recently, however, computer manufacturers such as Digital, Xerox, and Control Data, along with the government DARPA agency, have supported Common Lisp as the standard Lisp dialect. It is expected that the other dialects will eventually become obsolete in favor of Common Lisp.

Lisp is an interpreted language, making responses to commands immediate and interactive. The first interpreter was implemented on an IBM 704 in 1960. Since that time, Lisp has been implemented on such large systems as the IBM 370, Digital VAX, and Honeywell Multics. There are quite a few microcomputer interpreters for the IBM PC, CP/M computers, and even the Atari and Apple II series & Macintosh.

Lisp is very powerful when dealing with data structures, lists, and recursive problems. It also has a very organized structure and is an interactive language. On the negative side, Lisp looks confusing to the uninitiated. The syntax and coding format is also somewhat unusual compared with that of more standard languages.

In conclusion, Lisp is an important language for artificial intelligence programming. If you want to become involved in this challenging field, Lisp is a necessity. Following is a Lisp program that illustrates a function to calculate a Fibonacci

```
(DEFUN FIBONACCI (N)
  (COND ((= N 0) 1)
        ((= N 1) 1)
        (T (+ (FIBONACCI (- N 1) )
              (FIBONACCI (- N 2) ) ) ) ) )
```

A Lisp program that calculates a Fibonacci sequence.

sequence—such as 0,1,1,2,3,5,8,13,21,34 . . .—in which the result is the value of the next element; each next element is the sum of the preceding two.

Lisp Program Structure

Lisp programs are at first glance both organized and bewildering. Although the code appears symmetrical and ordered, the abundance of parentheses makes the novice quite confused as to how the program is arranged.

The structure of Lisp is designed to reflect the fact that the language is concerned primarily with lists. Each set of parentheses holds one list of information, whether it consists of words, numbers, or other lists. There is often nesting of lists, causing large numbers of parentheses.

Lisp is an interactive language, so you can interact with it in developing your programs. The language is interpreted, so each line in turn is inspected for errors and then translated. A Lisp program may consist of several functions, all of which start with the word DEFUN, which signals the beginning of a user-defined function. The entire Lisp language is based on functions, many of the commands built in to the language being "primitive" functions. It is difficult to illustrate a program shell for a Lisp program (since Lisp is coded in a very free format); consult the sample program to see what a complete program looks like.

Words and Lists

Most programming languages deal with numbers as their primary data type. This is not surprising, since the first computers were developed to solve mathematical problems and much of computing theory is mathematical. Languages such as BASIC, FORTRAN, APL, Forth, and machine language are concerned primarily with various calculations and manipulations of numbers and characters.

Lisp, on the other hand, works mainly with words and lists. Words are the same in Lisp as in English—groups of characters representing something of sense or nonsense. You can put a group of words into a list by writing them together, surrounded by parentheses:

```
(THIS IS A LIST) or

(VENUS SATURN URANUS PLUTO)
```

The two examples above both contain words in their lists, but what if a list contained nothing? That would be an *empty list,* which is designated by the symbol ( ) or by the designation NIL. The empty list has special properties and is important in Lisp programming. A note should be made that the smallest unit in Lisp is what is referred to as an *atom.* In the lists shown above, each word is an atom and cannot be divided further.

Symbols and Predicates

The terms *symbol* and *predicate* will occur frequently as you study Lisp. Symbols are used to represent things, whether they be names, functions, or some other identifier, as long as they are not strictly numbers. In the latter case, they are considered numeric data. Predicates are special functions that answer the question "true" or "false." For instance, the predicate ZEROP determines whether the number entered is equal to zero. If so, the result will be "T". Otherwise, the result will be "NIL". Symbols and predicates are mentioned frequently when you work with Lisp.

List and Arithmetic Functions

The names of some of the functions in Lisp may seem strange, but they go back to the days of the first Lisp interpreter. The notations used then have remained to this day.

The first two functions available are used very often in Lisp programming. They are CAR and CDR, which return parts of lists. The function CAR will return the first element of a given list, whereas CDR will return everything but the first element. You could give the two functions nicknames of "first" and "rest." These will work both on single lists (lists of words or atoms) and on lists of lists:

```
(CAR '(ACE THIS SHOT))
ACE
```

The CAR function here returns the first word of the list (ACE THIS SHOT). You will notice that the function name is itself contained within parentheses and precedes the information worked on. CAR also works on lists of lists:

```
(CAR'((JON AMY ) BILL))
(JON AMY)
```

We have two lists here, the first element being (JON AMY) while the complete list is ((JON AMY) BILL). The first list of two words is returned as the result.

The CDR function works in the opposite way from CAR, returning everything besides the first element. Therefore, in the following list:

```
(CDR '(BOZO RONALD CHUCKLES))
(RONALD CHUCKLES)
```

everything but the first element, BOZO, will be returned. The same thing applies to lists of lists:

```
(CDR '((ANDY CONNIE) ADRIENNE))
(ADRIENNE)
```

which here returns the second element of the two-element list. For lists of only one element, the result must be NIL:

```
(CDR '(A))
NIL
```

The values of CAR and CDR when they operate on NIL itself is defined to also be NIL. These two preceding functions are useful for taking apart lists. For putting lists together, there are the functions CONS, LIST, and APPEND. CONS, which is short for CONStruct, adds some item to the front of your list. For example:

```
(CONS 'A '(B C D ))
(A B C D)
```

is a simple way to add a character to the beginning of a list. If the list you are adding to is originally of value NIL, the new list will now contain the one element. The LIST function will take two different parts and put them together to form one list. The following example uses a form of LIST:

```
(LIST 'A 'B 'C)
(A B C)
```

This function will also put together three separate lists into one contained list. Before covering APPEND, you should see how

LIST works, since LIST and APPEND can be confused if this difference is not clear:

```
(LIST 'ABE '(BEN CHUCK) 'DAVE))
(ABE (BEN CHUCK) DAVE)
```

A new list is constructed of the input elements and lists. APPEND is used to make a list out of two existing lists, as in the following example:

```
(APPEND 'ABE (BEN CHUCK) 'DAVE))
(ABE BEN CHUCK DAVE)
```

The preceding functions are the primary ones used when you are dealing with lists. There are four more functions of importance when you deal with lists: LENGTH, REVERSE, SUBST, and LAST.

LENGTH returns the number of elements in a list, whether they be atoms or lists:

```
(LENGTH '(X Y Z ))
3

(LENGTH '((C D) (E F) (G H)))
3
```

REVERSE will reverse the elements of your list, regardless of the level of your list:

```
(REVERSE '(W X ))
(X W)

(REVERSE '((G H ) (I J )))
((I J ) (G H))
```

SUBSTR will replace a certain portion of a list with your indicated changes:

```
(SUBST 'G 'X '(X Y Z))
(G Y Z)
```

As you will notice, for every occurrence of X in the target list, the X should be replaced by G. The result is a new list.

Finally, we come to LAST, which will return a list containing the last element of the given list:

```
(LAST '(S T U))
(U)
```

You may have noticed in all the preceding examples that a quote preceded each of the lists or parts of lists being worked on. These marks are shorthand symbols for the function QUOTE, which serves to prevent each individual list or item from being evaluated. Without the quote, each list or item that is submitted to the Lisp interpreter would be evaluated by itself, making the use of functions difficult. Putting the apostrophe before each nonevaluated item is known as *quoting.*

Program Functions and Eval Notation

As was mentioned in the program structure section, a Lisp program consists of at least one user-defined function. Functions of this kind are characterized by the use of the DEFUN command, which stands for DEfine FUNction. Using DEFUN, you can create more complex functions through procedure abstraction (constructing new procedures by combining existing ones). By using primitive functions, you can create functions of your own. The general structure of a program function is as follows:

```
(DEFUN name (argument)
   (function lists))
```

By calling the function name followed by an appropriate argument, you will execute your newly created function. It was mentioned before that you can use primitive functions as part of your DEFUN declaration. There is a special kind of primitive function, known as the *predicate,* which always returns a true or false result. If the test value is true, LISP will return "T"; otherwise, the result will be "NIL". Some of the predicates available include:

ATOM	whether the data is an atom (or word).
LISTP	whether the data item is a list.
EQUAL	whether two items are the same.

NULL	whether the item is an empty list.
MEMBER	whether the item is a member of your list.
NUMBERP	whether the item is a number.
ZEROP	whether the item is equal to zero.
MINUSP	whether the item is negative.
EVENP	whether the item is an even number.
NOT	whether the item is NIL.
AND	whether all items are not NIL in a list.
OR	whether one item in a list is NIL.

In later sections you will see the importance of predicates, particularly when you are dealing with conditionals.

Another term that may be confusing when you read about Lisp is the reference to *eval notation.* All the examples given previously are given in eval notation, which means that all program statements are given in lists. Usually, the function name is followed by the operands.

Conditionals

One of the necessary aspects of programming is the ability to make decisions. Lisp has a set of functions, called *conditionals,* that make decisions based on the results of certain predicates. There are two forms of conditionals, the IF structure and the COND structure.

The IF structure is similar to IF..THEN structures in other languages. If there is the case where a certain condition is true, then this certain statement will be executed. As usual in Lisp programming, the statements are contained in lists. The following example is the definition for absolute value when written in a DEFUN statement:

```
(DEFUN ABS(Y)
   (IF (LESSP Y 0)  (MINUS Y) Y ))
```

This is a complete function for absolute value. If Y is less than zero, then the first condition will be executed (MINUS Y). The LESSP function determines whether the variable Y is less than zero. In the case where Y is positive or zero, the control will switch to the second function, which just returns the value of Y itself. You can also indicate the two conditions by specifying the results you desire for each condition:

```
(if t 'correct 'wrong)
```

Depending on the value of your variable, the system will return a value of either 'correct or 'wrong.

The conditionals just discussed are very simple ones. There is a more versatile form in the COND function, which can specify multiple cases for each condition:

```
(COND (condition  result)
      (condition2  result2)
      (condition3  result3)
      (T 'error ))
```

The COND is quite similar to the CASE structure in other languages, in that there are several conditions, each with a corresponding result. The use of the T (true) is like an "if all else fails" case, which will always be true if all other cases are not used.

Other Predicates and Functions

Lisp programming consists of combining functions together to form useful algorithms. There are several functions and predicates that are used frequently in Lisp and should be described.

One very important aspect of variables is *binding.* A variable that is part of a DEFUN function is unbound (has no value) before and after invocation of the function. During the time that the function is active, the variable becomes bound and takes on a value.

Many times you may wish to declare a *global variable,* which is one that has a value throughout your program. The SETQ function helps to accomplish this goal. SETQ will give values to variables outside of function calls:

```
(SETQ LETTERS '(A B C D E))
```

The variable LETTERS now has the value of the five letters indicated above and will evaluate to the value given.

The predicate BOUNDP will return T if the variable is bound and NIL if the variable is unbound. The function MAKEUNBOUND is available for those rare cases where you wish to unbind a variable.

Two other functions that are commonly used are CONSP and NCONS. The CONSP function determines whether a given list is any type of list except NIL. The NCONS function, on the other hand, enables you to make a list of the data you specify, whether it is an atom or another list:

```
(NCONS 'CONNIE)
(CONNIE)

(NCONS '(HENRY IRENE))
((HENRY IRENE))
```

Depending on your particular implementation of Lisp, you can use quite a number of primitive functions that are available in the language itself. For instance, a 512K professional version of Common Lisp for the IBM PC has several hundreds of primitive functions available.

Input/Output

Getting information into and out of a computer is known generally as input/output. The provisions for these operations are contained in the functions PRINT and READ, both of which are quite simple to use. The PRINT function simply takes the function argument and prints it to the screen:

```
(SETQ ACE 'CARD )
(PRINT ACE )
CARD
```

This is the most simple form of the function, and with more programming you can format data in whatever way you choose. The READ function works much like the command of the same name in Pascal, or the INPUT in BASIC. It asks for information interactively to be used in the program:

```
(DEFUN ASK ( )
   (PRINT 'NUMBER)
   (SETQ X(READ))
   (PRINT X ))
```

This little function prints a prompt for a number, then asks for the input "X(READ)", and finally prints out the result to the screen. These two are the most basic primitives available for input/output. Variants and other formatting functions are available—check your version of Lisp. In addition, Lisp supports the use of data files. Although file commands and programming techniques vary from system to system, in general special functions are used to write and read files. The OPEN function is used to open files for processing, whereas READ is used to obtain information from the data file. For file input, PRINT or a related function is available for writing data to files. The CLOSE command is used to close the file from processing.

Recursion

Recursion is a technique not widely known to beginning programmers, but it is extremely valuable for solving certain types of problems. *Recursion* in simple terms is a function that calls itself. Consider for a moment the problem of the factorial, often symbolized by n!. The factorial of 4 (4!) equals 4 * 3 * 2 * 1 or 24. Although this is not a very difficult problem to solve manually, when you are using the computer it is a bit more difficult.

Using recursion, you must multiply the current number by the product already accumulated to form the new product, all the way down to the terminal case. For 4!, the solution is represented as follows:

```
4!= 4 * 3!
        3!= 3 * 2!
                2! = 2 * 1!
                        1! = 1
```

In using Lisp to solve this problem, you must start with an input variable, such as N, times it by the factorial of the next lowest factorial until you reach the smallest case, which in the case of factorials is always 1. So, using recursion, you are always multiplying the current number by the result of calling the SAME function for a smaller case. The code is as follows:

```
(DEFUN FCTRL(N)
 (COND ((ZEROP N) 1)
       (T (TIMES N (FCTRL (SUB1 N ))))))
```

If the argument is 1, then the result is 1. Otherwise, the conditional structure will default to T and execute the recursive algorithm described above. Although recursion is difficult to implement in other languages, in Lisp it is quite simple.

Control Structures

Control structures are used to control something being done more than once. Some structures apply the same operation to each element of a list, whereas others concern a whole group of program statements.

Applicative operators allow you to take a function as part of your input in a new procedure. The applicative operator MAPCAR in Common Lisp will take as input both an input list and a function input. When this is executed, the input function will be applied to each element of the list. For example, consider this example:

```
< function defined previously: STAR--adds two to the number >

(mapcar 'star '(1 2 3 4))
(3 4 5 6)
```

The use of applicative operators is very useful for situations where you want to include another function in your new function. Another way to accomplish this is by writing a lambda expression. Although this method goes back to lambda calculus and the origins of Lisp, lamba expressions are simply applicative operators that have the specifics of the "visitor" function in the new function itself. For example, in an example where:

```
(mapcar '(lambda (n)(sqrt n)'(1 4 9 16 25))
(1 2 3 4 5)
```

and you wanted to find the square root of a list of numbers, the following lambda function would come in handy. The lambda expression contains the code for finding the square root of a given number, and the MAPCAR function applies it to all elements of the list.

From applicative operators we come to *iterative* or *repeat structures.* These are often called *looping structures* in other languages and are important whenever you want to do something over and over several times. The structures that will be discussed here are the PROG, LET, and DO forms.

The PROG is the most basic of the structures available and at the present time is used less frequently than the more powerful LET and DO. The general structure of the PROG as used in a function is as follows:

```
(defun newf(n)
  (prog (s)
  ( -- other statements )
  (                     )
  top-loop
  ( -- other statements )
  (                     )
  (if (zerop s) (go top-loop))))
```

This function shell has the DEFUN header, followed by the PROG statement, some other program lines, then the statement "top-loop," which indicates where control should return after each iteration is finished. The final statement of the program is a conditional statement directing execution either to terminate or to loop back to top-loop. At the end of the loop, the PROG function returns NIL, and execution ends. The special GO statement directs control to return back to the "tag" line, which in this case is top-loop.

The PROG structure is like a procedure in some languages, where a certain value is input to the program and then passed into the PROG as a local variable. In the above example, n is the argument for the entire function, but s is the local variable for the PROG structure. When you use the LET form, you can specify initial values for each of your local variables, like this:

```
(LET ((s 45) (t 96)))
```

This form, used with the PROG, is the most effective way to bind values to local variables. The final structure discussed here, DO, is a hybrid of the PROG and the DO and is therefore very useful. The general structure of a DO is as:

```
(DO ((VAR-1 value)
    ((VAR-2 value))
    ((condition) perform action)
    ( loop body )
    ( loop body ))))
```

which first allows you to define variables and initial values. Following that, there is the test condition to decide whether to go through the loop once again. Then follows the loop body, which contains the executable statements of the loop itself. Thus, the DO is the most versatile control structure, containing the best features of the PROG and the LET.

Other Features of Lisp

All the major aspects of Lisp have been covered here to give you a basic background in the language. Some of the other features available include property lists, more advanced list functions, and a host of other functions for various applications. Your interpreter system's reference manual and a textbook on Lisp programming should be consulted for more details on how to use Lisp effectively.

CONCLUSION

Despite first impressions, Lisp is an important language, whether or not you wish to become involved in artificial intelligence. The concepts of lists, functions, and recursion are very valuable if you wish to gain a greater understanding of computer science.

REFERENCES—LISP

Lisp, by Winston & Horn. A comprehensive college-level text on Lisp programming. (Addison-Wesley)

Lisp, by D. Touretsky. An easy-to-read text for nontechnical readers. (Harper & Row)

Lispcraft, by R. Wilensky. A comprehensive book combining both an introduction and a reference guide. (W. W. Norton)

Programmer's Guide to Lisp, by K. Tracton. A handbook on Lisp emphasizing applications examples. (TAB)

Lisp Programming, by I. Danicic. A concise textbook on Lisp 1.5. (Blackwell Scientific)

12 CHAPTER

LOGO

SOME PEOPLE MAY view computer languages as "dry" devices for representing mathematical formulas or keeping business records. However, with the introduction of Logo, that generalization was shattered. Here is a language that has a dual purpose—artificial intelligence research and education—both under the disguise of a friendly "turtle."

Logo, which is not an acronym but a derivation of the Greek word for "thought" or "word," is a language designed for both children and adults. A group of people, under the direction of Seymour Papert and working at Bolt, Beranek, and Newman, in 1968 started to design a language that would combine the theories of artificial intelligence with the latest learning theories of Jean Piaget. What resulted was an interactive, simple-to-use language that could teach children programming (using Turtle Graphics) and also be used to create artificial intelligence applications as in Lisp. Following the work at Bolt, Beranek, further research and development was done on Logo at the Massachusetts Institute of Technology; hence the common reference to a version of "MIT Logo."

Logo's main strength is its ease of use. With Turtlegraphics, a few simple commands can create a complex and beautiful geometric design. Very young children can be introduced to the computer using Logo, especially with the reinforcement of an immediate interactive response. On the more serious side, complex data structures, which may be difficult to use in other languages, can be created very easily (for example, lists and trees). Finally, Logo programs or "procedures" can be created via a building block approach. Different tasks can be defined as procedures, then tied together into a complete Logo software system.

Unfortunately, Logo is a specialized language that would not be suited to business applications or those requiring speed in execution. For instance, files are not well developed, in that direct reading and writing are not supported. Programming in Logo is different from that in a language like BASIC, since its emphasis is on lists and recursion.

The widest use of Logo is on microcomputers, particularly in schools. It has been recognized as a very effective tool for introducing computers to children and is available for many of the popular microcomputers.

All in all, Logo is a delightful language for graphics, for teaching, and for artificial intelligence use.

The following is a Logo program and graphics output; the graphics design uses only straight lines and 90-degree square corners, sometimes called *square spirals* or *squirals.*

```
TO SQUGRAPH :ANGLE
MAKE "SIDE 0
REPEAT 100 [FORWARD :SIDE RIGHT :ANGLE MAKE "SIDE
:SIDE + 2]
END
```

A Logo program and graphic output.

This will create different designs based on the angle input. The input was 90 since we are using square right angles. With a change in the angle, different interesting designs can be created.

Turtlegraphics

Turtlegraphics is undoubtedly the part for which Logo is most famous, allowing the user to draw geometric graphics figures without the use of coordinates. Instead, Cartesian plane degree measurements are used to direct the turtle to different parts of the screen. The name "turtle" came from past research in developing Logo; mechanical "robot turtles" were used. In the Logo language, the turtle is like a mechanical pen, which you can manipulate very easily using degree measurements and lengths. When you give the turtle the proper commands, it "draws" by leaving a "trail of ink" on the graphics screen. Unlike graphics systems in other languages, such as those using the PLOT command (which uses coordinates), the Logo turtlegraphics system is easy enough to be used by children.

The Cartesian plane system, as you may recall from your elementary school math, has 0 (or 360) facing up, with 90 facing right, 180 facing the bottom, and 270 facing toward the left. When you boot up Logo and type DRAW, the screen will clear and the turtle will appear on the screen in its "home" position. The turtle doesn't actually look like a turtle (with shell and little feet) but looks more like a colored triangle, with its head (tip of the triangle) facing straight up (degree 0).

The commands that we will discuss in this section are all ways of controlling the turtle. After the completion of any command that you enter, the system will stop, print a question mark, and await your response. In this way, you can interact with the turtle and make it do all kinds of things.

The first four commands that we will discuss move the turtle forward and backward or turn its head left and right. The command FORWARD will move the turtle's head the number of spaces you specify, such as FORWARD 50. The step number, 50, represents a predefined distance on the screen, so you'll have to get used to the system to judge how far a certain value will go. BACK does the exact opposite of FORWARD, moving the turtle backward in a straight line. This command also needs a distance operand. In order to turn the little turtle's head, you use either LEFT or RIGHT. In either case, the number attached after it will be the number of degrees that its head will turn. For instance, at the home position, a LEFT 90 will make the heading now 270, whereas a RIGHT 90 will face you in the direction of 90 degrees.

It may often be too tedious to move the turtle around until you reach the exact spot where it should start drawing something. For this you have SETX, SETY, SETXY, and SETHEADING. When you use SETX, the turtle will move horizontally until it matches the coordinates of X that you set. You can visualize the screen as a graph, with the center called the *origin* (0,0); using SETX 10 would move the turtle from its old spot (for instance, 1,5) nine spaces to the right to (10,5). SETY will do the same, changing the Y coordinate instead of the X. To set the exact location of the turtle, you would use the SETXY, as in SETXY 5 5.

For setting the heading of the turtle's head, there is a Logo command called SETHEADING, which will point the turtle in the direction you specify. SETHEADING 90 will point the turtle directly toward the right. Adding the word TOWARDS along with another directional operand, such as SETHEADING TOWARDS 50 (−40) would point the turtle in the direction of 50,−40.

There are also ways to affect the turtle and the screen. Sometimes you will want to move to a place without leaving an ink trail. Using PENUP, you can continue to move in draw mode without drawing anything. PENDOWN will allow the turtle to draw once again. PENCOLOR will allow you to select a color to draw in, such as black, white, green, violet, orange, or blue. If a monocolor monitor is used, this will result in different intensities of white. In addition, the background can be changed depending on your needs; you simply key in BACKGROUND followed by number of the desired color.

When you enter DRAW mode, you usually are presented with a split-screen format, the top being graphics and the bottom displaying text. There are options for a full graphics screen or a strictly text screen; just enter FULLSCREEN (graphics) or TEXTSCREEN (for nondraw programming). You can also clear away everything on a graphics screen by keying in CLEARSCREEN, or send the turtle back to its starting position by using HOME.

In cases where the head of the turtle is not desired, HIDETURTLE will draw what you instruct but will "hide" the turtle from view until you give the command SHOWTURTLE (which restores it to life).

These few paragraphs have covered the basic commands of Logo's Turtlegraphics. With these simple commands, it is easy to create marvelous, intricate geometric designs! In the next section, using the REPEAT statement and procedures, we can start and create beautiful art.

Creating Procedures

With the various commands illustrated in the previous section, simple pictures can be created. However, for more complex creations, you must build different "modules" and put them together in a procedure, which will be executed at one time. In essence, a Logo *procedure* is a program in which you specify the commands necessary to carry out a certain task. These not only can be run by themselves but can be called from other procedures. For instance, a procedure called LINE can draw a line, but the procedure called STICKS, which calls LINE repeatedly, could take that simple form and create a complex drawing.

Defining a procedure is easy. When you use the keyword TO, Logo will recognize that you wish to define a procedure. The system will move into editor mode, and you can then type whatever statements you wish to be included in your procedure, followed by the keyword END. Before you can leave editor mode, you must indicate your intentions either to define that procedure or to quit and start over. Once you have defined your procedure, you can invoke it by simply typing it in command mode or by including it in another procedure. A very simple procedure which draws a box could be defined as follows:

```
TO  BOX
    FORWARD 50
    RIGHT 90
    FORWARD 50
    RIGHT 90
    FORWARD 50
    RIGHT 90
    FORWARD 50
    RIGHT 90
END
```

You may have noticed how tedious it was to repeat identical statements so many times. Wouldn't it be better if you could just say, "Do these things X times"? Well, Logo has the REPEAT command that will do just that—repeat a group of statements a given number of times. The square program above could be simplified with the use of REPEAT:

```
TO BOX
   REPEAT 4 [FORWARD 50 RIGHT 90]
END
```

Notice how the statements that were written four times before can now be written just once, if included in brackets and preceded by a REPEAT 4 (repeat the bracketed code four times). Once a procedure has been defined, it's possible to modify its structure later with Logo's built-in editor. These procedures can also be saved onto the disk and also removed, at will. So, in a sense, Logo is a not only a language but an operating system.

Program Input

One drawback to a procedure like the one listed above is its static nature. Changes to the length or turn angles can be made only through editing and redefinition. However, with inputs (likened very much to parameters in other languages), you can set up a type of "variable" which can change at every invocation. For instance, suppose you wanted to use your previous example but this time allow the user to specify the length of each side before execution. This is easily done using colon input variables:

```
TO SHAPE :LENGTH
   REPEAT [FORWARD :LENGTH RIGHT 90]
END
```

Invocation of SHAPE:

```
? SHAPE 10
? SHAPE 90
```

In this example, you indicate a variable by typing a colon before the new variable name. This is repeated again in the executable REPEAT statement. When you finally want to draw your shape, the function name must be followed by a value for the variable. When you type SHAPE 10, you get a rather small box, but with SHAPE 90 you get a giant one. The values of variables can be manipulated with arithmetic operators (+, − , * , /), such as in this procedure using REPEAT:

```
TO POLYGON :LENGTH :TIMES :ANGLE
REPEAT :TIMES [FORWARD :LENGTH RIGHT :ANGLE]
```

This procedure will draw a polygon based on the length of each side (LENGTH), the number of sides (TIMES) and the angle between each side (ANGLE). For instance, for inputs of

50,6,45, you would get a six-sided hexagon with sides of length 50. These colon variables can be manipulated using addition, subtraction, multiplication (*), and division (/). In addition, more than one input can be accepted per function, and the procedure is basically the same. Just put in two colon variables on the first line of the procedure, then use them as you did before.

Repetez s'il vous plait: Recursion and Looping

The REPEAT command is a very useful tool for doing something over and over. The only problem is that it must be the same thing each time. Suppose you wanted to draw a large geometric design with a large square framing the entire screen. As you proceed closer to the center, the squares get smaller and smaller, until you finally stop in the middle. In a sense, you are making the same procedure (square) call itself, but each time with a smaller length value. This will continue until a stop point is reached. The technique just described is known as *recursion*, an important part of Logo programming.

The simplest form of recursion would involve a procedure calling itself. Without a change in value (for drawing a figure) the turtle would just continue to draw the same thing over and over, endlessly. This isn't very interesting, but a slight modification of the starting position would create a visually intricate design:

```
TO SPIRAL :LINE :TURN
   FORWARD :LINE
   RIGHT :TURN
   SPIRAL (:LINE + 4) :TURN    --recursive line calls itself
END                              4 added to LINE each repetition.
```

Using recursion, you can use very simple procedures to create wonderfully intricate geometric graphics. The only drawback to the programs illustrated so far is in a termination point. These programs will not stop until you terminate them manually. Wouldn't it be good if the procedure would know when to quit? Fortunately, there is STOP command in Logo, which is an easy way to direct the recursive procedure to stop executing. The code for a binary tree, using the stop command is shown below:

```
TO BINTREE :SIZE
     IF :SIZE < 5 STOP
     RIGHT 45
     FORWARD :SIZE
     TREE :SIZE * .75
     BACK :SIZE
     LEFT 90
     FORWARD :SIZE
     TREE :SIZE * .75
     BACK :SIZE
     RIGHT 45
END
```

This program draws a binary tree. The tree will draw two V-shaped branches pointing upward at 45-degree angles, after which a recursive call (TREE calls TREE) will draw another tree at the tip of the previous tree, except that this one is 25 percent smaller. The size of the new tree branches will decrease each time until SIZE is smaller than five. Although this is not the most graceful recursive example, it does show recursion in Logo and the use of the STOP command.

What about loops? Logo does have loops; however, the structure is rather simple compared with that of other languages. An example of a loop is shown below:

```
TO LOOP :LENGTH
   A:
   FORWARD :LENGTH
   RIGHT 90
   (:LENGTH + 5)
   IF :LENGTH = 75 STOP
   GO "A
END
```

The beginning of the loop is indicated by A:, and the end by GO "A. Notice that the beginning uses the name and a colon, and the GO command is followed by a quote and the name. In this example, you would input a length, which would be incremented by 5 each time around. The GO command directs the control to the A:. Whenever the length reaches 75, the procedure will STOP and terminate.

Sprites

Some versions of Logo offer a graphics feature known as the *Sprite*. Sprites are predefined objects that can be manipulated and displayed on the screen. These are very easy to use and usually include such shapes as balls, rockets, and trains. The user can change colors, set direction, speed, and heading, and even define his or her own personal Sprite images. They are not included in the basic versions of Logo and may require additional hardware to run.

Nongraphics Operations: Numbers

So far we have concentrated mainly on Turtlegraphics and how to draw, define procedures, and use recursion. Logo is also capable of manipulating numbers, lists, variables, conditionals, and even tree structures.

In general, Logo is comfortable working with real and integer numbers. With real numbers, you can perform addition, subtraction, multiplication, and division. The operators used are the standard ones (+, −, *, /), and the usual equations can be formed:

```
45 + 30
3 − 1
33 * 3
144/12
35.2 * 44.26
61.2/19.1
22.9+21.02
44.29−31.02
```

In addition, there is a limited set of built-in functions, such as COS (cosine), SIN (sine), ATAN (arctangent), and SQRT (square root). There are also provisions for scientific notation, in the usual form of mantissa, followed by E or N (positive or negative exponent) and the exponential power. A typical scientific notation figure could be: 2.465E40 or 3.1N20. Integers are also available, in much the same way as real numbers, with one notable exception for division. Since integer divisions will still return a real result, there are two commands, QUOTIENT and REMAINDER, which will produce an integer quotient along with the whole number remainder.

For games and other applications requiring the generation of random numbers, there exists the RANDOM function. The command RANDOM 6 will output a randomly chosen number from 0 to 5, which means that the lowest value could be zero, while the highest would be one below the number indicated (6).

The numeric capabilities of Logo, although simple, are useful for most problems you will encounter.

Words and Lists

In Logo, character text data are in the form of either a word or a list. Words are the more basic form, because they are put together to form lists. Although words and lists are simple concepts, they can be used to form complex trees and other advanced structures.

A *word* is what we usually know it to be—a string of characters, such as:

```
TREE   DOG   HARRY   DICK   BALL   FRIEND
```

Using the PRINT command, you can print out any word you want:

```
PRINT "HELLO
PRINT "TREE
```

and using the WORD command, you can put several words together into one:

```
PRINT WORD "HUCKLE "BERRY
```

or use the command for more than two inputs:

```
PRINT (WORD "HUCKLE "BERRY "PIE )
```

You may note the quote preceding each word and the space following "PIE. These both are required in LOGO.

While words are sequences of characters, lists are sequences of words. Several words are used to make up a list, which is usually enclosed in brackets ([]). A list can either be empty:

```
PRINT []
```

or have a number of words:

```
PRINT [PRAISE THE LORD]
```

The SENTENCE command will take several words and assemble them into lists. This is useful when you want to put together a number of separate textual items. For example:

```
PRINT SENTENCE "HAPPY "DAY
HAPPY DAY

PRINT SENTENCE [HOLY] [DAY]
HOLY DAY

PRINT SENTENCE [COLD] "DAY
COLD DAY

PRINT SENTENCE "HOT [DAY]
HOT DAY

PRINT (SENTENCE [TODAY] [IS] [A GOOD DAY])
TODAY IS A GOOD DAY
```

There are several functions that can be used with words and lists. For words, FIRST will output the first element of the output word, whereas LAST just does the opposite. BUTFIRST and BUTLAST will return everything except the first and last characters, respectively.

```
PRINT FIRST "SPECIAL
S

PRINT LAST "SPECIAL
L

PRINT BUTFIRST "SPECIAL
PECIAL

PRINT BUTLAST "SPECIAL
SPECIA
```

For lists, the functions FIRST, LAST, BUTFIRST, and BUTLAST work in the exact same way as for words, but in this case words will be output instead of characters. For example:

```
PRINT FIRST [ACE DEUCE KING]
ACE

PRINT LAST [ACE DEUCE KING]
KING

PRINT BUTFIRST [AX DOG BIRD]
DOG BIRD

PRINT BUTLAST [AX DOG BIRD]
AX DOG
```

Variables and Names

In other languages you are allowed to define variables and assign values to them. In Logo you can do this as well, using MAKE, the colon (:), and THING. These commands (or *primitives*, as they are also called) help you set up and retrieve values from a variable.

The MAKE command requires two inputs, the name of the variable and its initial value. To create variable LUNCH with the value "PIZZA, just type in the following:

```
MAKE "LUNCH "PIZZA
```

which will store "PIZZA in the variable "LUNCH. Although you have put the value "PIZZA in "LUNCH, perhaps you might want to check and make sure it's there. Along with the PRINT command, you now must use the "dots" command to find out the value of the variable:

```
PRINT :LUNCH
```

The command line above is pronounced "print dots-lunch" and will output the value in LUNCH. An alternate form of this, used whenever the colon is inconvenient, is the THING command. If you write:

```
PRINT THING "LUNCH
```

you will receive the value stored in "LUNCH. You can see that using the colon and using THING produce identical results.

Outputs

Logo offers the OUTPUT command (or primitive), which can print figures and messages that are not a result of some formula. Earlier, you could elicit a response from a function such as:

```
SQRT 144
12
```

which is a very simple procedure to print. However, for a more complicated formula, such as the factorial, the need for OUTPUT is clear, since it will evaluate an equation and return the result:

```
TO FACTORIAL :N
   IF :N = 1 OUTPUT 1
   OUTPUT :N * FACTORIAL :N–1
END
```

In this factorial example you would enter the number to be output. If the number is 1 (1 !) the procedure would output a 1. Otherwise, the procedure would perform a recursive call (N * (N − 1) !) and then output the final answer. In either case, the OUTPUT command prints out the desired result.

Conditionals

In Logo, just as in other languages, it's necessary to make decisions based on some condition. Logo offers the IF..THEN.. ELSE, TEST..IFTRUE..IFFALSE, ALLOF, ANYOF, and predicates.

The IF..THEN functions in the standard way, allowing choices to be made based on the IF condition:

```
IF :C = 0 PRINT [:C EQUAL TO ZERO] ELSE PRINT [:C IS NON ZERO]
```

If C equals zero, the output will be either the equal to zero or nonzero message. A variant of the IF..THEN is the TEST ..IFTRUE..IFFALSE structure, which performs a similar function:

```
TEST :C = 0
IFTRUE PRINT [:C EQUAL TO ZERO]
IFFALSE PRINT [:C IS NON ZERO]
```

Two Logo structures similar to the Boolean AND or OR are the ALLOF and ANYOF commands. The ALLOF performs the imperative command only if all conditions are true, and ANYOF if at least one is true. These both require a minimum of two expressions to be used:

```
IF ALLOF ( :N > 5 ) ( :N < 25 ) PRINT :N
IF ANYOF ( :N < 0 ) ( :N > 0 ) PRINT :N
```

Predicates are primitives that return the truth or falsity of a condition:

```
PRINT 5 > 0
TRUE
```

Predicates will return either a "TRUE" or "FALSE" result. In the above example, you get the result TRUE since 5 is indeed larger than 0. Some other predicates include NUMBER?, WORD?, LIST?, and THING?, which in each case will answer true if the data item in question is a number, word, list, or a variable with an assigned value.

CONCLUSION

We have presented the major parts of Logo—a language suited both for children exploring computers and for list-processing-type problems. The capabilities of Logo include much more than just the Turtle and graphics designs.

REFERENCES—LOGO

Logo for the Apple II, by H. Abelson. Comprehensive guide to Logo on the Apple. (Byte/MGH)

Turtlesteps, by P. Sharp. A colorful illustrated guide to Terrapin & Apple Logo. (Brady)

Explorer's Guide to Logo for the Apple 2, by Webb et al. A tutorial workbook for Logo. (Hayden)

Apple Logo, by Bailey et al. Hands-on guide to Apple Logo graphics. (Brady)

88 Apple Logo Programs, by M. Waite & Waite Group. Complete Apple Logo programs for fun and learning. Includes output (H.W. Sams)

Programming Apple Logo, by D. Thornburg. A guide to Logo; includes a full-color insert. (Addison-Wesley)
Apple Logo: A Complete Illustrated Handbook, by D. Berentes. A tutorial and handbook. (TAB)
Logo: An Introduction, by Burnett. A very basic children's workbook. (Creative Computing)

CHAPTER 13

MODULA-2

MODULA-2 IS ONE of the newest languages to appear in the computer community and is currently receiving a lot of attention. A descendent of the popular programming language Pascal, Modula-2 has a structure and form that resemble those of its parent, with several important differences. These differences separate the teaching language Pascal from the software development language Modula-2.

The name Modula-2 refers to the language's most significant feature, the module. Using both modules, low-level facilities, the process, and procedure types, it is possible to write major programs and those of a systems programming nature (compilers, operating systems, for example). Although much of the syntax may resemble that of Pascal, this language's new methods of organizing programs into modular units makes it more powerful and versatile than Pascal. Incidentally, the name Modula-2 is an acronym for MODUlar LAnguage-2.

Niklaus Wirth, the inventor of Pascal, experimented with the concept of a modular language when he created Modula,

Modula-2's direct predecessor. However, it was not suitable for widespread use, so he further developed and refined it until he created what we now call Modula-2. It was first implemented on a computer in 1979 and was released to the public in 1981. Since that time a good number of microcomputer implementations have been developed.

The most significant strengths of Modula-2 lie in the areas of modules, separate compilation, module libraries, low-level machine facilities, the process, and procedure variables.

In comparing Modula-2 to Pascal, you should be aware that whereas Pascal was designed as a teaching language, Modula-2 was intended for the professional software developer. The rigid structure of Pascal's declarations and structure is appropriate for those learning programming, while separate compilation and modules are useful features for more advanced users.

Since Modula-2 is so similar to Pascal, with the exception of certain special features and details, the emphasis of this chapter will be on the features that distinguish it from Pascal and similar languages. Although a study of Pascal is suggested before you approach Modula-2, this chapter will not assume any previous knowledge of the Pascal language.

Modula-2's strengths lie in its abilities for producing professional, system-oriented software. Although Pascal was good for students and for general programming needs, it required that all declarations be put together in the same place and that the program always be compiled as a whole. In addition it was difficult to interface machine-level operations, making systems programming difficult. Modula-2 addresses these problems and is very effective for systems development.

The special features of Modula-2 add a degree of complexity to programs, so the language is not suited for beginners. Beginning programmers might be advised to learn the more straightforward Pascal language before attempting Modula-2. In addition, the young age of the language is one reason why there is only a limited amount of information available for prospective users compared with Pascal.

In summary, Modula-2 is designed for a systems-oriented programmer who needs to develop major software projects. Although it is quite new, its popularity and increasing availability make it an important language to learn. In the future, it may be used on a large scale for different programming tasks. There are compilers available for such systems as the Apple II series, the IBM PC, CP/M, and the Apple Macintosh.

MODULA-2'S SPECIAL FEATURES

The Module

The module is the most important feature of Modula-2, because it is the basis of the language's structure. The module allows you both to separate visibility from existence and to control the visibility of objects (such as a procedure). In Pascal, all objects (such as procedures and variables) are programmed in block form, meaning that they can be used only within that procedure. Using the module, however, you can specify which variables and procedures can be used in a certain place in your program.

For instance, consider the example below, which works with variables both inside a program and in a procedure (Pascal):

```
PROGRAM outer(input, output);
VAR number1, number2: INTEGER;

PROCEDURE inner(number1:INTEGER);

BEGIN
  writeln(number1 * number2);
  number2 := number1;
END; /* inner */

BEGIN
inner;
END; /* outer */
```

This Pascal program, which contains the procedure "inner," is a potential source of problems. The procedure alters a value in the outer procedure (number2) although the number was not passed into the "inner" procedure. This situation is known as a *side effect* and should be avoided when programming. In addition, if number2 was not declared in "inner" by mistake, an error would be caused that is difficult to trace when you are debugging.

In Modula-2 the module helps you to avoid these problems by requiring you to identify what goes in and out of a module.

It is possible to declare a variable that can retain its value even after several procedure calls but that can be used only in the places that you specify. The following example should help to clarify the module concept:

```
PROCEDURE MATH;
 VAR a,b,c: INTEGER;

 MODULE MODL;
  IMPORT a,b;
  EXPORT c,PR;
  VAR a,b,g;

  PROCEDURE PR;
  BEGIN
   a := a + 5;
   c := a;
  END PR;

 END MODL;

END MATH;
```

The above example shows how the module controls the visibility of objects within the procedure MATH. The module does not really do anything except control visibility using IMPORT and EXPORT lists. Unlike a procedure or function, the module merely keeps track of what can be used by what and where; it does not execute anything. In the example above, the outer procedure MATH has three available variables a, b, and c. The module MODL controls the variables and procedures contained within this outer procedure. The IMPORT list specifies those variables that can be used within MODL, which in this case is (a,b). The EXPORT list, on the other hand, specifies what can be accessed from outside the module, as in the math module. MATH can use or "see" only the variable c and the procedure PR.

Modules contained in Modula-2 programs are not called as procedures are; rather, a module is executed automatically when its related enclosing procedure is called. A module can have in addition to its other statements a module body, which can contain executable statements. This body serves to initialize the module's variables and will begin to execute only before any of the modules themselves have been called.

Imported and exported identifiers can be given the "qualified" designation. These are used in situations where two modules are exporting identifiers with the same name. In this case, to prevent confusion and errors, the identifier can be qualified by your prefixing the module name before the identifier, as in:

```
MATH.MODL

SAMP.MODL
```

The concept of modules helps to divide a program into segments, each with its set of IMPORTed and EXPORTed procedures and variables.

Separate Compilation

In Pascal a complete program, regardless of its length, must be compiled as a single unit. Although this poses no problem for short programs, for longer ones it prevents a large project from being worked on by a programming team. Modula-2 is an improvement over Pascal in this regard, since modules can be developed and compiled separately.

Separately compiled modules have two main parts, a definition module and implementation module. The *definition module* specifies the objects to be exported from the module, and the *implementation module* specifies all the details of implementing each of the objects previously specified. This structure bears some resemblance to that of the Ada language's package. Each section, whether definition or implementation, is called a *compilation unit*, since it can be compiled separately. A separately compiled module can be used from a program by means of an import list. Modula-2's library is one example of a separately compiled module, as shown below:

```
MODULE Midtem;

    FROM library IMPORT writestring, writeint, writeln;

    (rest of module)

END midtem;
```

The ability to compile modules separately is an important aspect of programming in Modula-2. Before proceeding further, it is necessary to clarify the different uses of "module" in the language. The general description of modules covered the structure and other details of how modules work. Modules can be put together into one program and compiled together, or various sections can be compiled separately. *Program modules* are individual units that are executable programs in themselves, but several of these can be combined together to form a complete "program." *Utility modules* are stored in a module library for your use, such as for input/output, storage management, and arithmetic functions. These functions are not part of the Modula-2 language itself and must be imported into the program.

Low-Level Features

One limitation of Pascal lies in its inability to control systems-level operations. It would be very difficult to create a systems software package in Pascal, since it was intended primarily as a teaching language. Modula-2 is much better suited to these tasks, since it includes a library module, usually called SYSTEM, which includes procedures and modules for manipulating systems-level operations. The only drawback in using these features is that it reduces portability of your program.

The system module (named SYSTEM) includes the data types WORD and ADDRESS for working with machine-level data, as well as the procedures ADR, SIZE, and TSIZE. WORD is a data type that will accept different data types as arguments, a useful capability when you want to create a general-purpose routine for different-typed data. The ADDRESS data type will allow you to do arithmetic on pointers and addresses. The ADR function will return the memory address of a variable. SIZE and TSIZE return the number of storage units assigned to a certain variable.

Coroutines/Interrupts

Although Modula-2 does have concurrent processes, they are generally known as *coroutines*. Coroutines execute quasi-concurrently, meaning that the microprocessor is time-shared; it switches from one coroutine to another by a transfer statement. Only one coroutine executes at a time.

All the facilities required for using coroutines are found in the SYSTEM module. The identifiers available in this module are PROCESS, NEWPROCESS, TRANSFER, IOTRANSFER, and LISTEN. A process variable, which is in a sense a "pointer" to the process or coroutine, is declared by use of the PROCESS data type. Using the NEWPROCESS procedure, you can create new processes for use. Coroutines are called with the TRANSFER procedure. TRANSFER suspends execution of the preceding coroutine and starts execution of the designated new process. System interrupts come into the picture with IOTRANSFER and LISTEN. IOTRANSFER is similar to TRANSFER, except when an interrupt occurs after the call, execution will abruptly return to the old coroutine. IOTRANSFER is used most frequently in conjunction with a system's peripheral devices. LISTEN is used to change the priority of an executing process in relation to interrupts.

Procedure Variables

A procedure variable is a very special data type found in Modula-2. It takes on a procedure as a value. A typical declaration of a procedure variable could be as follows:

```
VAR A,B,C : PROCEDURE (X,Y,Z);
```

Procedures used in procedure variables can either have no parameters (empty parameter list) or have parameters just like any other procedure subprogram. In cases where parameters are totally excluded, the PROC standard predefined type may be used; it simply indicates a procedure declaration without a parameter list.

GENERAL FEATURES OF MODULA-2

Program Structure

The general structure of a Modula-2 program is in the form of the module, which was described previously. With this difference, program code generally resembles that of Pascal. An example of a short Modula-2 program follows.

Data Types

The data types available in Modula-2 differ from those in Pascal. INTEGER, CARDINAL, REAL, BOOLEAN, CHAR, and BITSET are the Modula-2 data types.

Although the integer and real types are very familiar, the others need some explanation. The CARDINAL data type represents whole numbers, but only if they are nonnegative. In other words, cardinal numbers are those whole numbers from

```
MODULE GREAT;
     From InOut IMPORT ReadCard,WriteCard,WriteString WriteLn;

VAR
     a,b, : cardinal;
BEGIN
     ReadCard (a);
     ReadCard (b);
     While a # b DO
     IF a > b THEN a:= a-b
     ELSE
     b := b-a
     END
   END;
     WriteString("gcd= ");WriteCard(a,6);WriteLn;
END GREAT;
```

A Modula-2 program computes GCD (greatest common divisor)

zero on up. BOOLEAN numbers are associated with the truth values True or False. The data type CHAR refers only to characters, not character strings. Modula-2's character set corresponds to that of the ASCII code, which is listed in an appendix in the back of this book. The data type BITSET is not a single value but a set of nonnegative integers on which special set operations can be performed.

Variables, Constants, and Assignment

In Modula-2 all variables and constants must be declared before being used. Constants, because their value cannot be changed, are given a value using the name, value, and an equals sign (=). Variables must have an acceptable name and type, separated by a colon. Unlike the case with Pascal, where constants and variables must be put together in one place, in Modula-2 these declarations can be put anywhere desired, although they must be declared before being used in a program statement. The assignment operator is the same as in Pascal (:=) and serves to remind programmers of the difference between assignment and equality. You may declare comments, which are not executed, by enclosing the comment line within the symbols (* *). Some examples of variable and constant declarations, as well as assignment, are given below:

```
VAR a,b: CARDINAL;        --variables a and b are cardinal numbers

CONST g = 4.235;          --constant declaration

a := 4;                   --assign 4 to variable a
```

Math and Comparison Operators

There are quite a number of operators in Modula-2, and some are not the same as in Pascal. The operators for math and comparisons are given below, along with a brief summary of their functions:

Operator	*Function*
+	addition
−	subtraction
*	multiplication
/	division
&	logical AND
=	equals
# or <>	not equal
DIV	divide two integers; whole number result
MOD	whole number division remainder
<	less than
>	greater than
<=	less than or equal to
>=	greater than or equal to

The above operators are used in arithmetic and logical expressions. DIV and MOD can be used only on whole numbers.

Procedures and Functions

Like its predecessor Pascal, Modula-2 allows you to create both procedure and function subprograms. Procedures and functions usually have the PROCEDURE header followed by the declaration of local variables, the BEGIN statement, all executable statements, and finally the END command. The form of the procedure is as follows:

```
PROCEDURE PROC ( parameters );
 VAR     < local variables >
BEGIN
     < procedure statements >
END
END PROC;
```

There is no separate function subprogram in Modula-2, but a form of the procedure known as the *function procedure* is available. Differing from standard procedures, function procedures can be called like built-in functions, with the function name used as part of another expression. For instance, you could call a regular procedure only like this:

```
ACT(d,n);
```

but with function procedures, you could use it as part of a mathematical expression:

```
c := 55.2 + ACT(d,n)
```

Since there is no PROGRAM header as in Pascal, modules are usually the highest level, with procedures contained within them. However, procedures can be developed and compiled as separate units in Modula-2.

Input/Output

As was mentioned previously, input/output facilities are not provided as part of the Modula-2 language itself, but rather are part of library modules called InOut and RealInOut. The appropriate commands must be "imported" from these modules. The language statements available are:

Read(c)	reads in a single character, c
Write(c)	outputs a single character, c
ReadString(s)	reads in a character string, s
WriteString(s)	outputs a character string, s

```
ReadInt(i)
ReadReal(r)                reads in an integer or real number

WriteInt(i)
WriteReal(r)               outputs an integer or real number
```

You execute these commands by simply putting the appropriate arguments into the statement as in the example below:

```
WriteString("hello !");
```

Modula-2 also has file capabilities, which are system-dependent and are described in detail in the Modula-2 system reference manual.

Conditional and Control Structures

The basic conditional statement in Modula-2 is the IF..THEN structure. In addition there are the following: the IF..THEN ..ELSE and the IF..THEN..ELSEIF..THEN..END. These can all be illustrated by examples:

IF..THEN

```
IF a=4 then
   writeString("top score !");
```

IF..THEN..ELSE

```
IF gpa > 3 then
   writeString("honor roll");
else
   writeString("graduation");
```

IF..THEN..ELSEIF..THEN..END

```
IF grade <0 then
   writeString("not so hot..");
elseif grade=0 then
   writeString("still poor");
else
   writeString("you pass")
end.
```

Another form of conditional structure available in Modula-2 is the CASE structure. Here, multiple choices can each be given an alternative:

```
CASE SCORE OF
   10: WriteString ("could do better");
   20: WriteString ("okay");
   30: WriteString ("fine");
   40: WriteString ("excellent")
END;
```

This code will print a different message for each score possibility. The CASE makes it easy to specify different conditions without needing to use many IF..THEN's.

Loop control structures enable you to control the repetition of certain segments of code. In Modula-2 there are three general loop structures—the FOR, WHILE, and REPEAT. There is also a LOOP loop, which is a very primitive eternal loop. The general structure of each is as follows:

FOR

```
FOR <counter> := <start> to <end> DO
    (loop body statements)
END
```

WHILE

```
WHILE <condition> DO

     (loop body)
END
```

REPEAT

```
REPEAT

    (loop body)
UNTIL (condition);
```

LOOP loop

```
LOOP
   (loop body)
END
```

The FOR loop is a counted loop, where you set up a start value, ending value, and counter variable. Looping continues until the counter reaches the stop value. The WHILE and REPEAT loops test for the truth of a certain condition, with WHILE testing at the top and REPEAT testing at the bottom. The LOOP loop is an eternal loop with no end. Modula-2 has a very rich set of control structures.

Other Features of Modula-2

Modula-2 supports both arrays and pointer variables. These are important for use in working with data structures. Arrays are declared as variables with a certain range and basic data type:

```
VAR C: ARRAY [1..10] OF INTEGER;
```

Pointers are somewhat different from those in Pascal: they use the word POINTER instead of Pascal's ^ or up-arrow. A pointer is often used to create a dynamic linked list of data. For instance, to set up a linked list of numbers, you would have to declare a pointer type and record type:

```
Listptr = POINTER TO LNode

LNode=
 RECORD
   dig: CARDINAL;
  next: Listptr
END
```

The LNode pointer links together a number of records of type LNode. This linked list can be increased or decreased as the need arises.

A further discussion of pointers would be quite technical. You can refer to textbooks on Modula-2 and data structures for more details.

Modula-2 also has provisions for records, files, and various other functions. Many of these are found in module libraries rather than in the language itself. Check your system's reference manual for details on the modules available.

CONCLUSION

Modula-2 is a "superset" of the Pascal language, since it has features designed to counteract the shortcomings and limitations of its predecessor, Pascal. Although its advanced capabilities are suitable for experienced programmers, Pascal is still recommended for beginners to programming. After you have mastered the necessary skills, Modula-2 is the logical next step. It is a new language destined to be used by professional programmers for years to come.

REFERENCES—MODULA-2

Since Modula-2 is such a new language, there are only a limited number of books available on this language. There is a good reference book by the inventor, Niklaus Wirth, along with a few by other fine authors.

Programming in Modula-2, by Niklaus Wirth. The definitive textbook on the language, which covers in a very concise style all major aspects of the language. Written in a somewhat technical style. (Springer-Verlag)

Modula-2 from Pascal, by Richard Gleaves. Designed for programmers already familiar with Pascal and wishing to make the change to Modula-2, this concise book points out the main differences between Pascal and Modula-2. (Springer-Verlag)

Modula-2, by Paul Chirlian. A beginning textbook on Modula-2. (Dilithium)

CHAPTER 14

PILOT

THE COMPUTER HAS been given an increasingly greater role in education in the last few years, particularly with the availability of inexpensive microcomputers. Computers are used both to teach programming and to teach academic subjects. The latter is known as CAI (computer-assisted instruction).

The PILOT language, which is an acronym for Programmed Inquiry, Learning Or Teaching, was created exclusively for use in preparing CAI lessons. Although some implementations of PILOT feature fancy functions such as sound and graphics, in general the language is quite simple and ideally suited for preparing lessons.

John A. Starkweather invented PILOT in the late 1960s at the University of California in San Francisco. Since that time its use has been restricted to educational program development, since that is its main strength; it cannot be used as a general-purpose language. There are several microcomputer implementations available.

DEVELOPING A PILOT LESSON

Programming in PILOT is unlike that in other languages. Instead of typing in some lines to do some calculation or print a simple message, you must plan a "lesson" in advance. Will it be multiple choice or fill-in? What will be the right (or wrong) answers? What will be printed and what will only be sent to the screen? How will grades be computed?

These are just some of the questions that you must answer before you actually code your PILOT lesson. For our example, let's create a State Capitals lesson. There will be five questions, each worth 2 points, and each is a multiple-choice question. If the answer is correct, an appropriate banner will be printed; otherwise the correct answer will be indicated.

First consider part of the "quiz" on paper:

```
1. The capital of New Jersey is:
   a. Newark
   b. Trenton
   c. Dover
   d. Pine Brook

   Your answer is: ( student types in the answer here )

< 4 more questions to follow >
    Your score is 00.       < total score printed here >
```

The above is just a format for an educational lesson (or possibly a test). It would be quite easy to code it into PILOT, since there are just a few commands to add:

```
T:    The capital of New Jersey is
T:    a. Newark
T:    b. Trenton
T:    c. Dover
T:    d. Pine Brook
T:
TH:   The answer is:
A:
M:    b.
T:
```

```
TY:  you're correct!
CY:  #X = #X + 2
TN:  sorry, didn't you know the answer is Trenton?
<  rest of quiz >
T:   your score is #X
E:
```

The above code represents the entire lesson, with the other four questions omitted to simplify the logic involved. The first several statements, preceded by a T:, just type out the question lines exactly as you specify. These are followed by a TH:, a prompt line which asks the user for the answer. The next line, A:, waits for the student to type in the requested information.

Now, in order to make a decision, the M: command is used. If the value in the input buffer (received via A:) matches the correct answer specified by the teacher, the YES flag is set, which in this case is 'b'. If not, the NO flag is set. Depending on the value of this flag, either the correct answer or wrong answer (TY: or TN:) message would be displayed. The variable #X is set up to compute score, by incrementing the value by 1, after which we come to four more questions, and the score and end (E:).

The above program represents a typical "lesson" in PILOT. Most lesson programs are not that much more complex than this, and, as you will see, the capabilities of the language are limited to those needed in CAI.

In terms of data, PILOT deals mainly with integers and character strings. Variables need not be declared but must be prefixed by the pound sign (#) for integers and the dollar sign ($) for character strings. For example, #C is an integer variable and $AGE is a character variable.

As we saw before, input/output is accomplished via the T: command (for TYPE) and the TH: (for TYPE HANG) where the user is being prompted for information. The difference between the two is that T: issues a carriage return after typing out the information and TH: does not. The combination of the TH: and the A: (ACCEPT) is similar to the INPUT statement of BASIC, where the user is prompted for information.

The MATCH statement (M:) is the "answer key" statement, which attempts to match the student's answer to the correct reply set up by the teacher. If the result obtained through the A: (ACCEPT) matches the correct answer, then the YES flag is set; otherwise a NO flag is set. On the basis of the value of this flag, you can either TY: (type if the result is YES), TN:

(type this if the result is NO), JY: (jump to another part of the program if YES) or JN (jump to another place if NO).

As was just mentioned, JUMP statements are available in PILOT. If you assign labels to places in the program, it is possible to branch to different places:

```
JY: *BOTTOM
*BOTTOM      T: this is where it starts!
T:
T:
E:      (end)
```

The last two major command structures in PILOT are *compute statements* and *logical expressions*. These calculations can be done with the C: for compute, followed by an expression, using the standard math operators. The logical operators are equal (=), not equal (<>), greater than (>), greater than and equal to (> =), smaller than (<), smaller than and equal to (<=), not (\ ), and or (!). For example, you could specify (a>5) or (b \= 6) as logical expressions.

In situations where you wish to continue looping through questions until the student gets its right, you can use the JUMP statement to go back to a previous question. The following is a short lesson segment that does this:

```
*BEGIN T: What is the first book of the Bible?
  :
  :    a. Genesis
  :    b. Leviticus
  :    c. John
  :    d. Revelation
  :
TH:   enter a, b, or c:
A:
M: a
TY: right ! you really know your stuff!
TN: sorry ! try again....
JN: *BEGIN
T:   very good ! time for another....
J: @P
PR: < next problem begins below >
```

This little Bible quiz will pose the same question again and again until the student gets it right. Here, if the question is not correctly answered, the JN statement will branch back to the question, which has the label *BEGIN. When the question is finally answered correctly, the J:@P statement will effect a jump to the next problem, marked by the statement PR: (PROBLEM).

From these simple parts, very effective CAI programs can be developed for all types of lessons. Some forms, such as Apple PILOT, even include graphics and other features to make the lessons visually stimulating. Although PILOT is not used as much as it used to be, it still is very well suited to what it was intended for, and it is a useful programming language for preparing interactive lessons.

REFERENCES—PILOT

One book on PILOT that is designed for novices is entitled *Pilot for Beginners*, by Christopher Lampton, published by Franklin Watts, 387 Park Avenue South, New York NY 10016.

15 CHAPTER

PL/1

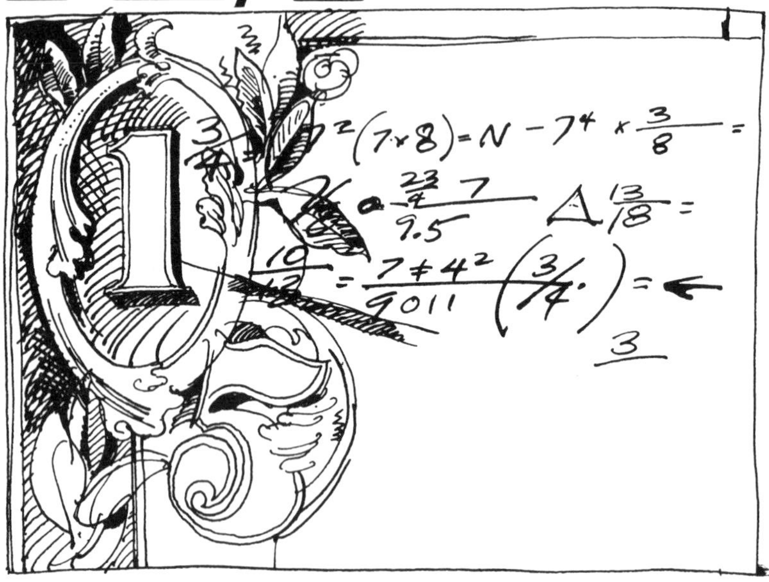

PL/1, SHORT FOR Programming Language 1, has been around since 1964. Developed through the joint efforts of a group of organizations and corporations, PL/1 combined the best features of FORTRAN and COBOL to form a "super-language," suitable for both business and scientific users. GUIDE, a business group, and SHARE, representing scientific users, got together with IBM to formulate PL/1.

What resulted was one of the largest languages ever designed. It has capabilities for dealing with a large number of data types, tables, files, structures, subroutines, functions, pointers/trees, and data processing "pictures." In fact, the full PL/1 compiler was the largest compiler ever written!

The designers of PL/1 hoped that Programming Language One would enjoy heavy use and would become accepted by a wide range of users. Unfortunately, acceptance by the computer community was less enthusiastic than was originally expected, probably because of the language's complexity, difficulty to learn, and lack of user support. COBOL and FOR-

TRAN, the two languages on which it was based, are still two of the most widely used languages today.

As was just mentioned, the language is very large and could easily take 1000 pages to describe in detail. Because of this, the discussion here will be of a general nature, omitting some of the lesser-used facilities. In addition, the language is not used often by microcomputer owners, because of the limited number of implementations available. There are only a few microcomputer PL/1 compilers on the market, the most notable being PL/1-80 (for CP/M-80) and PL/1-86 (for CP/M-86 systems). Because of memory limitations, only a subset of the PL/1 language is implemented.

The only practical way to use this language properly would be to use a mainframe compiler (such as PL/1-F, Optimizing PL/1, or PL/C) through a timesharing service. Through standard phone lines and modems, you can connect to an IBM 370 or similar mainframe and fully use the power of these full compilers. See the reference section on Timesharing for more details.

At the present time the main uses of PL/1 are in data processing and in colleges. Commercial businesses use its powerful numerical and character-handling capabilities for data processing, while colleges favor it because of its structured form and dual business and scientific nature. The PL/C compiler, developed at Cornell University, is a widely used implementation for students.

The main advantage of PL/1 is its power and versatility. There is so much that can be done using the language, from accounting and inventory packages to solving calculus and differential equations. What's more, it's extremely clear and easy to understand.

PL/1's drawbacks for the micro user are in availability and complexity. First, it would be difficult to obtain an implementation for your computer unless you had a large memory capacity and a special operating system (such as CP/M or UNIX). Also, timesharing costs on professional services can become expensive very quickly. Finally, there aren't many user or support groups for microcomputer PL/1.

Although starting out with PL/1 is easy, to become a competent PL/1 programmer might take years. However, despite these criticisms, PL/1 remains an important language that is worthwhile to learn and use.

```
LARGEST:   PROCEDURE OPTIONS (MAIN);
           DECLARE
             VAL FIXED (5,0),
             LARG FIXED (5,0);

           FLAG=0;
           ON ENDFILE(SYSIN) FLAG = 1;
           GET LIST (VAL);
           LARG = VAL;
           GET LIST (VAL);
COMPARE:   DO WHILE(FLAG = 0);
           IF VAL > LARG THEN
                LARG = VAL;
           GET LIST(VAL);
           END COMPARE;

           PUT DATA (LARG);
           END LARGEST;
```

A PL/1 program that finds the largest value among a set of data

Program Structure

PL/1's program structure is a very free one, allowing you a lot of choice in how to organize your code. Besides the line stating the beginning of the main routine (and program) written as PROCEDURE OPTIONS (MAIN) and its corresponding END statement, there is a great amount of flexibility for the rest of your text. Columnwise, there are no restrictions, so your statements can start in any column except 1 (which is reserved for systems directions). All procedures must be contained inside the main procedure, and usually subprograms are maintained as a separate entity, with a corresponding title header and END statement. Comments are contained inside the symbols /* */. The basic structure of a PL/1 program is as follows:

```
/* PL/1 PROGRAM SHELL */

NAME: PROCEDURE OPTIONS (MAIN);

        {DECLARATIONS}

        {STATEMENTS OR PROCEDURE}

PROC:   {PROCEDURE}
        END PROC;
PROC2:  {PROCEDURE}
        END PROC2;

        END NAME; /* END OF PROGRAM */
```

Data Types

PL/1's data types are complex in that there are subtle variations in each one; to use them effectively, you must choose the right one. While a simpler language might have FIXED, FLOAT, and CHARACTER, PL/1 has FIXED DECIMAL, FIXED BINARY, FLOAT DECIMAL, FLOAT BINARY, BIT, and CHARACTER. Each of these is best used in a certain capacity. Fixed decimal is usually used by commercial programmers, since it is the best form for monetary figure calculations. Fixed binary is used whenever faster speed is required for a calculation. Floating point numbers are best used where the number is very large or small and is difficult to represent with fixed numbers. Floating point decimal is used by scientific programmers and usually has 16 decimal digits precision maximum. Float Binary is used mainly where control of the precision bits is desired. Bit strings are simply strings of binary digits used for calculations or for keeping track of certain conditionals. Character is for single characters and data strings.

Variables and Assignment

In PL/1 you can define a variable name of up to 31 characters. The first one must be a letter, and after that they can be numbers, alphabet, or special characters ($,@, #, _). As you can see, it is very easy to form useful and descriptive variable names. The use of the underscore makes it much easier to read as well. Instead of taxrate, or txrte, you can declare it as tax_rate. All variables must be declared somewhere in the program, preferably at the beginning. Each name is followed by its type and the number of character lengths of a maximum value. Many variables can be declared together in one DECLARE statement:

```
DECLARE
    AMOUNT          FIXED(5,2),
    TAX_CODE        FIXED(5,2),
    FILE#           CHAR(4),
    YES             BIT(1);
```

PL/1 uses the equals sign (=) both for assignment and for equality. However, assignment concerns the transfer of a value into a variable, whereas equality is used basically in conditional statements. For example:

```
IF HIS_RATE = MAIN_RATE THEN .....          --equality

RATE = 4 ;
```

Math Operators and Comparisons

In general, the standard computer-math symbols are used, along with a few unusual ones such as NOT (¬) and OR (||). Here are some examples:

X + Y	addition
X − Y	subtraction
X * Y	multiplication
X / Y	division
X = Y	equality
X¬ = Y	not equal
X < Y	smaller than
X <= Y	smaller than or equal to
X > Y	larger than
X >= Y	larger than or equal to

X & Y	and
X || Y	or
¬X	not X

Built-In and User Functions

There are many functions available for use, depending on the particular system and compiler you are using. It would be impossible to list all the possible functions here, but here are a few of the most commonly used ones. The parameter variable (x) and parentheses are for ease of reading.

Function	*Function result*
ACOS	arc cosine
ASIN	arc sine
ATAN	inverse arctangent
COS	cosine in radians
COSD	cosine in degrees
EXP	exponential
LOG	logarithm (Base e)
LOG10	logarithm (Base 10)
LOG2	logarithm (Base 2)
SIN	sine in radians
SIND	sine in degrees
SQRT	square root
TAN	tangent in radians
TAND	tangent in degrees
MOD	returns the remainder of an argument

See your compiler's reference manual for a complete list of the PL/1 functions available.

Input/Output

There are two primary levels of input/output in PL/1: list and edit. The simpler form, LIST, does not allow any kind of formatting in the output. The basic forms, PUT LIST and GET LIST, print out information and read from a data list, respectively. Some of the variations are listed below:

PUT LIST	prints data on the next field available
PUT SKIP LIST	skips a line and prints at left

PUT PAGE LIST	goes to top of next page
GET LIST	gets data from data input
GET SKIP LIST	starts reading on a new line

The above LIST statements will take the information from input data without reference to columns. Output will also be printed in accordance with the default specifications preset by the LIST specification. However, many times there is a need to take information from certain columns only, and that is where the PUT EDIT and GET EDIT come in.

GET EDIT will take variable values from the input data based on what is contained in certain columns. For instance, you can assign the first five columns to variable NAME (alphanumeric) and the following three to an integer variable called AGE. The PL/1 code would look like:

```
GET EDIT (NAME,AGE) (X(5),A(5));
```

while the corresponding data lines may look like one of the following:

```
JAMES014
TIM  005
BILL 105
TANYA085
RONNY078
```

The use of PUT EDIT helps overcome the problem of output formatting. While PUT LIST statements will use a default location and length for your output, using PUT EDIT will allow total control over the appearance of your printed output. The appearance of the PUT EDIT syntax is very similar to that of the corresponding GET EDIT statement:

```
PUT EDIT (NAME,AGE) (A(5),F(3,0));
RONNY078
```

Although coding the PUT EDIT and GET EDIT is more time-consuming than their LIST counterparts, the potential for useful, formatted output makes it suitable for tables and charts, where format is crucial.

Conditionals

The conditions available in PL/1 include not only the familiar IF..THEN..ELSE but the IF..THEN..DO and a powerful CASE structure called SELECT.

For simple conditional structures, such as IF..THEN or IF..THEN..ELSE, it is necessary only to code these in the usual way:

```
IF (A=0) THEN
    PUT SKIP LIST ('A IS ZERO');
ELSE
    PUT SKIP LIST ('A IS NONZERO');
```

You can see that you must put a semicolon after each operational statement (the put skip list) but leave the conditional lines alone. In actuality you have above two statement lines, one for the IF and one for the ELSE. What about instances where you want to perform many commands for the IF..THEN or ELSE? Here, you must use DO groups, each of which corresponds to one of your conditional statements:

```
IF A=C
THEN
    DO;
        A=A-1;
        C=C+1;
    END; /* OF DO GROUP */
ELSE
    DO;
      A=A+3;
      C=C+19;
    END; /* OF SECOND DO GROUP—ELSE */
```

What if you have 36 different conditions? A string of IF..THENs would be tedious and unnecessary. Instead, PL/1's case structure known as the SELECT would be the best choice:

```
SELECT(WRITE_LETTER);
     WHEN (W) CALL WDPROCESS;
     WHEN (P) CALL PRINTLET;
     WHEN (E) CALL ENVELOPE;
END;
```

A letter-writing example is used here to illustrate SELECT. You could type 'W', 'P', or 'E' to perform a certain function of the program. In each case, a certain keypress would call a procedure indicated, making multiple conditions easy and straightforward. Unfortunately, SELECT is available only on certain PL/1 compilers.

Procedures

One of the strongest points of PL/1 is that it is an organized, structured language. The PL/1 PROCEDURE is an important factor in maintaining structure in a program of any size.

Procedures require two basic parts: a calling statement and the procedure subprogram itself. The calling statement, located in the main program, brings control to the procedure and remains there until execution is completed, after which there will be an automatic return to the main program.

```
CALL ADD(A,B,C);
```

In this line you are CALLing the procedure ADD and listing which variables are to be brought into your procedure. These values passed from the main program to the procedure are known as *arguments*.

The *procedure body*, located inside the main procedure, contains all the parts necessary to qualify it as an independent module—a header, variable declarations, and program statements terminated by an END:

```
ADD:        PROCEDURE (X,Y,Z) RETURNS FIXED(5,0);
            DECLARE (X,Y,Z) FIXED(5,0);
            SUM = X + Y + Z;
            RETURN(SUM);
            END ADD;
```

This procedure adds three numbers, which is the procedure called by the preceding CALL. First, let's examine the header line. Besides the procedure name (indicated by the label) we have the parameters X, Y, and Z. What relation do they have to the arguments indicated in the calling statement? A very close one, even though their names don't seem anywhere familiar. You use arguments to pass information into the procedure, and parameters to accept this information in as local variables. So, you can see that A corresponds to X, B to Y, and C to Z. Although A, B, and C are no longer used in ADD, they are still in memory and can be used, since they are global variables. X,

Y, and Z, on the other hand, are local to the procedure in which they are declared. In other words, while you use these in ADD without difficulty, you can't use them anywhere else. The differentiation between local and global variables is important when you are using procedures, since new and old values need to be kept separate. The variable SUM is returned back to the main procedure, so ADD could also be classified as a function procedure.

In our example procedure, we take the three values, accept them in parameters, declare them, then find their sum. The procedure is now complete, and control will return to the main program. Variables, constants, and expressions can be used as arguments in calling statements. When you are writing any programs, it is wise to break up the task into manageable smaller pieces, each of which can be implemented in a procedure.

There is no separate function subprogram in PL/1, but you can define a procedure that simulates a function. Several parameters are passed into the "function" procedure, after which one value will be returned. The difference between a standard procedure and a function procedure is in the RETURN statement. RETURN terminates the function and sends one value back to the main procedure. The different parts of the function are as follows:

```
A: ADDER(A,B);                            --calling statement

ADDER:      PROCEDURE(A,B);               --procedure header
            RETURN(A+B);                  --returns the sum back
            END CALC;                     --end of function procedure
```

String Handling

In PL/1 it is possible to work with both single characters and character strings. In the input/output section, we mentioned using both LIST and EDIT to output character information.

Before you can use a character string, it must be declared. Just like numeric information, it can be declared with the DECLARE statement:

```
DECLARE (SHORT) CHARACTER(80) VARYING;
```

or

```
DECLARE (LONG) CHARACTER(80);
```

The two DECLARE statements above are identical except for the variable name and the VARIABLE attribute. The first case would accept character strings of up to length 80. Shorter strings would be taken in their entirety, while longer ones would be cut short. Without the VARYING attribute, the string is taken to be of a fixed length. Shorter strings assigned to LONG would still be of length 80, with the remainder padded by blanks.

For working with strings, several built-in functions are available. The first, comparison, enables the determination of whether a given string is larger than another, based on its numerical character values. For instance, SON is considered less than SUN because of the O before U, and SUN is less than SUNLIGHT because of the lesser number of characters. Another handy function is LENGTH. This will return the length of a certain character string.

The three other widely used functions/operators for strings are concatenation (||), INDEX, and SUBSTR. The first will put two strings together exactly as you specify, and the second will find a certain string segment in a larger string. The SUBSTR function will take a specified substring from a base string.

The INDEX function can be used in the following way:

```
A='HELLO THERE'

B=INDEX(A,'THERE');
```

The INDEX function takes the target string, A, and attempts to find the beginning of the string patterns 'THERE'. If this is found, the computer will return the character location of where the pattern begins. In this example, the location is 7 (don't forget the space).

SUBSTR does the opposite of INDEX. Here you attempt to "extract" a certain string from another. Let's take 'GEORG' out of the following string:

```
S='SEE GEORGE RUN';

A=SUBSTR(S,5,5);
```

The SUBSTR function has three parameters—the target string, the start character position, and the number of characters your substring is to have. In this case, you take string S, start at character #5., and take only 5 characters. If the last parameter were omitted, everything after the start position would be taken ('GEORGE RUN'). As is shown here, it is easy to manipulate strings in PL/1.

Arrays

Arrays are very useful ways of storing a large number of generally similar data (integers, real numbers, etc.). PL/1's arrays, although powerful, are quite easy to use. Arrays can be created of integers, characters, and most other built-in types. More complicated types, such as structures, can also be used to form an array.

Arrays are declared just as regular variables are, except that after each variable name there must be a dimension number, showing how many elements are to be contained in a given array. If such a declaration were to include the INITIAL statement, then this array could be initialized:

```
DECLARE J(50) FIXED INITIAL(0);
```

This would declare an array of length 50, of which each element would contain a fixed integer. The first element would be initialized to zero. With arrays of more than one dimension the procedure is the same, except that each subscript must contain two values. To use an array, simply use the variable name J followed by the appropriate subscript (which can be a constant, variable, or expression).

```
J(35)=10;

J(I)=10          if subscript variable I equals 35

J(I+N)=10        if I + N equals 35
```

Structures

PL/1 doesn't have a RECORD structure but has a similar feature known as the STRUCTURE. Unlike the arrays just discussed, structures can hold information of varying types and still be known collectively by a specified name. Suppose you wanted to create a computer membership "card file" using PL/1. You can do this simply by making a declaration (under DECLARE) of the following:

```
DECLARE
   1    MEMBER,
          2  NAME CHARACTER(20),
          2  NO FIXED(5,0),
          2  DUES FIXED(5,2),
          2  ADDRESS,
             3  STREET   CHARACTER(60),
             3  CITY     CHARACTER(10),
             3  STATE    CHARACTER(2),
             3  ZIP      CHARACTER(5),
          2  AGE   FIXED(3,0);
```

You have declared the structure name, MEMBER, followed by a 20-character name, 5-digit membership number, a 5-digit (with 2 decimal place) dues amount, address, and 3-digit age. The address is a "minor structure" of MEMBER and contains the fields STREET, CITY, STATE, and ZIP, all character variables. Structures can contain numeric/character items by themselves or in arrays.

Use "dot notation" to assign values to structure variables. In other words, you must indicate both the structure name and variables, separated by a period or "dot." You could access a couple of variables defined above as follows:

```
MEMBER.NO

MEMBER.DUES

MEMBER.ADDRESS.CITY
```

The last example reaches down into the address substructure to access the city variable. It is also possible to assign one structure to another, as long as the types and fields are totally compatible, such as:

```
A = F;
```

Both A and F must have the exact same structure, except for the variable names themselves. It is also possible to move data in parts of one structure into another. Doing this, known as ASSIGNMENT BY NAME, allows movement of data as long as corresponding field variable names are identical, and often only a part of a structure is moved.

Files

PL/1 allows you to store information for future retrieval and use. Since most PL/1 compilers are on mainframe computers, you need to understand disk and tape storage before you can use files effectively. Most textbooks contain a detailed coverage of opening, closing, and other functions, as well as the techniques for indexed and sequential access files. You can consult one of these for file processing techniques.

Pictures

Anyone even vaguely familiar with the COBOL language would recognize the "picture" clause for specifying data formats. Instead of a general data format, such as FIXED(5,2) meaning five digits with two to the right of the decimal point, you can specify:

Decimal digits	9
Assumed decimal point	V
Sign of the variable	S
Zero suppressed when zero	Z
Decimal point	.
Commas	,
Blanks	B
Slash	/
Dollar sign	$
Asterisk fill (safety)	*
Credit (printed when value is negative)	CR
Debit (printed when value is negative)	DB
Alphabetic data	A

Any character	X
Any numeric digit	9

These work in the same way as COBOL's picture clauses.

With these specifiers, you can build little "picture clauses" to specify exactly what kind of information you want for a single data item, array, or structure. Here are some examples of picture clauses:

Picture Clause	Value	Result
AAAA	BAIT	BAIT
$$$$V.99	34.87	$34.87
$$,$$$V.9DB	−4004.35	$ 4,004.35DB
ZZZZ	0	<blank>

Picture clauses can be used in place of the standard format specifiers wherever a special definition is required (as in business output report formatting). If you are familiar with COBOL, you will feel right at home with PL/1's pictures.

CONCLUSION

Because of PL/1's size, it would be impossible to cover all of PL/1's features in any kind of detail. Therefore, a survey of the main capabilities have been offered here. Feel free to consult the reference books listed for more information on PL/1. If you are serious about learning PL/1, a good compiler to start with is the subset compiler PL/C, which features debugging and error diagnostics and is easier to use than standard PL/1.

REFERENCES—PL/1

There are quite a few PL/1 books on the market, some on the full PL/1 language and others on a subset such as PL/C.

General Books on PL/1

Programming the PL/1 Way, by Dan Smedley. An interesting handbook of the PL/1 language, the structure of computers, and other related topics. Half the book consists of an extensive data processing glossary. (TAB)

PL/1 Structured Programming, by J. K. Hughes. A very complete textbook of over 800 pages on how to program in the PL/1 language. Includes examples and problems. (John Wiley)

Structured PL/1 Programming with Business Applications, by C. J. Rockey. An introductory textbook on the basics of PL/1 programming. (William C. Brown)

PL/C and Subset G Compilers

Problem Solving and the Computer, by Shortt & Wilson. An easy-to-read textbook on programming using the PL/C student compiler. (Addison-Wesley)

PL/I on Micros, by Bruce H. Hunter. A book specializing on Subset G, used on mini and microcomputers. (Scott, Foresman)

16 CHAPTER

PROLOG

ARTIFICIAL INTELLIGENCE IS a topic of interest and concern to our technological society. Advocates cite the advantages of machines being able to think like humans but with great logical speed and accuracy. Opponents fear the replacement of human beings by mechanized machines. Regardless of your personal opinions on this expanding field of computer science, artificial intelligence, or AI, is here to stay.

Besides robotics, the most publicized aspects of computers, another important aspect of artificial intelligence is creating expert systems. An expert system is a very intelligent computer program that can simulate the reasoning and technical knowledge of a human expert. Medical diagnosis is one area where an expert system has been developed and used. In simple terms, a medical expert system can accept patients' symptoms and then make an accurate diagnosis as to the probable ailment. The vast amounts of technical information and logical relationships have all been programmed into the system, making the computer a useful tool for practicing physicians. However, the process is quite complex, especially when one attempts to tie together complex relationships and arrange the data in a meaningful way.

Getting back to computer languages and AI, for years Lisp (List Processor) was the language of choice for artificial intelligence research. It was not until the early 1970s that any language was available to challenge Lisp's premier position, and that language is named Prolog. Prolog, which is an acronym for PROgramming in LOGic, is ideally suited to use in artificial intelligence since its strength is in defining and working with logical relationships between pieces of information. Large databases of logically related information are the backbone of artificial intelligence, as in the expert system application mentioned above.

Prolog represents an entirely different type of programming from most programming languages. It is concerned mainly with defining certain objects and the relationships between them. The language is based on the theories of propositional calculus.

Prolog was invented early in the 1970s by Philippe Roussel. Roussel, working at the Artificial Intelligence Group at the University of Marseille, developed the first Prolog compiler in 1972. Since that time, the language was used in the AI community, but its popularity did not spread to the majority of computer users. In the last few years the great interest in artificial intelligence has sparked interest in Prolog. In addition to mainframe implementations, there are now at least a dozen microcomputer implementations for such systems as the IBM PC and CP/M computers. Books on programming in Prolog are beginning to appear as well. Prolog was widely publicized when Japan used it as the language for its fifth-generation computer project.

Although the language is very effective and efficient for applications such as math logic, expert systems, and the understanding of natural language, it is not a general-purpose language and cannot be used like BASIC or Pascal. The syntax and programming style of Prolog are quite different and, for this reason, may not appeal to most computer users.

Prolog is a language for researchers in artificial intelligence. Since AI is still a relatively young field, the use of Prolog may be very important in the years to come.

Prolog Program Structure

Prolog programs do not follow any preset structure or organization, but rather are lists of relationships between different objects. There are generally three aspects of programming in Prolog: declaring facts about objects and their relationships, defining rules about these relationships, and asking questions about these objects and relationships. Prolog programs can be visualized as a database, with all the interrelationships defined and specified exactly. A user of a Prolog program can ask questions and receive an "intelligent," logical answer.

You can see how Prolog would be useful in artificial intelligence, such as in the creation of expert systems. After you have programmed in all the medical knowledge equal to the level of that of a medical school graduate, you could list your symptoms as "runny nose, fever, sore throat" and receive the diagnosis "common cold."

Facts and Queries

In Prolog the object is to specify both objects and the relationships between them. These are represented by English-like statements clearly defining the relationships desired for your needs. In other languages, certain relationships (for instance, larger than or equality) are defined, and you generally can manipulate only data from these relationships. In Prolog you can define the relationship you desire, whether it be father-of, colder-than, or meaner-than. Here are some examples of relations that you can define:

```
pig fatter—than cow

Leroy meaner—than junkyard dog

Bob cold—as ice
```

In all of these examples there is one condition and two operands. Depending on the syntax used, the condition can either precede the operands (the usual syntax) or be positioned between the two operands. For the sake of simplicity, the code shown here is presented in the Micro-Prolog dialect using a special front-end system called SIMPLE, which allows the coding of facts in the latter method.

To start, you should define some facts about the data in your "fact database," which at this point comprises your program. For example, suppose you define some family relationships:

```
(Clark father—of Rusty)
(Clark father—of Audrey)
(Ellen mother—of Rusty)
(Ellen mother—of Audrey)
(Clark husband—of Ellen)
(Ellen wife—of Clark)
(Rusty brother—of Audrey)
(Audrey sister—of Rusty)
```

This is a definition of a simple family structure with a husband, wife, and two children, Audrey and Rusty. This information is entered into the Prolog interpreter system using an editor-type system, with provisions for interactively entering and retrieving information. In the statements above, the two operands surround the hyphenated relationship operator. In the above example, you have entered some facts into your database.

There are certain commands for retrieving specific facts from the information given. The simplest, LIST, prints out the relationships that you have just specified, in the form in which you entered them. You can be more selective and list the conditions relating to a certain relationship only, such as wife-of. The built-in interpreter editor allows you to save, load, and delete clauses, groups of conditions, and even entire logic files (programs).

The statements just listed are more of a systems nature than pure Prolog. We now come to queries, which are ways of retrieving the information needed from a database. The first command is IS, which in some dialects is indicated by the question mark (?) symbol. In Micro-Prolog, the query could be as follows:

```
is (Clark father—of Rusty)
YES
```

which will return the English word "yes." This case asks about the specific case of whether Clark is the father of Rusty. Suppose you wanted to find out whether anyone was the father of Rusty without naming Clark specifically. Here, you can use a variable to replace "Clark," which is like a "wildcard"—anything can be in that location as long as the rest matches. Trying it on the system, you would get:

```
is(x father—of Rusty)
YES
```

So, since there is one instance in the database, Prolog will return YES.

In the preceding cases, you asked whether a condition was true or not. Now suppose you want to get back some actual information from your database by querying for the actual data items. The requests here must use the WHICH command and a type of "receiving variable" indicated by the variable name and colon:

```
which (x:x father—of Rusty)
Clark
No (more) answers
```

The variable x is set up to represent the item you wish to retrieve and is placed both at the beginning and at the proper place in the query. The language will return "Clark" as the only result available from the database. The "No (more) answers" indicates that the retrieval is done. You can liken these query commands to those found in a database system.

The command shown above is of the simplest form possible. A more complex form would apply if you wanted to find out who was the mother of someone in the family. Another way to phrase it would be "Is x the mother of anyone (y) ?" The Prolog query is as follows:

```
which(x: x mother—of y)
Ellen
No (more) answers
```

The x is the variable sought, while y represents any answer possible. Since Ellen is the mother of both Rusty and Audrey, she is returned as the result. With the use of more complex query conditions, you will be able to retrieve data that you need, regardless of the size or complexity of your Prolog database.

Mathematical Operations

For you number-crunching mathematicians, Prolog does provide a number of numerical commands. These include SUM, INT, TIMES, and LESS. These are all relations and must be coded in the same format as the family facts above.

The SUM relation requires three operands, designated as the two addends and the solution. You can test the truth of an addition or find out the sum of the numbers. To test if 2 + 2 equals 4, simply use the IS command:

```
is(SUM(2 2 4))
YES
```

or if you want Prolog to find the answer, use which:

```
which(x: SUM(3 3 x))
6
No (more) answers
```

By rearranging the arrangement of the variables, you can find out the difference:

```
which(x:SUM(x 5 25))
20
No (more) answers
```

Numbers used in Prolog can be either positive or negative, and either integer or floating-point. The INT command is used for either testing for integers or converting between types:

```
is(36 INT)
YES
```

This example answers the question "is 36 an integer?" The answer of course is yes. To convert a real to an integer, you simply change the query around:

```
is (3.77 INT X)
3
No (more) answers
```

This converts 3.77 to an integer by dropping the decimal portion.

TIMES is used both for multiplication and division:

```
is(TIMES(6 6 36)
YES
```

This example functions by testing whether 6 times 6 is 36. Multiplication can be performed as follows:

```
which(x:TIMES (2 2 x))
4
No (more) answers
```

which is like the example of the SUM relation. By reversing the operands, you can divide two numbers:

```
which(x:TIMES(x 2 12))
6
No (more) answers
```

The LESS is used only for checking whether the value of one data item is less than that of another. This is used both for numbers and for characters (which are compared by dictionary order):

```
is(CARL LESS CARLY)
YES
```

Since the first word has one less character than "CARLY", it is considered less in value; hence the relation is true.

Rules

We have covered how to declare facts and make queries about that information. You may have noticed how tedious it is to declare every condition, since every fact is unrelated. In Prolog you can define rules that have a much greater range.

In the example above about the family, you can define a rule about "parents." In the facts you have so far, you defined the father and mother relations for the two children. Suppose you wanted to make the more general rule that mothers and fathers are "parents" of the children. Defining a rule would make this easy:

```
(x parent—of y if x father—of y)
(x parent—of y if x mother—of y)
```

By adding these two rules to the set of facts already submitted, you make the concept of the "parent" part of the logical database. Using the WHICH query, you now can find out information about the parents.

```
which(x: x parent—of Audrey)
Clark
Ellen
No (more) answers
```

Rules are considered conditional statements in that they are based on another condition being true. The conditions are specified with the IF statement, as well as the logical AND.

Lists

Prolog, unlike FORTRAN or COBOL, consists of relations arranged in an ordered format inside parentheses. These parentheses may remind you of Lisp, and indeed lists are part of the Prolog language.

In the relations defined so far, you have defined only one condition, such as (John studies math). With lists, you can define a number of subjects for John. For example:

```
(John studies (math science history))
```

where John now has a trio of courses. When you retrieve this information, the list containing the courses will be returned:

```
which(x: John studies x)
(math science history)
No (more) answers
```

Using compound conditions and multiple lists, you can create complex relationships. Lists can be used as data items just as single objects can, and therefore Prolog is useful for list processing.

Complex Logic and Other Prolog Features

The conditions and relationships defined so far were rather simple. In real life, more complicated conditions are needed, and so Prolog provides the NOT, ISALL, OR, and IS-TOLD.

In all the conditions that have been presented thus far, each of the statements has been a positive one. The question being asked was always, "Is something this way?" By using the NOT condition, you can specify when something is fulfilling the negation of a statement. For instance, suppose you make the following condition:

```
which(x: x brother—of Rusty & x brother—of Audrey & x son—of Clark &
not x son—of Ellen)
```

Here, you are looking for the names of any illegitimate sons (or sons from a previous marriage) in this family. Although this boy is the brother of Rusty and Audrey, he is the son of Clark but not Ellen. The NOT represents the negation of a condition.

The ISALL condition is useful where there are multiple results for a "which" query. Normally, answers will be listed individually followed by a "no (more) answers." When you use ISALL, all the answers will be put together in a list. When you have this information in list form, a variety of other functions can be applied to this data. An ISALL conditional structure showing parents relation follows:

```
(x,y) parents—of Z if
      Z isall (z:x father—of z and y mother—of z)
```

The OR condition helps to put several statements together. By putting together several conditions, you can create complex relationships. Often the & symbol is used for convenience, as in our example for the NOT condition.

The IS-TOLD is an interesting condition which implements an interactive question structure in a Prolog program. The questions themselves are quite similar to those with WHICH and IS, but instead of your putting the question to the system, the system asks you the question during the execution. For instance:

```
all(mark x is z score: (mark x) is—told & z=(x/5))
```

is an IS-TOLD structure which will ask the user for the value of x and then proceed to return the result of the set calculations:

```
mark X ? ans 20
mark 20 is 4 score
```

This condition is extremely useful when you want to communicate with your program's user in an interactive mode.

It is useful to mention that all comment statement lines must be preceded by the comment symbol /*. Comments are not evaluated but are for documentation purposes only.

The basic concepts of Prolog have been presented, from which you can explore further with a good understanding. Consult one of the books listed in the back for more detailed information on how to program in Prolog.

CONCLUSION

Prolog is a very new and special language which is designed to express relationships rather than numerical computations. It is not a general-purpose language, but rather one for use in artificial intelligence, logical problems, and other special situations. Because of the recent interest in artificial intelligence, the language has become more widely recognized. Its place in the microcomputer community is increasing, with a number of fine implementations on the market today. Prolog may be an important part of the growing Artificial Intelligence field in the years to come.

REFERENCES—PROLOG

There are very few Prolog books available at the present time, but more should be on the way very soon, because of the recent interest in artificial intelligence.

Programming in Prolog, by Clocksin & Mellish. An introductory but comprehensive guide to the language, from both the program development and program execution aspects. (Springer-Verlag)

Programming in Micro-Prolog, by Clark & McCabe. A complete tutorial guide to the Micro-Prolog interpreter for use on microcomputer systems. Includes examples of application programs and details of the Micro-Prolog syntax. (Prentice-Hall)

Beginning Micro-Prolog, by Richard Ennals. A beginning textbook on Prolog, specifically concentrating on the Micro-Prolog interpreter. (Harper & Row)

Part IV

STATISTICAL LANGUAGES

SPSS
SAS

These chapters are not designed for the novice but rather for readers with some interest and background in statistics. Keep this in mind when you start this section.

CHAPTER 17

SPSS

SPSS, AN ABBREVIATION for Statistical Package for the Social Sciences, is a very powerful system for analyzing statistical data. Unlike most of the languages covered in this book, SPSS is not considered a true language by many people, since it is in reality a collection of programs all tied into one system. Through the use of a simple coding format, raw data can be analyzed and statistics produced in the form of graphs, charts, tables, and even graphical displays.

Even though it can be called either a language or a software package, we will keep with the nature of this book and call it a language. Because the standard SPSS reference manual is over 600 pages long and includes many complex statistical procedures, we will merely describe the major statistical areas covered; you should consult reference manuals and books for specific coding details.

SPSS was developed by a group of political science professors and researchers at Stanford University in 1965. They found it extremely difficult to complete their research and scholarly activities using just a library of different statistical programs. It was very time-consuming to learn a large number of languages/programs and transfer data between incompatible programs. In addition, there was the problem of limited documentation, different source languages, and the need to write programs for file management and other "housekeeping" chores.

The introduction of this large "package" of statistical programs known as SPSS was welcomed by the academic and research community, and by 1970 it was in use at over 60 different computer installations. Since that year, through the cooperation of statisticians, social scientists, and researchers, the number of features available has doubled and the language is now in use in over 600 installations on more than a dozen different systems. The developers of SPSS have included in their reference manual a section entitled "A Programmer's Guide to SPSS," allowing programmers to add procedures to their SPSS systems, provided they possess a strong knowledge of FORTRAN. One of the future goals is to develop a truly interactive form that would give immediate results, instead of requiring the long waits associated with batch runs.

Some of the statistical analysis capabilities provided in the SPSS language are descriptive statistics, crosstabulation, breakdown description, hypothesis testing, correlation, scattergrams, analyses of variance, and regression. All of these can be used through simple commands typed into a SPSS command file. The power of SPSS is apparent whenever it is used, since a few lines of commands can generate pages of charts and statistics.

For many years, the SPSS package could be used only through mainframe or minicomputers through batch processing. A complete job deck, including a command file, data, and JCL (job-control language), had to be submitted to the computer for processing, after which a printout would be produced for inspection.

In order to use SPSS on large systems, it probably would be most feasible to subscribe to a timesharing service that offers SPSS or the newest version, SPSS-X. Through a modem, your personal computer could act as a remote terminal, sending jobs to the host computer for processing and receiving back the runs on your screen or printer.

Just recently, microcomputer versions of the language were released for the IBM PC and DEC Professional 350. Known as SPSS/PC and SPSS/Pro, respectively, these versions have many of the capabilities of their mainframe counterparts and should be valuable to those who want to use SPSS but don't have access to a mainframe system.

SPSS is a very specialized language for statistical applications. It will take your raw data and give you all the statistics you may ever want in the form of neat charts and tables. It was not designed as a general-purpose language, but as a tool for analysis and research.

The SPSS Command File

The SPSS Command File is a synonym for an SPSS "program." Here, you specify exactly the format of your data and what operations you want to have performed on it. The English-like language is simple and easy to understand.

Each line of an SPSS command file consists of two fields. The left field, columns 1-15, is called the *Command Field* and lists the general commands that you wish to execute. Columns 16-80 make up the *Specification Field* and hold the operands or the specifications for each major command. In the command field, you tell SPSS what you want to do (frequencies, crosstabs, regression, etc.) while you give the specifics for your data in the specification field.

Regardless of the analyses that you wish to perform for your data, there is certain information that you must tell the system first. These are the RUN NAME, DATA LIST, VARIABLE LABELS, NUMBER CASES, and any special characteristics of the data that you need to specify. After that you can indicate what you want done with your data. Consider the example below, which will output the frequencies and descriptive statistics for the data you provide:

```
RUN NAME        GRADES
DATA LIST       FIXED (1)/1 STU 1-3 GRADE 4-5 LEVEL 6-7
N OF CASES      5
VAR LABELS      STU, STUDENT NUMBER/
                GRADE, FINAL GRADE FOR COURSE/
                LEVEL, CLASS LEVEL/
VALUE LABELS    LEVEL (01) KINDERGARTEN (02) ELEMENTARY
                (03) JUNIOR HIGH (04) SENIOR HIGH/
FREQUENCIES     GENERAL=GRADE
OPTIONS         8
STATISTICS      ALL
READ INPUT DATA
0016503
```

```
0029501
0039904
0048202
0058802
FINISH
```

This is a complete SPSS command file that will produce a great deal of information from the small amount of data given. The file is given the name GRADES and first proceeds to describe the data format. Under DATA LIST, it first indicates by FIXED (1)/1 that all the data will conform to the format specified and that there is only one record per case. Following that, you list what columns hold what information. The computer will take your data strictly on the basis of the columns, so coding of your input information is crucial. You then give more descriptive labels to your variables and can explain what coding scheme you use to record the school level. Finally comes the meat of SPSS—in just three short lines, you have asked for frequencies (how many in each category, in this case, grades) with option 8 (bar charts), and the statistics command. Since you coded ALL for statistics, you will be given the following: mean, standard error, median, mode, standard deviation, variance, kurtosis, skewness, range, as well as minimum and maximum. Following these commands are the input data, followed by a FINISH. As you can see, SPSS will do a lot for you with a minimum of programming. Usually, there is the basic command (such as FREQUENCIES and CROSSTABS) followed by a set of auxiliary commands, such as OPTIONS and STATISTICS.

The rest of this chapter will cover the most basic statistical features offered in the language. While the command file instructions (such as FREQUENCIES and STATISTICS) will be covered, it would be unnecessary to actually continue listing entire programs. Since users of SPSS are usually familiar with statistical concepts, we will give only a very brief description of the statistics background of each command.

Frequencies

Using FREQUENCIES, you can find out how many there are in a certain category, depending on what you select. In the preceding example, you could find out how many students were in a certain class group, or how many of the group got a certain grade. Using OPTIONS, you can print a bar chart, include missing values, or change the sorting of tables (ascending or descending). Using various STATISTICS options, you can obtain statistics mentioned previously (mean, standard error, etc.). The general format is:

```
FREQUENCIES      GENERAL= variable names specified
OPTIONS          option numbers
STATISTICS       selected or ALL
```

Crosstabs

In using frequencies, you could work on only one variable at a time. But suppose you wanted to test a scented envelope against a plain one as to mail response rate. One bunch was colorful and scented while the others where white and sterile, and an equal number were sent to men and women. To analyze the results, you would need to correlate the envelope color with the gender. That is where crosstabs come in—you want to be able to see how many responses you get for each arrangement: white/men, color/men, white/women, color/women. Assuming the variables were ENVELOPE and GENDER, you could set up crosstabs as follows:

```
CROSSTABS            TABLES=ENVELOPE BY GENDER
```

Using the option command, you could select an index, omitting percentages, or include missing variables. The STATISTICS option allows the inclusion of chi-square, Kendall's tau, contingency coefficient, and Somers' d.

Hypothesis Testing

Using hypothesis testing, you can draw some conclusions about a population or sample. SPSS allows you to test hypotheses about the equality of two means for variables on a ratio or interval scale. The command T-TEST will compute the Student's t-statistic for testing this significance. An example of this is given below:

```
T-TEST      GROUPS=( division of groups )/VARIABLES=(test var.)
OPTIONS     (option #)
```

Scattergrams and Correlation

One valuable part of statistics is the ability to correlate (or show the relationship between) certain factors. A simple example would be the relationship between age and learning ability. SPSS allows two methods of analysis—the scattergram and the Pearson Correlation. The first is a graphical method of presentation, displaying dots wherever one case resides, depending on a visual scale. The second attempts to show a relationship based on the position of the dots, using the technique known as the "correlation coefficient." These have the general form:

```
SCATTERGRAM        (first variable) WITH (second variable)
OPTIONS            (option number)
STATISTICS         (option number)
```

The options include different arrangements of grid lines and plot formatting. Statistics available include the intercept, slope Pearson r, and R Squared.

```
PEARSON CORR       (variable names)
OPTIONS            (option number)
STATISTICS         (option number)
```

The Pearson coefficient correlations can be printed in tabular form.

Analysis of Variance

In comparing data, there is often a need to determine if differences in certain groups (such as the public acceptance of three brands of Cola) are due to chance or true differences. The analysis of variance or ANOVA is used to examine this aspect by testing to see if several population means are equal. In SPSS there are two basic variation analysis commands: ONEWAY and ANOVA. ONEWAY can handle one dependent variable and one independent variable; ANOVA is more powerful and can handle several dependent variables and up to five independent variables.

The syntax of both ONEWAY and ANOVA are given below:

```
ONE WAY            (dependent variable) BY (independent variable)
                   (minimum,maximum values)
                   RANGES=
```

< options for ranges >

LSD—least significant difference
DUNCAN—Duncan's multiple range test
SNK—Student-Newman-Keuls test
TUKEYB—Tukey's alternate procedure
TUKEY—Honestly significant difference
LSDMOD—Modified LSD
SCHEFFE—Scheffe's test

OPTIONS	(option number)
STATISTICS	(option number)

syntax for ANOVA:

ANOVA	(dependent variable) BY (independent variables)
OPTIONS	(option number)
STATISTICS	(option number)

Regression

Regression is one of the most versatile methods of data analysis. Although it is an advanced statistical concept, in general it involves fitting a "regression line" not only to describe the data but also to attempt to draw inferences about the population. Although it is beyond the scope of this book to describe the statistical concepts involved, it is important to mention SPSS's regression capabilities.

SPSS's procedure NEW REGRESSION is a powerful program that will create a regression model based on the variables indicated. Dependent variables labeled on a separate line from the complete list, VARIABLES, are preceded by the word DEPENDENT. The variables can be analyzed through a FORWARD, BACKWARD, or STEPWISE method. Other regression options include STATISTICS, residual analysis, scatterplots, and provisions for missing cases.

NEW REGRESSION	(variables)
	DEPENDENT= (dependent variables)
	BACKWARD/FORWARD <method subcommands>
	STATISTICS= (choices)
	RESIDUALS= (options)
	CASEWISE= (options)
	SCATTERPLOT= (options)

Consult the reference materials listed below to learn about the many other statistical analysis procedures through the SPSS language.

REFERENCES—SPSS

Because SPSS is a specialized analysis language used mainly in research and academics, its use is not widespread. Hence, only a few books, written in reference-manual format, are currently available. In order to use a mainframe version, you must consult your system's operating manual for details on job control language and other such details. Most of the books listed here were written in cooperation with SPSS Inc., the firm involved with marketing and developing SPSS for all types of systems.

For current information on SPSS, contact:

SPSS INC.
Suite 3300
444 North Michigan Avenue
Chicago IL 60611
(312) 329-2400

Reference Materials on SPSS

SPSS 2/e, by Nile et al. The basic guide and reference manual to SPSS, it covers the language in detail. Starting with basic concepts and control cards, it progresses through data modification, files, descriptive statistics, crosstabs, correlation, regression, covariance, and descriminants. Includes a useful section on job control language and how to implement new procedures into SPSS's code. Designed for serious users of SPSS. (McGraw-Hill)

SPSS Introductory Guide, by Norusis. A supplement to the reference manual listed above, this follows more of a tutorial approach and features examples drawn from real studies, followed by syntax charts. (McGraw-Hill)

SPSS Primer, by Klecka. A short manual for those who don't need the full SPSS language but only the basic features. Documents the 1975 Release 6 version. (McGraw-Hill)

SPSS Update 7–9, by Hull & Nie. Covers new procedures available in this new release: time series, graphics, report writing, etc. (McGraw-Hill)

SPSS Pocket Guide: Release 9, by Hull & Nie. A quick reference guide for SPSS programmers. (McGraw-Hill)

Reference Materials on SPSS-X

SPSS-X User's Guide, by SPSS Inc. A guide to this advanced version of SPSS which includes among its topics matrix manipulation, plotting, scaling, clustering techniques, and log-linear analysis. (McGraw-Hill)

SPSS-X Advanced Statistics Guide, by Norusis. For advanced researchers and statistics students. (McGraw-Hill)

SPSS-X Graph Builder, by SPSS Inc. Covers the techniques for using SPSS-X's interactive graphics features to create charts, maps, and plots and graphs. (McGraw-Hill)

SPSS-X Reference Handbook, by SPSS Inc. A quick guide to SPSS-X for experienced programmers. (McGraw-Hill)

SPSS-X Basics, by SPSS Inc. A beginner's guide to SPSS. (McGraw-Hill)

Reference Materials on Specific Implementations of SPSS

SPSS/Pro, by SPSS Inc. A guide to the SPSS package available for the DEC Professional 350 microcomputer. (McGraw-Hill)

SPSS-11, by N. Morrison. A guide to the version of SPSS package available for the DEC PDP-11 minicomputer. (McGraw-Hill)

18 CHAPTER

SAS

SAS, AN ACRONYM for Statistical Analysis System, is similar to SPSS in that it is more of a specialized software package than a general-purpose programming language. SAS was developed in 1966 by the SAS Institute, and up to the present time the same company still markets the product and related documentation.

SAS allows users to analyze raw statistical data and produce meaningful output in the form of charts, graphs, and tables. The system was designed to require a minimum of programming, allowing the user instead to concentrate on the problem at hand. Besides descriptive statistics, correlation, frequencies, and tabulation, SAS also supports bar charts, block charts, pie charts, plotting, and the printing of schedule calendars.

The SAS language has a simple program structure and most of the procedures are simple to use. With a few lines of command code (procedures), pages of statistics or charts can be produced for each variable or set of variables. It is, however, a specialized language and cannot be used like the majority of programming languages. Although SAS is easy to use and powerful, one potential drawback lies in getting access to a SAS system compiler. At the present time, SAS is available only on mainframe or minicomputers such as the IBM 370, DEC VAX, Data General Eclipse, and Prime series 50. A timesharing service must be used with these systems. In the near future, a microcomputer version will be released by the SAS Institute.

In general, SAS is very useful for the purpose for which it was intended, statistical analysis, and it is used widely in the academic, scientific, and research communities.

Program Structure

An SAS program consists of two main parts, a data section and a command (procedure) section. The data section both describes and lists the data to be analyzed, and the procedure section indicates the type of analysis to be done.

Since SAS is almost always used on large systems, the following example will include some OS JCL (job control language) statements to show how SAS is run on an OS IBM 370 system.

```
    //GEORGE JOB ( 4736514,G405),'REPORT'
    //*PASSWORD CURIOUS
    // EXEC SAS
    //SYSIN DD *
     DATA CLASS;
      INPUT NAME $ MIDTERM FINAL;
      CARDS;
    POPEYE    85  34
    OLIVE     92  85
    WIMPY     66  31
    BRUTUS    21  12
    SWEETPEA  99  98
    ;
     PROC SORT;
      BY NAME;
     PROC PRINT;
      TITLE GRADE STATISTICS;
    PROC MEANS MAXDEC=2;
/*
//
```

This program, complete with the JCL statements, could be run on an IBM OS mainframe computer through a timesharing service. In the example, all job control commands are preceded by // or /*, and SAS commands are sandwiched between these control statements. The first two lines, which are JCL statements, specify the accounting data, such as username, password, bin, and titles. The next two lines tell the operating system to EXECute the SAS software and prepare to accept the program (data set) immediately afterwards. For those not familiar with large computer facilities, the bin denotes the "mailbox" where the computer operator would put your program listing after it is printed on the university or computer center printer.

In our example, we find two main sections, the DATA step and PROC (procedure) step. All SAS programs follow this binary structure, regardless of whether the program is simple or complex. In this example, we use in-stream data, with the data located in the program itself. It is also possible to obtain data from disk, tape, or other data sets, and to do so would require a different DATA step. In the in-stream example, you first indicate the DATA name, "CLASS", followed by the INPUT or data list of variables, which in this case is MIDTERM and FINAL. The command "CARDS;" signals the beginning of the data cards, at the end of which you must code a semicolon (;).

So, with in-stream data, all the necessary information is found in the source program itself. After this DATA step comes the actual analysis, which is accomplished by calling a number of procedures, each of which is designed to do a different type of analysis. In the above program three basic procedures are used: SORT, PRINT, and MEANS. You tell SAS to sort the entire data set by name alphabetically, then print the title "GRADE STATISTICS", followed by descriptive statistics in table form (mean, standard deviation, standard error, sum, variance, etc.). The output, which will take several pages, will be a report of sorted data and a table of descriptive statistics.

When you finally use SAS on a mainframe or through SAS/PC, a microcomputer implementation currently available for the IBM PC, you will see the power that SAS provides for statistical research. A few PROC calls would produce pages of valuable statistical data, all computed from the data you provide. It would take a very lengthy program in a standard programming language to provide the same output that a short SAS job could.

Since every SAS program consists of two parts, the DATA step and PROC step, we shall discuss these in more detail.

The DATA Step

The DATA step is concerned mainly with the data to be processed in this SAS program. In the previous example you saw how data can be included in the SAS program itself, with the DATA, INPUT, and CARDS commands. In the DATA step there are a number of commands available for use. They fall into four main categories—file handling, action, control, and information.

The *file handling* commands control the input and output of data from the SAS program. Each of these commands is listed below and described briefly.

CARDS	Cards will follow this command.
DATA	Start a data set for this program.
INFILE	Identifies the external file containing the data to be processed.
INPUT	Describes the data records in the data file (or cards).
MERGE	Merges two data sets into one.
PUT	Output formatting command.
UPDATE	Master file update.

When working with file data of any type, you may want to modify your data, read only certain cards, or perform error checking. The following *action* commands enable you to perform these functions.

ABORT	Stops execution of the job.
CALL	Calls a routine (not for PROC).
DELETE	Deletes the current data observation (data line) from processing.
ERROR	Prints an error message on the SAS Log (listing).

LIST	Lists the input lines in the output.
STOP	Terminates the creation of the current data set.

Usually, statements in a DATA step are executed sequentially. However, as in any language, there arises the need to transfer control for more complex analyses. SAS has a number of *control* structures for this purpose.

DO	When DO is used with an END it becomes a loop structure of the form DO..END.
DO X = Y TO Z BY 3	A DO structure similar to the FOR loop structure in BASIC.
DO OVER;	This will repeat the same command for every element in an array.
DO WHILE	Repeats while a certain condition is true.
DO UNTIL	Repeats until a certain condition is true.
END	END of a DO group.
GOTO	Jumps to a labeled location.
IF..THEN/ELSE	The familiar conditional structure.
LINK..RETURN	A simulated subroutine structure, with the LINK branching to a labeled line then returning back to one statement after the LINK.

The final category of SAS data step commands is known as *information* commands; they concern names, formats, and operations on the data.

ARRAY	Declares a set of variables to be processed the same way, as in an array.
BY	The data are processed in groups or keys, such as "BY NAME" in our example.
DROP	Drops certain variables from processing.
FORMAT	Formats for printing and storing data.

KEEP	Variables to be kept in a data set for analysis.
LABEL	Labels are associated with variable names.
LENGTH	A SAS variable's storage length.
RENAME	Renames variables in a data set.

Using the statements listed above, you can set up the exact format you would like to use and the data to be processed.

The PROC Step

The PROC step is where you specify exactly the analysis that you desire for your input data. By simply specifying the correct PROCedure, you can obtain descriptive statistics, correlation, regression, variance, descriminants, and even graphic bar and pie charts!

Since a detailed description of each of the different procedures would be very lengthy, we will cover here only the various procedures in general, describing the statistical analyses performed for each one.

Descriptive Statistics

CORR	Correlation coefficients.
FREQ	Frequency and crosstabs.
MEANS	Univariate descriptive statistics.
SUMMARY	Calculates descriptive statistics and outputs the results to a new data set.
TABULATE	Creates tables of descriptive statistics.
UNIVARIATE	Simple descriptive statistics for numeric variables.

Reporting

PRINT	Prints out values from a SAS data set.
FORMS	Prints mailing labels and forms.
CHART	Prints a variety of charts: bar, block, pie, etc.

PLOT Prints out scatter plot graphs.

CALENDAR Prints out a calendar of events and dates.

Utility Procedures

APPEND Puts one data set at the end of another, making one new data set.

BMDP Calls a BMDP program to analyze a SAS data set.

BROWSE To read but not modify a SAS data set.

CONTENTS Prints descriptions of the contents of a SAS data set.

CONVERT Converts files used in the software systems BMDP, DATA-TEXT, OSIRIS, and SPSS to SAS data sets.

COPY Makes copies of SAS data sets.

DATASETS Operates on data sets, by listing, altering, and deleting SAS data sets

DELETE Deletes data sets from the disk or tape library.

EDITOR An editing system for use on SAS data sets.

FORMAT Defines new formats for output (labels, numbers).

OPTIONS Lists all SAS system options and current states.

PRINTTO Defines SAS procedure output.

SORT Sorts a data set by the variables you indicate.

Advanced Statistical Procedures

Each field is indicated by its SAS procedures.
Multivariate statistics: CANCORR, FACTOR, PRINCOMP
Matrix: MATRIX
Regression: REG, RSQUARE, RSREG, NLIN, STEPWISE
Analysis of Variance: ANOVA, GLM, NESTED, NPAR1WAY PLAN, TTEST, VARCOMP
Clustering: CLUSTER, FASTCLUS, TREE, VARCLUS
Categorical: FUNCAT, PROBIT
Scoring: RANK, SCORE, STANDARD
Discriminant: CANDISK, DESCRIM, NEIGHBOR, STEPDISC

Since these techniques may be "foreign" to those without a statistical background, descriptions are not given. Instead, you can refer to the SAS *User's Guide* for detailed information on each of these advanced procedures. A beginner's guide can be found in the BASICS volume, and the advanced procedures are located in the advanced user's *Statistics* volume. Contact the SAS Institute (Box 8000, SAS Circle, Cary NC 27511-8000) for more information on these and other SAS publications.

The material presented above is not a complete guide to the SAS language, but rather an overview. However, you can certainly see SAS's value to researchers and anyone who wants statistical analyses quickly, neatly, and easily.

REFERENCES—SAS

All SAS software, documentation, and other information are marketed and distributed by the SAS Institute, the organization that originally developed the complete SAS system. The institute distributes the software for mainframe and minicomputer systems and in the near future will be releasing a microcomputer implementation. SAS utility programs and graphics software are also available. A complete range of documentation in the form of manuals is available directly from the institute.

Finally, telephone technical support, training seminars, a newsmagazine (*SAS Communications*), and SUGI (SAS User's Group International) memberships are available. For more information, you can contact the SAS Institute at:

SAS INSTITUTE INC.
SAS CIRCLE
Box 8000
Cary NC 27511-8000
(919) 467-8000

Part V

OTHER LANGUAGES

Obscure Languages
SNOBOL4
RPG II
ICON
Smalltalk

CHAPTER 19

PAST, PRESENT, AND FUTURE LANGUAGES

THE LANGUAGES INCLUDED in this book are used and supported by a moderate to large number of users. In addition, most of them are available in microcomputer implementations. Those not readily available can be used through a modem and a timesharing computer system.

Besides these major languages, there exists a large number of languages that enjoy only limited popularity. Some of these are known only within certain industries or are more "academic" and used in scholarly studies. In the 1960s, for example, over two hundred languages were invented, but only a handful of them ever became widely used. A second group has enjoyed a small yet steady acceptance. Third are the new "specialty" languages that require programming but are not considered languages if we try to relate them to BASIC or FORTRAN. A fourth group of languages exists: Those that are not yet available, but will become important in the future.

Some of the obscure languages mentioned in the first group above are listed below, along with their application categories:

Category	*Language*
Scientific	Ariel, JOSS, PROSE, Speakeasy, VECTRAN
Data Processing	I-D-S/I, UTLTYCODR
List Processing	LAMBIT/L, TREET
General Purpose	AED, BALM, Coral 66, MUMPS, Oscar, SAIL
Engineering	COGO, NASTRAN, STRESS
Graphics	ARTSPEAK, LG
String Processing	COMIT-II, VULCAN
Mathematics	AMBUSH, GAMMA, UHELP
Accounting	ABLE
CAI	FOIL, LYRIC, PLANIT, TUTOR
Simulation	CSSL, DYNAMO-III, CELLSIM, SIMSCRIPT
Social Science	CROSSTABS, DATA-TEXT, TROL
Systems Programming	BLISS, CHILI, PROTEUS

These are just a few of the languages available. There are many more, so many that often languages are represented as a huge Tower of Babel. For more information on the obscure languages, consult a programming language textbook or book on programming language history.

The second group of programming languages consists of those that are not used widely at the present time but are still somewhat "alive" in the computer community. The languages in this group are SNOBOL4 and RPGII.

SNOBOL4, a special language designed to work effectively with character strings, was invented by Ralph Griswold. This special-purpose programming language is used almost entirely for string processing applications. Developed in 1962 at Bell Labs, the first version was named simply SNOBOL. A later version, known as SNOBOL3, had many improvements over the original version, and in 1969 SNOBOL4, the most advanced form, was released. SNOBOL4 has a number of statements for pattern matching and replacement, which are useful for working with characters and strings. There are versions for both large machines and the IBM PC. The small SNOBOL4 program that follows gives you an idea of what SNOBOL4 code looks like; it counts the number of words in an input file.

```
*        WORD COUNTING PROGRAM
*
         &TRIM = 1
         UPPER = 'ABCDEFGHIJKLMNOPQRSTUVWXYZ'
         LOWER = 'abcdefghijklmnopqrstuvwxyz'
         WORD = UPPER LOWER
         WPAT = BREAK(WORD) SPAN(WORD)

NEXTLN   LINE = INPUT                      :F(DONE)
NEXTWD   LINE = WPAT                       :F(NEXTWD)
         N = N + 1                         :NEXTW
DONE     OUTPUT = +N ' words'
END
```

This program will accept data in a data file and print out the number of words in the file. In the listing above, the declarations are at the top, followed by the executable code underneath. You will notice that the colon statements (such as :F(DONE)) are to the right of everything else. They are not comments, but branching statements. The first two lines in the code are comment statements. See the reference section for details on SNOBOL4 books and software packages.

RPGII stands for "RePort Generator II," which is a rather simple language for creating organized business reports. It will calculate figures and other business tasks and output reports to your specifications. The somewhat complicated coding structure is helped by the use of special coding forms. RPGII is not generally available for microcomputers, with the exception of Baby/34 by California Software Products, which allows you to simulate IBM System/34 operations and develop RPGII programs. Books on RPGII are included in the reference section of this book.

The third group of languages we mentioned are actually software packages that require programming to be used. They could be categorized as "business application languages." They are generally used to create database programs for business use.

One such language is dBASE II, marketed by Ashton-Tate Company. Business information can be stored away and retrieved by use of a simple database language. dBASE II is used to create business applications programs and is also classified as a "database management program." It uses an English-like language code, a sample of which is shown here:

```
ERASE
? "DO YOU LIKE COMPUTERS ? (Y/N) ";
ACCEPT TO ANSWER
IF ($ANSWER,1,1) = "Y"
   ? "HOORAY!"
ELSE
   ? "BOO FOR YOU!"
ENDIF
RETURN
```

This program will clear the screen (ERASE) then ask you whether you like computers. If you do, the system will print "HOORAY!" Otherwise, it will print "BOO FOR YOU!" The program then ends. dBASE II was designed to be able to run on both 8-bit and 16-bit computers including CP/M and the IBM PC. A more powerful and faster version, designed to take advantage of the large memory available on the IBM PC and compatibles, is known as dBASE III. Besides being faster, dBASE III includes a helpful ASSIST command as well as help menus. The documentation, file sizes, and number of files available for use are all increased and improved. It is more user-friendly than dBASE II, and more powerful. It is also available from Ashton-Tate.

Some other programs, less known than dBASE II and dBASE III, are ADAPT (Application Development And Productivity Tool) by Wilmes Systems, Versaform, MACLION, The Sensible Solution, and R:Base5000 by Microrim. See the language reference section for more details about these programs.

The final group of languages consists of those that are not yet widely available but are destined to become very important in the near future. These are ICON and Smalltalk.

ICON is a new language that is the immediate descendent of SNOBOL4 and is designed by the same inventor. ICON has many of the features of SNOBOL4 but also includes some of the more conventional language control structures. In addition, some expressions in ICON may have an infinite number of different results. Also, there are facilities for logic programming. More information on ICON can be found by obtaining Griswold's book, *The Icon Programming Language* (Prentice-Hall, 1983) or by writing to ICON Project, Department of Computer Science, University of Arizona, Tucson AZ 85721.

Smalltalk, which is also referred to as the Smalltalk-80 system, is an object-oriented language. In simple terms, an object is a memory location that holds a pointer to some variables instead of holding the values themselves. Computation in Smalltalk involves sending "messages" to objects, which in turn will elicit a response using "methods." These are rather abstract topics, which require further explanation. The textbook *Fundamentals of Programming Languages* by Horowitz (Computer Science Press, 1984) has a chapter on Smalltalk and object-oriented languages. Other new languages of this type include Object-C and Neon.

Although this is a brief coverage of the other languages available, it serves to complete this book's comprehensive coverage of the major programming languages available.

Part VI

REFERENCE SECTION: LANGUAGE AVAILABILITY

CHAPTER 20

LANGUAGE SOFTWARE

THE PRECEDING SECTIONS have described the capabilities, character, and structure of seventeen programming languages, most of which you are likely to encounter frequently in both personal and professional computing. Those chapters are designed to give you a feel for the language; some relevant reference books were suggested so you can gain proficiency in programming in that language.

This section is a comprehensive reference section on the programming language software (compilers and interpreters) available for both the major microcomputers and the major operating systems available. The sections will be categorized by computer or operating system, then will be divided into subheadings for each language. First come headings for BASIC, COBOL, FORTRAN, and Pascal, and then the other languages that are available. For each language, you will be given the product name, manufacturer, product description, and, when available, the list price and memory requirements for each of the packages.

A list of addresses and phone numbers for each of the companies mentioned in this chapter is provided in the appendix entitled "Directory of Book and Software Publishers," so that you can write or call for more information. This section should help you locate the right language software for your computer.

APPLE COMPUTER SOFTWARE

Among the most popular computers available, those in the Apple family are known for quality and software support. Although there is probably more software written for Apple computers than for many others, there are only a limited number of language software packages available. Apple computers can be divided into three main categories—the Apple II series (including the II, II Plus, IIe, and IIc), the Apple III, the Lisa, and the Macintosh.

The computers in the Apple II series can generally all run the same software, but the Lisa and Macintosh can run only programs specifically written for those systems. The Apple III can run both its own programs and those of the Apple II series (in emulation mode).

Although the Apple DOS language software choices are somewhat limited, with the addition of a Z-80 CP/M card the choices can be greatly expanded. This section will cover Apple II DOS, Apple II CP/M, Apple III, Lisa, and Macintosh software. Apple compatibles such as the Franklin Ace and others can run Apple programs without any difficulty.

Apple II Series (DOS and ProDOS—II, II Plus, IIe, IIc)

BASIC

Since the Apple computer comes with two versions of BASIC included, there usually isn't the need to buy a BASIC interpreter unless a more powerful dialect is sought. Most systems from the II Plus on come with Applesoft BASIC built into ROM (read-only memory) and Integer BASIC on disk. You can use either of these versions; however Applesoft (which, unlike Integer, has real numbers) is much more versatile.

Recently, the desire for faster programs has led to the development of "BASIC compilers." These are not compilers in the true sense, like a Pascal compiler, but simply take a prewritten Applesoft or other BASIC program and create a speedy binary file from it. These are quite effective but often create a very large object code file. Some BASIC compilers for the Apple are listed below. Some of the compilers are true compilers in that they take the BASIC code and translate it into machine language. Contact the appropriate manufacturers for details about their BASIC compilers.

MACROSOFT
Microsparc Inc.
48K minimum, requires Microsparc's ASSEMBLER program

Translates Applesoft programs into machine language. Allows you to access graphics and sound routines through special BASIC commands.

Integer BASIC Compiler
Galfo Systems

Compiles Integer BASIC files into binary files.

EINSTEIN COMPILER
Einstein Corp.
48K Apple

A compiler for Applesoft BASIC files, which creates very fast binary files. The compiled files are usually somewhat larger than the original BASIC files.

TASC
Microsoft Corp.
48K memory

TASC translates Applesoft BASIC files into machine code, allowing for faster execution. Supports graphics and program chaining.

Other special forms of BASIC are available for the Apple:

BASIC A+
Optimum Systems
48K Apple

An enhanced version of BASIC.

SB STRUCTURED BASIC
U-Microcomputers

A BASIC interpreter for the Apple.

Following are some educational software packages:

HANDS ON BASIC PROGRAMMING
Eduware/Peachtree Software
48K minimum

A complete computer-based instructional program on how to program in BASIC. Includes a 299-page workbook and interactive software to make learning BASIC programming easy.

BASIC BUILDING BLOCKS
Micro Education Corp. America (MECA)
48K minimum

A fully interactive guide to BASIC programming. It will lead you through the learning process with examples and sample executing programs. A special feature allows you to see how your programs execute, useful for debugging and studying how programs work.

COBOL

There are at the present time no COBOL compilers for the Apple II series. However, with a Z-80 CPU and CP/M, it is possible to use COBOL on your Apple. See the next section on Apple CP/M.

FORTRAN

APPLE FORTRAN
Apple Computer Company
64K, minimum of one disk drive

Based on the same (UCSD) system as Apple Pascal, this implementation of FORTRAN is the only one available for the Apple without additional hardware. However, for owners of the II or II+, a RAM card is required to bring the memory space up to 64K.

Pascal

APPLE PASCAL
Apple Computer Company
64K and at least disk drive

A version of Pascal based on the UCSD P-system. It can be run with either one or two drives but requires at least 64K. Some significant extensions include an assembler, Applestuff utilities, and a Turtlegraphics facility for creating graphics pictures.

KYAN PASCAL
Kyan Software
64K plus one disk drive

A complete Pascal package, it features an optimized machine code compiler, full screen editor, files, assembler, and graphics support.

UCSD PASCAL COMPILER
Softech Microsystems
64K minimum

This professional UCSD system compiles Pascal into p-code for running on the UCSD P-System. A version of UCSD Pascal release IV.0, which is quite slow on Apple II computers.

VISIBLE PASCAL
John Wiley & Sons (software)
64K memory

A unique product that teaches Pascal using a special Pascal interpreter. The code and output are displayed simultaneously, and features allow you to see both the code and graphics as the program is executing. Includes an editor and provisions for graphics and music. This interactive Pascal package does not require Apple Pascal but runs independently.

PASCAL LEVEL 1
On-Going Ideas
48K minimum

A subset of Standard Pascal, designed as an inexpensive Pascal development system.

PASCAL LEARNING AIDS
Minnesota Educational Computing (MECC)
48K minimum

Educational materials, including a tutorial program and manual, help users to learn how to program in Pascal.

Ada-APL

There are currently no implementations of Ada or APL for the Apple II series, although there may be in the future. CP/M versions of Ada are available for the Apple; see the Apple CP/M section.

Assembly/Machine

Built into the Apple computer is a Monitor program that allows you to program in machine code. Memory locations can be examined and changed as needed. When you are running Integer BASIC, there is a small "mini-assembler" that can be used to create some elementary assembly language programs. For anything beyond the most simple programs, a full assembler is required.

APPLE ASSEMBLY LANGUAGE PROGRAMMING
Hayden Books/Software
64K, comes with guidebook

This complete book-software package includes a full assembler/disassembler, which was specially designed for use with the book written by Malcolm Whapshott. Starts from the basics and works into more advanced features such as interrupts and macros. Come with reference charts and solved exercises.

THE ASSEMBLER: MACRO-ASSEMBLER/EDITOR
MicroSparc Inc.
48K or 64K, comes with detailed manual

This program, created by Alan D. Floeter, has both a powerful editor (including Global Search and Replace) and a macro-assembler (which allows you to create and store macros). An easy-to-use assembler, especially for beginners.

MACHINE LANGUAGE DEVELOPMENT SYSTEM
Micol Systems
Apple II+, IIe, IIc

A complete machine language development system, including a text editor, macro-assembler, and monitor system.

MICOLMON
Micol Systems
Apple II+, IIe, IIc

A powerful machine language monitor for debugging and machine-level manipulations. Gives you control over your computer's lower levels.

MERLIN
Southwestern Data Systems
Separate versions for 48K and 64K

A powerful macro-assembler and editor, MERLIN supports 6502, 65C02, and Sweet-16 op-codes. Also comes with a macro library and utility programs. The company also markets an assembly debugger known as Munch-a-Bug. An excellent assembler.

LISA 2.5
Sierra On-Line
48K minimum memory

One of the best choices for beginning assembly language programmers, the Lisa was written by Randall Hyde. It is covered both in Robert Mottola's book *Apple Assembly Language Programming*, Hyde's own book, and Maurer's *Apple Assembly Language.* Designed for novice programmers, it keeps both the editor and assembler in memory simultaneously, making development and testing simple. However, this arrangement limits the size of program object files.

S-C ASSEMBLER
S-C Software
Minimum of 24K, tape or disk

One of the first assemblers developed, S-C attempts to make assembly programming as painless as BASIC. An interface is provided to the Apple machine language monitor to make all aspects from development to final run contained within the S-C program.

ORCA/M
The Byte Works
Apple II+ or IIe/c

A powerful assembler for the Apple II series, which is a complete development system modeled after the IBM 370 assembler. It includes its own operating system, over 150 macros, a subroutine library, 400-page reference manual, utilities, and support for the 65816 and 65802 CPUs. A ProDOS version is also available for the newer versions of the Apple II.

APPLE TOOL KIT ASSEMBLER
Apple Computer Company
48K memory minimum

This is included as part of a complete utility package for the Apple. It can be used for both small and large programs. Includes an assembler, editor, and command interpreter.

MAC/65
Optimized Systems Software

A macro-assembler, editor, and debugger system which will be available soon for the Apple II series.

MDS-MICROPRODUCTS 6502 DEVELOPMENT SYSTEM
Microproducts
48K memory

A professional-level editor/assembler, disassembler, and debugger system.

C

AZTEC C65 C COMPILER
Manx Software
Dos 3.3

A professional version of the C language-version 7, includes VED editor, Shell, Unix, and math libraries.

C/65
Optimum Systems Software

This implementation of C will be available shortly.

Forth

MVP FORTH PROGRAMMER'S KIT
Mountain View Press
48K disk, Programming Aids Kits also available

A complete development package, MVP Forth includes the Forth operating system, editor, Forth assembler, tools, utilities, course, and the book *Starting Forth* by Leo Brodie. Also includes the guide "All about Forth."

MASTER FORTH
Micromotion
48K disk; also available: Hi-Res/Floating Point

A version of the Forth-83 standard, this Forth package includes a full-screen editor, micro-assembler, file primitives, and an option for hi-res and floating-point features.

FORTH II
Artsci, Inc.
32K memory

A Forth development system for the Apple which includes in the language provisions for graphics, sounds, and disk/tape I/O.

FORTH DEVELOPMENT LANGUAGE
Information Unlimited Software
48K memory

A language system following the F16-19 standard. Includes an editor, screen filing system, and Forth compiler.

FIG-FORTH
On-Going Ideas
48K memory required

A FIG Forth compiler for the Apple that includes a screens disk, 6502 assembler, decompiler, editor, and control features for Apple cursor, printer, and screen displays.

FORTH-79
On-Going Ideas
48K memory

This version is similar to the above package except that the Forth-79 dialect is supported.

ISYS FORTH
Illyes Systems

A fast implementation of the Forth-83 standard, which includes two editors for program development. ISYS is designed for speed and will execute programs very quickly. Written by Robert F. Illyes.

MMS FORTH
Miller Microcomputer Systems

This is the form of Forth mentioned in the Forth chapter. It includes the 79-standard as well as other enhancements. MMS carries a complete line of Forth software and materials.

Lisp

P-LISP
Gnosis Inc.
48K

An implementation of the P-Lisp dialect for the Apple.

Logo

APPLE LOGO
Apple Computer Company
48K

A version of Logo for the Apple, it features such enhancements as color graphics.

KRELL LOGO
Krell Software Corp.
64K (optional KINDERLOGO)

Krell Logo, an MIT-authorized version, is a complete learning package for the Apple II Series. It comes not only with the Logo language, but also with an educational adventure, "Alice in Logoland," a disk of utilities, a wall chart, computing journal, and a technical manual on Logo. Available in sets of 10, 20, and 40 for schools. A companion disk to Krell Logo, Kinderlogo is designed to teach children how to use Logo.

TERRAPIN LOGO
Terrapin Inc.
64K memory

An enhanced version of MIT Logo which contains the language, utilities disk, tutorial, words and lists manual, and MIT technical manual.

APPLE LOGO
Logo Computer Systems
64K memory requirement

An Apple version designed by the Logo Computer Systems Corp.

TERRAPIN LOGO
Unicom Systems

An alternate version of Terrapin Logo.

EZ LOGO
Minnesota Educational Computing Consortium (MECC)

An instructional program for learning to program in Logo.

Modula-2

MODULA-2
Volition Systems
64K

A version of Modula-2 based on UCSD P-system which may be purchased with or without a special ASE (Advanced Systems Editor). Includes a disk of library modules for use in developing programs.

PILOT

APPLE PILOT
Apple Computer Company
64K

A lesson-development system for creating CAI educational lessons. Includes graphics and sound enhancements.

APPLE SUPERPILOT
Apple Computer Company
64K

An improved version of Apple PILOT, with greater capabilities.

PL/1-Prolog-SAS-SPSS

There are currently no implementations of these languages for the Apple computer. It is suggested that you either purchase a Z-80 CP/M system or use these languages through timesharing services.

APPLE II CP/M (Z-80 CP/M-80 5¼-inch Apple format)

BASIC

MICROSOFT BASIC-80
Microsoft Corp.
48K memory, on CP/M system disk

A greatly enhanced version of BASIC, including a host of commands and features not found in Applesoft. Usually available as part of a complete Softcard system. Also known among CP/M users as MBASIC. GBASIC is also available, for graphics applications.

CBASIC
Digital Research Corp.
48K memory.

This version of BASIC is compiled rather than interpreted, with a CBAS compiler and CRUN execution module. A fast and powerful form of BASIC.

COBOL

COBOL-80 COMPILER
Microsoft Corp.
48K memory

A powerful microcomputer compiler and development system, with special features for taking advantage of the micros' special features, such as screen display/input. A professional system, with compiler, various programs, and utilities.

NEVADA COBOL
Ellis Computing
48K memory minimum

A subset of COBOL which is priced very reasonably. Includes most of the major commands and features.

CIS COBOL
Micro Focus
48K memory minimum

CIS stands for Compact, Interactive, Standard COBOL, which is designed for use on microcomputer systems. It is based on the 1974 × 3.23 standard, with extensions for use on microcomputers.

FORTRAN

FORTRAN-80 COMPILER
Microsoft Corp.
44K memory

Based on the 1966 ANSI standard, FORTRAN-80 supports the complete language with the exception of the COMPLEX data type. A complete development package.

NEVADA FORTRAN
Ellis Computing
48K memory

An inexpensive implementation of the FORTRAN language. Although not a professional/commercial package, it is useful for learning and programming in FORTRAN.

RATFOR
Software Toolworks
48K memory minimum

Designed to work with FORTRAN-80, this package allows structured programming in FORTRAN, as well as other enhancements.

Pascal

TURBO PASCAL
Borland International
48K memory minimum

A very fast and inexpensive Pascal compiler system. It includes not only the compiler but a built-in Wordstar-like editor and a menu-driven system. Can be purchased together with a Tutor program and Utility program.

Ada

JANUS ADA
R R Software
48K memory minimum

A microcomputer implementation of Ada which is a subset of the complete language.

SUPERSOFT A
Supersoft Inc.

A subset version of Ada developed by Marantha Software Systems and marketed by Supersoft Inc.

APL

There are currently few APL interpreters for the Apple CP/M system, in part because of the difficulties of implementing the APL character set on the Apple screen.

APL/V80
Vanguard Systems Corp.
64K memory

An APL interpreter system, with built-in functions and operators. Also allows the Apple computer to be used as a remote APL terminal.

Assembly/Machine

For Apple CP/M, there are a number of assemblers available. The first group can usually be obtained on a CP/M or CP/M Plus system disk, or from a language software package:

ASM assembler—usually provided with CP/M
MAC assembler—a macro-assembler for CP/M
RMAC assembler—relocatable macro-assembler for CP/M

One inexpensive compiler available separately is:

UVMAC Z80 MACRO ASSEMBLER
Software Toolworks

UVMAC is an absolute macro-assembler for Z-80, which accepts the full set of Z-80 mnemonics. It also includes an AS version, which doesn't support macros but compiles twice as fast.

C

TOOLWORKS C/80
Software Toolworks
56K memory minimum

This is a very inexpensive, yet powerful C compiler. It supports virtually the full C language. By itself, it doesn't support float or long data types, but with the addition of another float/ long package, that can be implemented as well. Compiler produces code for AS, RMAC, or Macro-80 assemblers.

SUPERSOFT C
Supersoft Inc.
48K memory minimum

A full, professional implementation of the C language.

AZTEC C
Manx Software Systems
48K memory minimum

A professional package for C program development.

BDS C
BD Software
24K minimum

A full implementation of the C language, known for its fast execution speed and extensive library of functions. Although it is not a standard implementation of C, it features very fast compilation speed.

Forth

Forth interpreters are available under Apple DOS.

Lisp

MULISP ARTIFICIAL INTELLIGENCE DEVELOPMENT SYSTEM
Microsoft Corp.
48K

A Lisp development system for Apple CP/M. A professional package for Lisp programmers and artificial intelligence researchers.

LISP/80
Software Toolworks
48K

An implementation of the Interlisp dialect, with more than 75 functions, editor, documentation, and Eliza program.

MULISP
Soft Warehouse
56K memory

This is similar to the Microsoft version of MuLisp.

Logo

The Logo packages available for the Apple are usually in the standard DOS format rather than CP/M.

Modula-2

See Apple DOS for Modula-2 compiler systems.

PILOT

NEVADA PILOT
Ellis Computing
48K

A version of PILOT-73, written by John Starkweather, PILOT's inventor.

PL/1

PL/1 is not available in Apple CP/M, but only in standard 8-inch CP/M and CP/M-86.

Prolog

MICRO-PROLOG
Logic Programming Associates (U.K.)
48K

A microcomputer version of Prolog which is one of the few commercial products available for CP/M. Package includes the interpreter, sample programs, manual, and tutorial book.

SAS-SPSS

No Apple versions of SAS-SPSS are available, for DOS, or CP/M.

Apple III

The Apple III, in emulation mode, can run Apple II software. Therefore, most of the programs listed for the Apple II can be run on the Apple III.

APPLE BUSINESS BASIC
Apple Computer Company
128K, SOS

This powerful form of BASIC is used for both business and scientific applications, with extended data types, advanced file handling, and long variable names.

APPLE III PASCAL
Apple Computer Company
128K, SOS

An implementation of UCSD Pascal for the Apple III.

Apple Lisa

RM/FORTRAN
Ryan-McFarland Corp.

A full implementation of the ANSI FORTRAN-77 standard.

Apple Macintosh

The Macintosh is a new computer system, and software is currently being written for it. Listed below are some language packages currently available. More should be released in the months to come.

Pascal

UCSD PASCAL
Softech Microsystems
128K or 512K Macintosh

A professional package that offers access to the Macintosh routines, windows, mouse, and, menus.

APL

PORTAAPL
Portable Software
256K memory

With a few exceptions, PortaAPL follows the IBM/ACM standard and is a powerful implementation of APL.

C

MEGAMAX C
Megamax Inc.

A C compiler system for the Macintosh.

HIPPO-C Levels I and II
Hippopotamus Software
128K for Level I

A C compiler available in two versions—one for the personal and beginning user (Level I) and one for professional developers (Level II). Includes an editor, linker, on-line tutorial, debugger, and shell command processor.

CONSULAIR C
Consulair

A C compiler for the Macintosh.

AZTEC C
Manx Software Systems

See listing under Apple DOS and CP/M.

Lisp

EXPERLISP
ExperTelligence
512K Macintosh

A version of the Lisp language for the Macintosh.

Logo

EXPERLOGO
ExperTelligence Inc.

A powerful implementation of Logo, it includes not only Turtlegraphics but 3-D Bunny Graphics, which are fast-moving "turtles."

ATARI COMPUTERS

The following language software is written exclusively for the Atari 400/800 and higher series such as the 800XL and 1200XL.

BASIC

BASIC XL
Optimized Systems Software
16K minimum

A BASIC interpreter for the Atari computer system.

COBOL—FORTRAN—Pascal

There are no COBOL, FORTRAN, or Pascal language packages available in commercial form for the Atari series of computers.

Ada-APL

Because of limited memory space and keyboard limitations, Ada and APL are not currently available for the Atari.

Assembly Language

MAC/65
Optimized Systems Software
48K minimum

A macro-assembler system, including an editor, assembler, and BUG/65 debugger.

C

C/65
Optimized Systems Software
48K minimum

A C compiler for the Atari computer systems 600XL, 800XL, and 1200XL.

Forth

VALFORTH
Valpar Inc.

A Forth interpreter system for the Atari family of computers.

Lisp

Lisp is not available on Atari computer systems.

Logo

ATARI LOGO
Logo Computer Systems

A version of the Logo language for the Atari series of computers.

COMMODORE COMPUTERS

This section covers software for the Commodore series of computers such as the Commodore 64 and Commodore 128.

BASIC

SIMON'S BASIC
Commodore Inc.
Commodore-64, 64K

Expands Commodore BASIC with 114 additional commands and graphics.

SUPER EXPANDER 64
Commodore Inc.
Commodore-64, 64K

Graphics and music extensions for the C-64 BASIC.

TINY BASIC
Abacus Software

A small subset of the BASIC language for the Commodore-64 and Vic-20.

INTRO TO BASIC
Commodore Inc.

An instructional tutorial for the BASIC language.

BASIC
Commodore Inc.

A BASIC interpreter with a tutorial section.

COBOL

There are at the present time no COBOL compilers for the Commodore-64 or Vic-20 systems.

FORTRAN

There are currently no FORTRAN compilers for either the Commodore-64 or Vic-20 systems.

Pascal

PASCAL-64
Abacus Software
64K, for Commodore 64

A Pascal compiler supporting most of the basic features except sets, records, and pointers.

PASCAL
Commodore Inc.
Commodore-64

A PASCAL compiler for the Commodore-64.

Ada

Ada, because of its young age, is available for only a few systems, which does not include the Commodore series.

APL

APL is very difficult to implement on the Commodore because of the need for a special character set and keyboard.

Assembly/Machine

ASSEMBLER 64
Commodore Inc.

Includes two machine language monitors, editor, loader, and support routines. A complete development package.

MAC/65
Optimum Systems Inc.

A 6502 macro-assembler for the Commodore-64 computer.

C

C/65
Optimum Systems Inc.
48K

A C compiler for the Commodore-64 computer, the source code of which is compatible with a number of other systems.

Forth

FORTH
Commodore Inc.
Commodore-64, 64K

A Forth-79 standard, including enhancements for the Commodore-64 computer.

FORTH
Abacus Software

A Forth compiler system for the Commodore-64 and Vic-20.

FULL FORTH PLUS
CGRS Microtek
32K

A Forth system, compiling and testing words separately. Includes a screen editor for program development, and allows the use of floating-point numbers.

Lisp

There are currently no Lisp interpreters available for Commodore systems.

Logo

LOGO
Commodore Computers
Commodore 64, 64K

A version of Terrapin Logo for the Commodore, which includes sprites, sounds, and Turtlegraphics.

Modula-2

Because of its very young age, Modula-2 is not yet implemented on the Commodore series of computers.

Pilot

PILOT
Commodore Inc.
Commodore-64, 64K

A version of PILOT for the Commodore-64.

PILOT II
Tamarack Software
Commodore-64, 64K

An advanced PILOT interpreter, including files, turtlegraphics, sprite editors, color, and sound. Includes a package of programmer's aids.

VANILLA PILOT
Tamarack Software
Commodore 4000, 8000, 9000, C-64, Vic-20, 32K

A complete PILOT system, including turtle graphics and a development TRACE command.

PL/1—Prolog—SAS—SPSS

These languages are not available for any Commodore computers, but may be accessed through a model and timesharing.

PROMAL

PROMAL
Systems Management Association
Commodore-64, 64K

An implementation of the new language PROMAL

RADIO SHACK COMPUTERS

The microcomputers marketed by Radio Shack Inc. include the Tandy 1000, Tandy 2000, Model 4, and Model4P. Older models include the Models I, II, and III.

The Tandy 1000 and 2000 are IBM-compatible machines running the operating system MS-DOS. Compatible software is listed under the IBM PC section.

The other systems require special software that is listed here by language.

BASIC

Tandy/Radio Shack systems usually come with BASIC interpreters standard. There are BASIC compilers available for those who wish to speed up their programs. These are listed below, along with their respective systems:

BASIC COMPILER
Tandy/Radio Shack
Tandy 2000/1200/1000 System

COMPILER BASIC
Tandy/Radio Shack
Model 12

BASCOM BASIC COMPILER
Tandy/Microsoft
Model 12

XENIX BASIC INTERPRETER
Tandy/Radio Shack
Model 6000/16B
Advanced BASIC interpreter

BASCOM-4
Tandy/Microsoft
Model IV

SDOS 6800/6809 BASIC COMPILER
Software Dynamics
TRS-80 Color Computer
Includes and requires the SDOS operating system

A powerful BASIC compiler which supports an enhanced form of BASIC. It must be used together with SDOS (Software Dynamics Operating System). SDOS includes an editor and assembler.

COBOL

COBOL COMPILER
Tandy/Ryan McFarland
Tandy 2000/1200/1000

COBOL DEVELOPMENT SYSTEM (Ansi-74)
Tandy
Tandy 12/16/6000

XENIX COBOL
Tandy/Radio Shack
Tandy 6000/16B

COBOL-4
Tandy/Radio Shack
Model 4 (I and II versions available)

FORTRAN

MICROSOFT FORTRAN
Tandy/Microsoft
Tandy 2000/1200/1000

FORTRAN
Tandy/Radio Shack
Tandy Model 12

FORTRAN 4
Tandy/Radio Shack
Model 4 (versions for I and III also)

Pascal

MICROSOFT PASCAL
Tandy/Microsoft
Tandy 2000/1200/1000

PASCAL MT+
Tandy/Microsoft
Tandy Model 12

PASCAL-2
Tandy/Radio Shack
Model 6000/16B

ALCOR PASCAL
Tandy/Alcor
Model 4(also for I, III)

Ada

For those systems that support MS-DOS or CP/M, there are programs that may be available for your system. Check these two sections for more details.

APL

There are currently no implementations of APL written specifically for Radio Shack computers. MS-DOS IBM PC interpreters may be used on those systems that run the operating system.

Assembly

MACRO ASSEMBLER
Tandy/Microsoft
Tandy 2000/1200/1000

ASSEMBLY LANGUAGE DEVELOPMENT
Tandy/Radio Shack
Tandy Model 12

ASSEMBLY LANGUAGE DEVELOPMENT SYSTEM
Tandy/Radio Shack
Tandy Model 4

C

LATTICE C
Tandy/Lattice
Tandy 2000/1200/1000

TRS-80 MODEL 4 C
TANDY/Radio Shack
Tandy Model 4

Forth

ALTERNATE FORTH
Alternate Source
Model I, III, 4
48K

MMS FORTH
Miller Microcomputer Services
Model 4

Lisp

Check the MS-DOS (IBM PC) section for Lisp interpreters.

Logo

For 1000/2000 systems that run MS-DOS, check the IBM PC section for additional software.

Modula-2

For the 1000/2000 series, check the IBM PC section for Modula-2 compilers available (MS-DOS).

Prolog

For the MS-DOS 1000/2000 systems, see the IBM PC section.

SAS and SPSS

These two languages are not available in any form for Radio Shack computers, with the exception of timesharing systems through a modem.

Those packages designated as "Tandy/Radio Shack" can be purchased from Radio Shack stores. The firms listed as Tandy/(other firm) can be obtained either from Tandy/Radio Shack or directly from the manufacturer.

IBM PC, INCLUDING THE PC, PCJR, XT, AND AT

The IBM PC, a powerful microcomputer for business and professional applications, is supported by an impressive number of language software packages for most major languages. There are available packages for both large-scale organizations and the home user. Most of the packages are written in the operating systems available for the IBM: PC-DOS and MS-DOS.

BASIC

Listed below are BASIC interpreters and compilers that are not included with the IBM PC computer and must be purchased separately.

MEGABASIC
American Planning Corp.
64K memory

MEGABASIC is a very powerful form of BASIC, since it allows you to access "packages" of programs and data from memory, access one megebyte of memory, and execute your programs many times faster than most BASICs through the use of a run-time semicompiler. An enhanced and powerful form of BASIC.

CBASIC
Digital Research
48K minimum

A compiled form of BASIC, which executes programs quickly and features a structured form of the language.

CBASIC COMPILER
Digital Research
48K minimum

This is an enhanced version of the above CBASIC. Some of the features include 32K strings, labels, and relocatable object files.

CBASIC-86
Digital Research
48K minimum

A 16-bit version of CBASIC, designed for commercial business application programming. A version featuring 16-decimal arithmetic, file processing, and advanced string processing.

BASIC COMPILER
IBM Corp.
64K minimum

Compiles BASIC programs into machine language files.

BASIC INTERPRETER
IBM Corp.
for IBM-PCjr

An MBASIC interpreter system.

PROFESSIONAL BASIC
Morgan Computing
256K minimum

A powerful version of BASIC that can use the computer's full memory and the 8087 math co-processor. Includes a window-oriented system of trace screens for analyzing program flow, as well as enhancements for effective programming. The most powerful feature of Professional BASIC is the program execution tracing feature.

BETTER BASIC
Summit Software Technology

This BASIC system offers a large number of new, extended features. It includes a configuration file, increased number of data types, a greater choice of loops and string functions, as well as user-defined types. Files and graphics are supported, and it runs quickly. Also available are a math module and run-time system at extra cost.

BASIC COMPILER AND RUNTIME UNIT
Softech Microsystems

A BASIC compiler system for the IBM PC.

BASIC INTERPRETER (BI-286)
Control-C Software
128K

A business-oriented BASIC interpreter for the IBM MS-DOS. Includes ISAM and other file operations. Also available in multiuser version.

RM BASIC
Ryan/McFarland Corp.

A BASIC language package for the IBM PC. Features powerful line-editing commands, matrix math, graphics, and other professional features.

PLUTO BASIC
Southwest Data

This is a microcomputer version of BASIC, quite similar to minicomputer versions. Includes a number of useful functions and procedures and is designed for business users. The interpreter can interpret files from MAI/BASIC Four and CMC BASIC systems.

TBASIC
Transera

A compiled BASIC with a similarity to ANSI or Tektronic BASIC. Has matrix capabilities as well as powerful graphics.

TRUE BASIC
True Basic Inc./Addison-Wesley

Developed by Kemeny and Kurtz, the originators of the BASIC language, True BASIC, this "semicompiler" system corresponds to the new ANSI BASIC standard. Structured programming, free-form code, and a greatly improved set of loops, control structures, and graphics commands make this much more powerful than the original version. Also has powerful error handling.

WATCOM BASIC
Watcom Inc.

This version was originally developed by the University of Waterloo for larger machines but is now available for microcomputers. The system includes an editor, a matrix handling package, graphics, and network capabilities. It also supports the 8087 math co-processor.

87 BASIC
MicroWay

A version of the Microsoft BASCOM interpreter, designed to work with the 8087 math co-processor.

MTBASIC
Softaid Inc.

A multitasking package, with characteristics of both an interpreter and compiler. It has a built-in editor, is fast, and offers multitasking features. A very unusual BASIC software package.

BASIC B
Sparry Software

This compiler compiles quickly, uses virtual screens, and supports ISAM file programming. At the present time, floating point is not supported.

COBOL

CIS COBOL
Micro Focus

CIS stands for Compact, Interactive, and Standard COBOL. This version is the minicomputer version of COBOL implemented on microcomputers. This dialect is based on the ANSI 1974 X 3.23 standard.

LEVEL II COBOL
Micro Focus

This is a mainframe-level COBOL for professional users. It is a professional system and includes close to 600 pages in documentation.

PERSONAL COBOL
Micro Focus

A complete development package with editing and interactive capabilities. Includes full-screen editing, forms generation, and control of program execution for debugging purposes.

PROFESSIONAL COBOL
Micro Focus

This is a very complete and professional package for software developers. It includes the full language and even includes a communications section. The system is completely menu-driven and allows screen design and use of an animator. The extensive help menus make programming very easy.

LEVEL II COBOL
Digital Research Inc.

Designed jointly by Digital Research and Micro Focus, Level II is similar to the Micro Focus version above except that Digital Research features an access manager and display manager for the compiler.

PC COBOL
IBM Inc.

An implementation of the 1974 ANSI standard of COBOL.

MBP COBOL
Software and Systems Technology

This extremely fast COBOL offers execution speed and easy screen design. Because of the size of this program, it is best used on a hard disk system. The newest version, 9.00, includes several improvements and added features.

MICROSOFT COBOL
Microsoft Corp.

A good professional-level COBOL compiler, available in several versions.

RM-COBOL
Ryan-McFarland Corp.

An easy-to-use compiler which compiles quickly and has been used to prepare several professional software packages.

REALIA COBOL
Realia Inc.

This is reputed to be the fastest microcomputer compiler. It runs mainframe-level COBOL. Designed for users with experience in using COBOL effectively.

WATCOM COBOL
Watcom

This is a special form of COBOL, designed for students learning how to program in COBOL. There is another professional package available only to educational institutions; it must be licensed on a yearly basis.

FORTRAN

FORTRAN COMPILER
Supersoft Inc.

Supports the 1964 ANSI standard with extensions. Supports complex arithmetic and character variables. A RATFOR preprocessor is available.

MICROSOFT FORTRAN
Microsoft Inc.

A compiler which supports the full 1977 standard. Includes 8087 support. Includes a number of generic intrinsic functions.

DR. FORTRAN 77
Digital Research Inc.

A full implementation of ANSI FORTRAN-77, packaged as a complete development environment.

PC FORTRAN
IBM Inc.

ANSI FORTRAN-77 compiler for the IBM PC-DOS.

PCP FORTRAN
IBM Inc.

An enhanced version of the PC FORTRAN, PCP is designed for professional software developers.

WATCOM FORTRAN INTERPRETER
Watcom Corp.

A useful system for beginning FORTRAN students, because of the interpreted (rather than compiled) source code. Diagnostic error messages help the user learn from errors. Comes with program disk and manuals.

Pascal

UTAH PASCAL
Ellis Computing

An MS-DOS version of this inexpensive Pascal compiler.

TURBO PASCAL
Borland International
48K minimum

A very fast yet inexpensive compiler for the IBM PC. Includes a menu-driven system and a Wordstar-type built-in editor. Easy to use.

PASCAL MT+
Digital Research Inc.

Based on the ISO standard, MT+ translates source code directly into object code.

PASCAL COMPILER
IBM Inc.

A Pascal compiler for the IBM PC.

UCSD PASCAL
Softech Microsystems

A UCSD-Pascal development system for the IBM PC.

SBB PASCAL
Software Building Blocks

A complete Pascal development system for MS-DOS IBM PC.

PASCAL COMPILER
Whitesmiths Ltd.

A professional Pascal system for the IBM PC.

MICROSOFT PASCAL COMPILER
Microsoft Inc.

Offers the full language and extensions to the ISO standard.

PROFESSIONAL PASCAL
Microtek Research

A powerful Pascal package for the IBM PC, designed for serious software developers.

Ada

JANUS ADA
RR Software

A subset of the Ada language, used by many organizations for their ADA program development.

SUPERSOFT A
Supersoft Inc.

"A" is a subset of the Ada language developed by Marantha Software Systems.

APL

APL*PLUS/PC
STSC Inc.
192K

A complete APL system for the IBM, which supports the APL*PLUS version of APL. Includes character ROM, several manuals, Gilman/Rose's book, and APL software. STSC is also marketing a subset of the full system called Pocket APL.

SHARP APL/PC
I.P. Sharp Associates

An implementation of Sharp APL for the IBM.

APL
IBM Inc.

An APL interpreter, requiring the 8087 math co-processor to function, along with the color graphics adapter.

PORTAAPL
Portable Software

This APL interpreter does not require addition of a special ROM or keyboard but will provide the necessary characters from software.

WATCOM APL
Watcom Co.

This APL interpreter system includes a ROM chip for implementing the character set, as well as labels for the keyboard. The system comes with reference manuals on APL and on how to operate the system.

Assembly Language (Assemblers)

MACRO ASSEMBLER
IBM Inc.
128K minimum

A complete assembler system which allows the formation of macros. Supports 80286 and 8087 computer systems, as well as a pre-processor and library manager.

PASM 86
Phoenix Software Products
An assembler for the IBM PC

C

LATTICE C
Lattice Inc.
128K minimum

A powerful and widely used IBM C compiler. It runs under MS-DOS and produces 8086 code. The full Kernighan and Ritchie C is supported, and it includes several enhancements as well.

OPTIMIZING C86 COMPILER
Computer Innovations
128K memory

A PC/MS-DOS full C compiler with various extensions and an extensive C86 library.

MICROSOFT C
Microsoft Inc.
256K minimum

A very fast and professional C compiler for MS-DOS. Includes a compiler, runtime library, linker, and library manager. Source code from Xenix or Unix can be transported to Microsoft C.

MWC86
Mark Williams Company

The MWC C86 is a professional C compiler for MS-DOS developers. It is widely used because of its speed, small memory space requirement, and user-friendly command structure. The system includes a CSD source debugger to trace and understand program problems.

INSTANT C
Rational Systems
320K

A system designed to save time in program development. It has a very fast compile time, absence of link time, and an integrated editor.

WIZARD C
Wizard Systems

A C compiler system for the IBM PC.

C COMPILER
Supersoft C
MS and PC DOS

A powerful, full C compiler, complete with compiler, utilities, and more than 135 library functions. A professional development package.

AZTEC C/PRO
Manx Software Systems
PC and MS DOS

An optimized C compiler which supports the full 7C version of the C language. The system includes math, screen, and graphics libraries, as well as an assembler, and the option of a /PRO feature upgrade.

C
C-Systems

A C compiler system for the IBM PC.

DE SMET C
C Ware
MS-DOS

This is a fast compiler, which supports the complete C language. The development package includes a compiler, assembler, linker, librarian, and editor. A symbolic debugger is also included.

SMALL-C
Datalight
PC or MS-DOS

Although not as complete as professional versions, Small-C is suitable for smaller-scale applications. Includes source code, I/O, and standard libraries, and the option exists for purchasing a source-level debugger.

C COMPILER
IBM Inc.

A C compiler for the IBM PC.

C COMPILER
Whitesmiths Ltd.
PC or MS-DOS

This professional compiler supports the full C as defined by Kernighan and Ritchie. It includes support files, extensive documentation, and a large C library.

Forth

HS/FORTH
Harvard Softworks

This complete Forth package includes such features as graphics, music, management support, co-processor support, optimizer, and assembler. It executes very fast and includes both the Forth-79 and Forth-83 standards.

PC/FORTH
Laboratory Microsystems Inc.

Based on the Forth-83 standard, this application development system includes an interpreter/compiler, editor, decompiler, utilities, and multitasking facilities. There is an advanced version known as Forth+.

MMS FORTH
Miller Microcomputer Services

The MMS versions of Forth development packages for the IBM PC.

MVP FORTH
Mountain View Press
Programmer's Kit

This FIG-Forth source offers a programmer's kit, including disk, documentation, *Starting Forth* book, and source code/glossary. A variety of other books and software are available directly from MVP.

ASSIST
Macmillan Inc. (software)

A Forth-like language for the IBM PC.

Lisp

MU LISP
Microsoft Inc./Soft Warehouse
128K

A Lisp interpreter developed by the Soft Warehouse and distributed by Microsoft. It includes a good editor, fast execution, and tutorials.

UO LISP and LEARNING LISP
Northwest Computer Algorithms

A newly revised and complete Lisp development system. It includes an editor, compiler/optimizer, RLisp, Lisptex, Lisp interpreter, and an option to purchase the Learning Lisp package.

GOLDEN COMMON LISP
Gold Hill Computer Inc.
512K

A complete Common Lisp development package, including a GMACS editor, the "San Marco Lisp Explorer" (an instructional system), Lisp textbook, reference manual, on-line documentation, and multitasking features.

IQ LISP
Integral Quality Inc.
PC-DOS

A Lisp development system, which has close to 200 primitives, I/O support, 8087 support, graphics, and a Lisp library.

BYSO LISP
Levien Instrument Co.
128K

A subset of McCarthy's Lisp 1.5.

LISP/80
Software Toolworks

An inexpensive version of Lisp, designed for medium-size applications.

Logo

IBM LOGO
Logo Computer Systems/IBM
128K

Designed by Logo Computer Systems and marketed by IBM. A complete package including Turtlegraphics. Includes a reference manual and an "easy introduction."

DR. LOGO
Digital Research
192K

An implementation of Logo for the IBM PC, which includes the software and full documentation. Also includes an introductory manual for a basic coverage for beginners.

Modula-2

MODULA-2
Volition Systems
64K

A UCSD p-code compiler system for Modula-2, including compiler, interpreter, utilities, and library modules.

MODULA-2
Logitech
MS, PC-DOS

A native-code compiler which compiles source code into machine code. It includes multitasking features, low-level access, symbolic debugger, plus special Logitech modules. Includes professional customer support.

MODULA-2 SOFTWARE DEVELOPMENT SYSTEMS
Interface Technologies

A full implementation of the Modula-2 language. Includes an editor, linker, compiler. An easy-to-use development system for Modula-2, and reasonably priced.

PILOT

PILOT is not used on IBM computer systems.

PL/1

PL/1-86
Digital Research Inc.

A subset of the PL/1 language for use on the IBM PC. Includes compiler, documentation, and utilities.

Prolog

PROLOG-86
Solution Systems
MS-DOS/PC-DOS, 96K minimum

An interpreter for the IBM PC, adapted from the UNSW interpreter by Clause Sammut.

PROLOG-1
Expert Systems International
MS-DOS/PC-DOS

A Prolog interpreter system for the IBM PC. Includes disk, manual and sample programs.

SAS

SAS/PC
SAS Institute

A version of SAS for the IBM PC. Includes graphics and other powerful features.

SPSS

SPSS/PC
SPSS Inc.
IBM PC/XT with hard disk

A large, twelve-disk system implementing the mainframe language SPSS on the IBM PC. Includes the major analyses, including report and graphics capabilities.

OTHER LANGUAGES

MINNESOTA SNOBOL4
Berstis International
128K minimum

A complete implementation of the SNOBOL4 string processing language, developed by Viktors Berstis.

SNOBOL4+
Catspaw Inc./Prentice-Hall

A book and software system for running the SNOBOL4+ language. Available through Catspaw or Prentice-Hall, it includes a complete guide to the language and the language system.

GAUSS
Applied Technical Systems

A specialized matrix programming language for doing mathematical and statistical tasks. There are also programs for statistics and data handling. The mathematical capabilities of C or FORTRAN are included in Gauss, but Gauss is capable of handling matrices as data items.

THE SENSIBLE SOLUTION
O'Hanlon Computer Systems

A business-oriented specialty language which handles database management, screens, field masking, editor, and debugger.

ADAPT
Wilmes Systems
192K, MS-DOS

A business applications language, specializing in forms, data entry, and information records. The English-like language can be used for a variety of business tasks.

DBASE II
Ashton-Tate

This widely used and powerful database management language is used to store and analyze information for business applications. It is "programmed" with its own language and includes a tutorial and utility programs.

DBASE III
Ashton-Tate

A more powerful version of DBase II, which is available only for the IBM PC. It enhances the powers of its predecessor and offers many additional professional capabilities.

RBASE 5000
Microrim

A powerful database management language package for business data filing and manipulation.

CP/M OPERATING SYSTEM

The software in this category is written for the widely used microcomputer operating system CP/M. The letters stand for Control Program/Microcomputers. This operating system, used on many different kinds of computers, supports a very wide selection of software in all application areas. The operating system itself was written and developed by Digital Research of Pacific Grove, California.

We will center on the CP/M-80 and the CP/M-86 operating systems here. The first is generally used on Z-80, 8080, and 8085 type microprocessors (8-bit), while CP/M-86 is used on 16-bit machines such as the IBM PC. The major language compilers and interpreters available are listed, along with some general information about each program. For more detailed information about each product, you might contact the companies themselves. They will be able to help you determine if the program is the right implementation for you.

CP/M-80

BASIC

MBASIC INTERPRETER
Microsoft Corp.
5¼-inch disk format for standard CP/M
or Apple CP/M

An extended form of BASIC that supports many advanced features such as structured programming and advanced strings. The compiler version translates programs into machine code, making programs run three to ten times faster than an interpreted version.

CB80 and CBASIC
Digital Research Inc.
8-inch disk formats for CP/M

CBASIC is a form of BASIC that is suited for business applications because of its efficient memory use, compiled translation, and business-related features. It is the leading form of BASIC for business programs. CB80 is an enhanced form of the language.

BI-280
Control-C Software

An implementation of Business BASIC II, which is a popular minicomputer level BASIC. It allows micro users to create minicomputer-level programs.

HAI*BAS BASIC
Holland Automation

A commercial form of BASIC suitable for business applications.

ZIL
Softmart Inc.

A form of BASIC that comes in both interpreted and compiled forms. Used for making control programs.

BASIC-Z
Software Source

This includes a compiler/editor, tree structures, sort/merge, and automatic terminal configuration.

COBOL

MICROSOFT COBOL-80
Microsoft Corporation
5¼-inch disks for Apple and standard CP/M

A widely used form of the COBOL compiler for microcomputers. Comes with a compiler, editor, and various utilities.

CIS COBOL
Digital Research
8-inch disks for standard format

Based on the ANSI'74 COBOL, this COBOL compiler software system has Cobol features of larger machines while retaining interactive features of the microcomputer.

CIS COBOL and LEVEL II COBOL
Micro Focus Inc.
5¼-inch and 8-inch disks for standard format

These two powerful forms of COBOL are minicomputer and mainframe computer compilers that are designed to run on microcomputers. CIS is based on ANSI '74, as well as Level II, which is a full mainframe version. Includes various programming tools.

RM COBOL
Ryan McFarland Corp.
5¼-inch and 8-inch disks for standard format

A widely used COBOL compiler which is used on a large number of machines and microprocessors.

NEVADA COBOL
Ellis Computing
5¼-inch or 8-inch disks for various formats

A subset of the COBOL language, this inexpensive form of the language is available for many different microcomputers.

FORTRAN

MICROSOFT FORTRAN-80
Microsoft Corp. (Mic)
5¼-inch or 8-inch Apple or standard CP/M

A widely used and powerful form of the FORTRAN IV language. Includes compiler, linker, and various utilities.

FORTRAN COMPILER
Supersoft Inc.
Standard CP/M

A full implementation of ANSI 1966 FORTRAN including many advanced features. A professional package.

NEVADA FORTRAN
Ellis Computing (Ell)
5¼-inch or 8-inch CP/M

A low-cost subset of FORTRAN ANSI-1966. Includes one disk and manual.

Pascal

PASCAL/MT+
Digital Research
8-inch standard CP/M

Pascal MT+ compiler is a version of ISO Standard Pascal, translating Pascal into object code. Included is a Speed Programming Package, which helps in debugging.

TURBO PASCAL
Borland International
5¼-inch and 8-inch CP/M

An inexpensive form of Pascal, this compiler is based on Standard Pascal, with some changes. A speedy and efficient form of the language, written in popular microcomputer CP/M formats.

Ada

JANUS ADA
RR Software
5¼-inch and 8-inch CP/M

Janus Ada is a subset of the Ada language, which includes most of the features feasible for use on a microcomputer. Includes a compiler, library, assembler, linker, and disassembler. Used in many educational and scientific environments.

AUGUSTA
Laboratory Microsystems
5¼-inch and 8-inch CP/M

A subset of the Ada language developed by Computer Linguistics.

APL

PORTAAPL
Portable Software

An APL interpreter system for CP/M which does not require a special chip, keyboard, or color/graphics adapter.

C

C/80
Software Toolworks
5¼-inch and 8-inch CP/M

A low-cost C compiler which is a complete implementation of the language except for floats and longs.

C COMPILER
Supersoft
5¼-inch and 8-inch CP/M

A professional full version of Unix version 7 Standard C. Includes over 135 library functions.

BDS C
BD Software
5¼-inch and 8-inch CP/M

This compiler is a fast and efficient version of C. It includes overlays, library, sample programs, and a symbolic debugger.

WHITESMITHS C
Whitesmiths Ltd.
5¼-inch and 8-inch CP/M

A full-language compiler, with extensive utilities and library. A professional package for serious programmers.

C COMPILER AND MICROSOFT C
Infosoft
5¼-inch and 8-inch CP/M

A 3-pass C compiler that supports a subset of C. It generates 8080 type object code.

AZTEC C
Manx Software Systems
5¼-inch and 8-inch CP/M-80

A full C compiler for professional program development.

ECO-C
Ecosoft Inc.
8-inch CP/M, other formats available

A professional C development system, producing code for Macro-80 or SLR assemblers. The package includes over 100 library functions, manual, and C programming guide.

Forth

POLY FORTH
Forth Company
5¼-inch and 8-inch CP/M

A complete, professional development environment developed by the Forth Company, related to the original Forth developers. Includes a complete version of Forth including debugging aids and an assembler.

JIB RAY FORTH
Jib Ray Company
8-inch CP/M

A Forth compiler, well supported and documented, with excellent special features.

Z80 FORTH
Laboratory Microsystem
8-inch CP/M

A complete application development system including interpreter/compiler, assembler, screen editor, and decompiler.

FORTH 79 V2
Micromotion
5¼-inch and 8-inch CP/M

A professional system based on the Forth-79 standard, it features portable programs, an interactive environment, screen editor, assembler, and tutorial.

STACKWORKS FORTH
Stackworks
8-inch CP/M

A powerful yet simple-to-use Forth interpreter/compiler.

TASK FORTH
Shaw Laboratories
5¼-inch and 8-inch CP/M

A professional yet low-cost Forth system, including a Novice Programmer Protection Package, screen editor, and hierarchical file system.

Lisp

MULISP/MUSTAR
SoftWarehouse (Swh)
5¼-inch and 8-inch CP/M

This Lisp pseudo-code interpreter and compiler is based on Lisp 1.5 and extensions. The MuStar portion is an editor and debugger.

TOOLWORKS LISP/80
Software Toolworks
5¼-inch and 8-inch CP/M

This interpreter is based on the Interlisp dialect, including over 75 functions and editor and library.

TLC LISP
The Lisp Company

A version of Lisp for CP/M-80, which is also listed in the IBM PC section.

U-O LISP
Northwest Computer Algorithms

A Lisp development package with interpreter, extensive documentation, utilities, and other useful additions. A separate Learning Lisp tutorial package is also available.

PILOT

NEVADA PILOT
Ellis Computing
5¼-inch and 8-inch CP/M

Based on the PILOT-73 Standard. It includes a full-screen editor.

STOK PILOT
Stok Inc.
8-inch CP/M

The Stok interpreter supports a superset of the PILOT language.

PL/1

PL/1-80
Digital Research
8-inch CP/M

This compiler is based on the ANSI Subset G, which produces 8080 object code. It includes such features as pictures, fixed/float, and binary, and it comes complete with the compiler, linker, librarian, and assembler.

RPGII

RPGII
Software West
8-inch CP/M

Based on IBM system 8 RPGII, it includes compiler, utilities, execution aids, manual. It supports the full language.

Other languages not listed are not available at this time for the CP/M-80 Operating System. They may be available in the near future.

CP/M-86

BASIC

BI-286
Control-C Software
Standard CP/M

A basic interpreter supporting Business BASIC II, a previously exclusive minicomputer language.

CB-86
Digital Research
5-inch and 8-inch disks

A native code compiler for BASIC programs, which supports the compilation of separate program modules.

CBASIC-86
Digital Research
5-¼-inch and 8-inch disks

A 16-bit version of CBASIC, with extended mathematics, file processing, and string processing.

PERSONAL BASIC
Digital Research
5¼-inch and 8-inch disks

An advanced BASIC interpreter designed for novice users. Includes a tutorial, development, testing, and debugging aids. Friendly environment for persons new to BASIC.

BASIC-Z
Software Source
256K disks CP/M

A native code compiler with various features and extensions. Includes sort/merge, BCD mathematics.

MEGABASIC
American Planning Corp.

See the IBM-PC listing.

COBOL

CIS COBOL-86
Digital Research
5¼-inch or 8-inch disks

Based on ANSI '74 COBOL, this compiler has many mini and mainframe features as well as microcomputer extensions.

LEVEL II COBOL-86
Digital Research
5¼-inch and 8-inch disks

A mainframe-level compiler for microcomputers. Full ANSI74 COBOL.

CIS COBOL and LEVEL II COBOL
Micro Focus Inc.
5¼-inch and 8-inch CP/M

Like their CP/M-80 counterparts, CIS and Level II are the 16-bit versions of these powerful minicomputer-level and mainframe-level compilers. They are professional compiler packages.

RM/COBOL
Ryan McFarland Inc.

A 16-bit version of this popular microcomputer compiler for professional and business use.

Pascal

TURBO PASCAL
Borland International

See the listing under Apple CP/M or CP/M-80.

PASCAL/MT+
Digital Research
5¼-inch and 8-inch

An 8086 version of ISO Standard Pascal Compiler, which includes a complete development system. Includes a Speed Programming Package enhancement.

SBB PASCAL DEVELOPMENT PACKAGE
Software Building Blocks

Pascal compiler system.

Ada

JANUS/ADA
RR Software

See the listing under CP/M-80.

APL

IDEAL-APL
Alan Pearson Ltd.
5¼-inch and 8-inch

A CP/M version of APL interpreter for microcomputers.

PORTAAPL
Portable Software

A CP/M-86 version interpreter for 16-bit computers. Runs APL without a special keyboard, chip, or graphics adapter.

C

C COMPILER
Digital Research
8-inch CP/M and other formats

A complete implementation of Unix v.7 C, with linker, assembler, librarian, and library.

CC-86
Control-C Software
8-inch CP/M and other formats

This full C compiler compiles source code into object modules. Includes floating point and many functions.

SUPERSOFT C
Supersoft Inc.
5¼-inch and 8-inch

Includes most of Unix v.7. It is a high-quality professional compiler package.

CP/M-86 C
Telecom

A native code C compiler, featuring the full v.7 language, along with the Unix library.

MWC
Mark Williams Co.
Needs two 243K drives

The full C language is implemented, with an I/O library, linker, and assembler.

C-86 C COMPILER
Computer Innovations
5¼-inch and 8-inch

A 16-bit version complete C language package.

WHITESMITHS C
Whitesmiths Ltd.
5¼-inch and 8-inch

A professional, full version of the C language. Includes a set of utilities and a Unix C I/O library.

LATTICE C
Lifeboat Associates
5¼-inch and 8-inch

A high-quality and fast 16-bit C compiler for large, professional applications. Includes many development tools.

INSTANT-C
Rational Systems

A C compiler with very fast compilation and execution, full screen editor, symbolic debugging, and automatic recompilation features.

DE SMET C
C Ware

See the listing under IBM PC software.

AZTEC C
Manx Software Systems

A professional-level C compiler system featuring the complete C language. Includes an extensive library. See also IBM and Apple sections.

Forth

MVP FORTH
Mountain View Press

See the listing under Apple or IBM PC, FIG-Forth system.

PC/FORTH
Laboratory Microsystems

See the listing under CP/M-80. Complete Forth system.

Lisp

SUPERSOFT LISP
Supersoft Inc.

Lisp interpreter system for CP/M-86.

MICROSOFT MU-LISP
Microsoft Corp.

Lisp Artificial Intelligence System.

TLC LISP
The Lisp Company

A Lisp interpreter and development system for CP/M-86.

GOLDEN COMMON LISP
Gold Hill Computer Company

A professional Common Lisp package, including hundreds of functions, documentation, Lisp books, and a "lisp explorer" program.

Modula-2

MODULA-2
Logitech Inc.

Native code compiler for CP/M-86. Professional system.

Prolog

PROLOG-86
Solution Systems

A Prolog development system for CP/M-86.

Other languages not listed are not available for CP/M-86.

21 CHAPTER

TELE-COMMUNICATIONS UNIX, AND OTHER SYSTEMS

TELECOMMUNICATIONS SERVICES

Microcomputers can be used to run most programs needed by personal computer users, since many microcomputer versions of languages are comparable to their mainframe counterparts. However, in some cases a more powerful version of a language or one that is unavailable in a micro format is needed. With the advent of the "telecommunications revolution," any microcomputer with a modem and communications software can access mainframe computers throughout the world.

It is fascinating to think that one can just dial a phone number, most likely a local one, type in a few commands, and instantly be connected to a computer in California, Virginia, London, or Tokyo! Networks such as Tymnet, Telenet, and others connect your home computer to hundreds of computer systems around the world.

There is an abundance of computer services available, but here we will concern ourselves only with those that offer programming language timesharing. That is, we "share" the use of the computer concurrently with many other users. Systems are set up for either batch or interactive processing. In *batch* mode a program is written with an editor, then submitted to the appropriate compiler for translation and execution. We receive the results in the form of a printout or other form of output. *Interactive* systems enable the user to put in a program, see the results immediately, and then make any changes or create a hard copy printout.

The telecommunications services we will present here are grouped into "popular" and "professional" services. *Popular* services are designed for the home user or hobbyist, and the charges reflect this orientation. *Professional* services are designed for large-scale business users and often offer databases and prewritten application programs.

Pricing is usually grouped into the following general areas:

1. *Connect time.* This refers to how long you stay connected to the computer service. It is usually measured in a figure per hour.
2. *CPU usage.* There may be a separate charge for the time that you use the computer's central processing unit. This is usually much higher per hour than the connect charge.
3. *Storage.* Many services add a charge for the amount of information you store in your files on the computer. For example, to store 10,000 80-character records on a system at a rate of $0.16 per 1,000 characters a month would come to $128.
4. *Communications costs.* The costs of using a communications network such as Tymnet, Telenet, or the company's own network may be listed as a separate charge.
5. *Initiation charge.* This is the cost of opening up an account and obtaining user id#s, passwords, and manuals. This can be in the range of from none to several thousands of dollars.
6. *Minimum monthly charge.* Some services charge a minimum every month you're a user. That means that if there is a $15 minimum, even if you use none or less than $15, you will still be charged the minimum. Some companies have no minimum, while others can have a minimum of hundreds of dollars.

To get started, call or write the company and explain what service you are interested in. They will send you information about their service and details on how to sign up.

Popular Services

COMPUSERVE and THE SOURCE

These two services, probably the most popular and well known of the ones mentioned, previously had language programming, but they no longer offer them to regular users. They do offer a wide range of other services, however.

DELPHI
3 Blackstone Avenue
Cambridge, MA 02139
(800) 544-4005

Founded in 1980 by Wes Kussmaul, this service originally started out with an electronic version of the Cadillac Modern Encyclopedia and eventually expanded into other services, such as electronic banking, shopping, and travel, along with games, gateways to the Source, Dialog, and Official Airline Guides. Last but not least, on its VAX it features computer languages such as BASIC, COBOL, FORTRAN, and Pascal. There is a subscription fee and also a straight hourly connect charge, which varies from day to night. There is no monthly minimum.

DATA-NET
4515 Culver Road
Rochester, NY 14622
(716) 244-9210

Data-Net, a relatively new service from Arm Associates, features news/information, application programs, shopping, mailgrams, e-mail, and of course the programming languages C, Pascal, BASIC, COBOL, and FORTRAN. It has no subscription fee and is billed by a straight hourly charge. There is a small minimum per month, though.

FINREPORT COMPUTER SERVICES
One Moody Street
Waltham, MA 02154
(617) 647-5550

Twilight, a service from FinReport Computer Services, offers mainframe computing on their mainframe IPL 4460 computers, running VM/CMS operating system. Languages supported include COBOL, APL, PL/1, BASIC, FORTRAN

IV, and VS FORTRAN. This service is available only in evenings and includes half a megabyte (500,000) storage, Tymnet network access, and technical support, all for a flat fee of $10 an hour, with a two-hour monthly minimum.

JOHN DRAPER'S PROGRAMMING NETWORK
182 Caldecott Lane
No. 126
Oakland, CA 94618
(415) 540-7058

A new service, formed in September 1984 by John T. Draper, it is designed to support and help fill the needs of programmers. It contains tips on programming, job placement, computing resources, and program development. The service carries a subscription fee, monthly minimum, and hourly connect time charge. Network used is Tymnet.

THE SOLUTION
5701 Prescott Avenue
Lincoln, NE 68506-5155
(402) 483-2238

A strictly programming service for software developers and hobbyists. It features a Unix System III with the languages C, COBOL, SNOBOL4, FORTRAN, Assembly, and Lisp. It features extensive on-line documentation on the Unix system. There is a subscription fee, a minimum charge, and both prime- and nonprime-time rates.

Professional Services

APL Services

These computing services offer primarily the programming language APL as a part of an APL Language System. Services usually charge for connect time, CPU usage, and storage.

I.P. SHARP ASSOCIATES
2 First Canadian Place
Suite 1900
Toronto, Canada M5X 1E3
(416) 364-5361

IPSA offers computing services in the form of its Sharp APL Service. The company, formed by Ian Sharp in 1964 as a software company, has grown to become one of the world's largest APL timesharing companies in the world. The services operate on IBM and Amdahl mainframes located in their Toronto data center. Sharp features a worldwide communications network as well as connections to major public networks.

STSC INC.
2115 East Jefferson Street
Rockville, MD 20852
(301) 984-5000

STSC Inc., formerly Scientific Time Sharing Corporation, is a service offering APL timesharing through its APL*PLUS System. Operating on IBM 370 and 4300 computers, its APL system includes application-specific programs and programming productivity tools. The firm has its own telecommunications network and also offers microcomputer versions of APL. There is no initiation fee, although there is a monthly minimum.

THE COMPUTER COMPANY
1905 Westmoreland Street
Richmond, VA 23230
(804) 358-2171

The Computer Company offers primarily APL services in a form known as APL.SV. It operates on IBM 370 and Amdahl 470 computers and includes PL/1, COBOL, and FORTRAN in batch mode. The service is available nationwide through the Tymnet network.

TSR, INC.
777 Northern Boulevard
Great Neck, NY 11021
(516) 487-0101

This company, previously named Time Sharing Resources, offers APL service through its IBM 3031 and 370 computers, as well as the languages BALassembler, BASIC, COBOL, FORTRAN, and PL/1. It features a private communications network, an enhanced version of APL, and many utilities and applications programs.

General Timesharing Services

MDCSS, INC.
7535 East Hampden Avenue
Suite 200
Denver, CO 80231
(303) 695-1500

MDCSS was formed in 1984 from McAuto, Computer Sharing Services, and Tymshare. It offers programming languages through DTSS (Dartmouth Time Sharing System), which is an interactive system. Languages offered include BASIC, COBOL, FORTRAN, PL/1, ALGOL, APL, Lisp, SNOBOL4, and the GMAP assembly language. Numerous application programs are offered. The company has a private worldwide telecommunications network and uses Honeywell, Cyber, and DEC VAX computers.

CONTROL DATA CYBERNET
8100 34th Avenue South
Box 0
Minneapolis, MN 55440
(612) 853-8100

Control Data Corporation, one of the world leaders in the computer industry, offers timesharing services through its Cybernet division. Operating out of its main data center in Minneapolis, as well as data centers throughout the world, on CDC Cyber computers, Control Data offers a wide range of computer services. The programming languages offered include BASIC, COBOL, FORTRAN, ALGOL, and Pascal. CDC does not charge any initiation fee nor any minimum monthly charge. The company operates its own worldwide communications network.

COMPUTER SCIENCES CORP. INFONET
650 North Sepulveda Boulevard
El Segundo, CA 90245
(213) 615-0311

Computer Sciences Corporation, a major computer services company, first started in 1959 and began its Infonet remote computing services in 1970. Besides offering a complete range of application-specific programs, it has programming languages including COBOL, FORTRAN, Assembler, BASIC, and APL. CSC operates a worldwide private network system.

IBM INFORMATION NETWORK
P.O. Box 30104
Tampa, FL 33630-3104
(813) 872-3826

An independent unit of IBM, Inc., the network offers a wide range of languages for clients' use. From its headquarters in Tampa, Florida, through IBM mainframes, it uses two main systems, the MVSPS and the VMPS. The MVSPS offers the languages Assembler, COBOL, FORTRAN, and PL/1. The VMPS offers APL, RPGII, Pascal, and BASIC in addition to the languages in the MVSPS system. There are many forms of each programming language for the user to choose from. Services use both a private IBM network and the Telenet network. There is a minimum monthly charge.

UNITED INFORMATION SERVICES
5454 West 110th Street
Overland Park, KS 66211
(913) 341-9161

UIS, a division of the Control Data Corporation, offers computing services in the form of Apex, Supra, Dec-10, and Centra Services. The Apex service uses CDC Cyber computers and offers the languages FORTRAN, BASIC, COBOL, SNOBOL4, Pascal, and APL. The Cray service uses a Cray-1 computer and supports FORTRAN and Assembler. The Dec-10 and Centra (IBM) services offer the languages mentioned above, as well as those available for each specific machine.

COMPUSOURCE
Raleigh Federal Building
1155 Kildaire Farm Road
Cary, NC 27511
(919) 469-3325

Compusource, a computer services firm specializing in IBM services, offers the languages PL/1, Assembler, FORTRAN, COBOL, and Statistical (SPSS, SAS) languages. Its IBM mainframes are available by direct dial-up or through the Tymnet network. There is no initiation charge, but there is a minimum monthly charge.

Educational Computing-Based Systems

EDUNET
P.O. Box 364
Princeton, NJ 08540
(609) 734-1878

Edunet is a network based on university computer systems that is available for colleges, research, and nonprofit organizations. In addition to computing services, electronic mail is also available. The university systems represented and the languages available are listed below. Services on a specific system may be available to individuals; however a subscription to the entire Edunet is not.

Carnegie-Mellon (DEC-20): APL, BASIC, COBOL, FORTRAN, Pascal, C, SPSS.
University of Chicago (IBM, DEC): FORTRAN, PL/1, COBOL, WATFIV FORTRAN, SNOBOL4, APL, BASIC, Lisp, Macro Assembler.
City University of New York (IBM, Amdahl): Assemblers, FORTRAN, COBOL, PL/1, APL, Student Compilers in Assembler, PL/C, BASIC, Pascal.
University of Colorado (CDC Cyber): FORTRAN, Assembler, Pascal, BASIC, Assembler.
Cornell University (IBM 3081): COBOL, ALGOL, Assembler, Assist, FORTRAN, Lisp, Pascal, PL/1, SNOBOL4, BASIC, APL.
Dartmouth College DTSS (Honeywell): BASIC, PL/1, FORTRAN, COBOL, Pascal.
University of Delaware (Burroughs): ALGOL, COBOL, FORTRAN, PL/1. (DEC-10): APL, BASIC, FORTRAN, Lisp, Pascal, SNOBOL4.
Massachusetts Institute of Technology (Honeywell, IBM): BASIC, FORTRAN, PL/1, APL.
University of Michigan (Amdahl): ALGOL, APL, Assemblers, BASIC, COBOL, FORTRAN, Lisp, Pascal, PL/1, SNOBOL4.
Wayne State University (Amdahl): ALGOL, APL, Asssembler, BASIC, COBOL, FORTRAN, Lisp, SNOBOL4.
Western Michigan University (DEC): ALGOL, BASIC, COBOL, FORTRAN, Icon, Lisp, Assembler, Pascal, RPG, SNOBOL4.
University of Minnesota (CDC Cyber): ALGOL, APL, BASIC, COBOL, FORTRAN, Lisp, Pascal, SNOBOL4.
North Carolina TUCC (IBM 3081): Assembler, COBOL, FORTRAN, Pascal, PL/1, RPGII, SNOBOL4, APL.

Notre Dame University (IBM 370): COBOL, Assembler, FORTRAN, Pascal, PL/1, BASIC.
Rice University (NAS 9000): ALGOL, Assembler, COBOL, FORTRAN, Lisp, Pascal, PL/1, APL, SAS, SPSS.
University of Southern California (Dec-20): Pascal, FORTRAN, ALGOL, Lisp, Bliss, SNOBOL4, Simula, COBOL, SPSS, PILOT.
Stanford University (IBM 3081): APL, Assembler, BASIC, COBOL, FORTRAN, PL/1, SNOBOL4.
Stockholm University (Amhdalh 470): FORTRAN, PL/1.
University of Wisconsin (Univac 1100): ALGOL, APL, Assembler, COBOL, FORTRAN, Lisp, Pascal, PL/1, SNOBOL4, Spitbol4.
Yale University (IBM 4341): Assembler, FORTRAN, PL/1, SNOBOL4, APL, BASIC, COBOL, Watbol, Pascal.

NEW JERSEY EDUCATIONAL COMPUTER NETWORK
3900 Park Avenue
Edison, NJ 08820
(201) 549-9700

NJECN, a private nonprofit corporation, is the central computing network for educational institutions in New Jersey. Founded in 1969, it was the first statewide network in the United States. The service owns two mainframes, an IBM 3033 for batch computing and a 370/168 for interactive computing through CMS. Languages offered include ALGOL, APL, Assembler, COBOL, FORTRAN, Lisp, Pascal, PL/1, PL/C, SAS, SPSS, and special student and "fast-batch" compilers. The network is reached through dial-up lines in New Jersey.

Unix Operating System

Listed below is software for Unix-based microcomputers such as the AT&T-PC and 68000 systems. Contact the manufacturers for more information about the product's compatibility to your system.

BASIC

CBASIC COMPILER
AT&T/Digital Research

An enhanced form of the CBASIC compiled form of BASIC.

GW-BASIC INTERPRETER
AT&T/Microsoft Corp.

An advanced form of BASIC including graphics and music, editor, and communications support.

PHILON FAST-BASIC/C
Philon Systems

A BASIC compiler system.

BASIC-68K
Plessey Microsystems

BASIC interpreter software.

68000 UNIFLEX C
Technical Systems Components

BASIC language and control system.

SMC THOROUGHBRED BASIC
Science Management Corp.

Business BASIC compiler.

LPI BASIC
Language Processors Inc.

A compiled BASIC, compatible with Microsoft BASIC.

COBOL

MICROSOFT COBOL
Microsoft Corp.

The most advanced version of COBOL available through Microsoft, it is based on the Level 2 ANSI '74 standard, which is identical to mainframe implementations.

ACT COBOL 74
Advanced Computer Techniques

A full Level 2 standard compiler.

LPI COBOL
Language Processors Inc.

A full COBOL compiler system.

FORTRAN

MICROSOFT FORTRAN
Microsoft Corp.

This is a version of FORTRAN based on the ANSI X3.9-1978 standard. It includes, among other features, an extensive subroutine library.

ACT FORTRAN 77
Advanced Computer Techniques

Generates native object code based on the FORTRAN-77 x3.9-1978 standard.

Pascal

PASCAL/MT+
AT&T/Digital Research

A native code compiler for the full ISO standard of Pascal. The system includes the compiler, linker, run-time library, disassembler, and program debugger.

MS-PASCAL
Microsoft Corp.

An ISO standard compiler with various extensions. A native code compiler.

I.PAS 8000
Ithaca Intersystems

Pascal compiler system.

ACT PASCAL
Advanced Computer Techniques

Superset of the ISO standard Pascal.

LPI-PASCAL
Language Processors

Pascal compiler system.

C

DIGITAL RESEARCH C
AT&T/Digital Research

A complete implementation of the C language, version 7.

LPI-C
Language Processors

C language compiler.

VANDATA Z80 C
Vandata

C development system.

Forth

FORTH-68K
Plessey Microsystems

Forth compiler and interpreter for FIG Forth-79.

Logo

DR.LOGO
AT&T/Digital Research

A professional Logo program development package.

PL/1

PL/1
AT&T/Digital Research

A subset of PL/1 based on the G ANSI standard. A complete development package.

LPI-PL/1
Language Processors

ANSI G Subset compiler system for PL/1.

OTHER SYSTEMS

Timex-Sinclair

This very small system supports a special version of BASIC, as well as the following machine-level programming packages:

ZEUS ASSEMBLER
Softsync Inc.

This assembler package includes a full screen editor, mini monitor, and full assembler. (cassette)

ZEUS MONITOR AND DISASSEMBLER
Softsync Inc.

A monitor system for editing, debugging, and disassembly of machine code files. (cassette)

Texas Instruments (Professional) Series

The Texas Instruments Professional, Portable Professional, and Pro-lite are IBM-compatible machines and will run programs written for the IBM PC, as long as they are created for MS-DOS or CP/M-86. For more information on software available, consult the reference sections for the IBM PC and CP/M-86.

IBM Compatibles

For any computer designated as an "IBM-compatible," you should consult the IBM PC section for obtaining the software you need.

Other Systems (computers not covered here)

Consult the software directory for your particular system to locate the language software for your needs.

APPENDIX

LANGUAGE/APPLICATION SUMMARY CHART

This chart summarizes the information found in the language chapters and gives you a brief outline of each language's characteristics in a capsule form.

BASIC	Interactive programming, interpreted. Designed for beginners to programming. Best for developing short, quick programs.
COBOL	Specialized for business data processing. Very English-like, easy to understand. Powerful for reports and file processing. A compiled language, rigid format.
FORTRAN	The first programming language. Best suited for mathematics and science. A compiled language, must follow column restrictions.

Pascal	Designed as a teaching language. Structured form, many advanced features. A compiled language, free form.
Ada	Developed by U.S. Department of Defense. Complex software development language. Many advanced features. Not yet widely available.
APL	Very powerful and concise language. Uses a special keyboard and character set. Works with vectors, arrays, and matrices. Suitable for math/science and business.
Assembly/Machine	The machine's native language. Complex and difficult to learn. Requires knowledge of hardware. Most powerful and fastest of all languages. Assembly—uses mnemonic codes. Machine—uses numerical object codes.
C	Very flexible middle-level language. Allows manipulation of hardware. Fast execution, small memory requirement. Uses the "function library" for I/O and special function needs. Associated with the Unix system.
Forth	Unusual, specialized language. Fast execution, peculiar syntax. Popular among a group of fans. Available in the public domain. Uses stacks and postfix notation.
Lisp	List-processing artificial intelligence language. Works with primarily lists and words. Uses many sets of parentheses. Offers powerful recursive capabilities.
Logo	Simple, yet powerful artificial intelligence language. Turtlegraphics. Simple "primitive" functions. Useful for serious research in artificial intelligence.
Modula-2	Advanced descendent of Pascal. Module concept for program structure. Low-level manipulation commands. Multitasking and advanced features.

Language Availability Chart

Language	Apple	Atari	Commodore	Radio Shack	IBM	CP/M	Unix	Telecommunications
BASIC	X	X	X	X	X	X	X	X
COBOL				X	X	X	X	X
FORTRAN	X			X	X	X	X	X
Pascal	X		X	X	X	X	X	X
Ada					X	X		
APL	X				X	X		X
Assembly/ Machine	X	X	X	X	X	X	X	X
C	X		X	X	X	X	X	X
Forth	X	X	X	X	X	X		
Lisp	X	X	X	X	X	X	X	X
Logo	X	X	X	X	X	X		
Modula-2	X			X	X	X	X	
PILOT	X	X	X		X	X		
Pl/1					X	X		X
Prolog*					X	X		
SAS					X			X
SPSS					X			X

X = implementation(s) available now.

PILOT	Creates lessons for computer-assisted instruction. Simple structure and syntax.
PL/1	A large, powerful general-purpose language. Full PL/1 was the largest compiler ever built. Suitable for business and science/math.
Prolog	Logic-oriented artificial intelligence language. Creates a database of relationships. Useful for creating expert systems and for artificial intelligence research.
SAS	Statistical Analysis System. For performing statistical analyses.
SPSS	Statistical Package for the Social Sciences. For performing statistical analyses.

Availability is reflected by at least one implementation in this book's reference section.

ADVANCED BOOKS

This section is designed for those who wish more of a technical and theoretical grounding in concepts relating to computer languages and programming. The books are categorized into general topics.

I. Programming Languages

Programming Languages, by A. Tucker, 2/e (1986). A revised edition of a book originally published in 1977, it covers languages from the viewpoint of structure and applications. It includes the new languages Pascal, Prolog, C, Ada, and Modula-2. (McGraw-Hill)

Fundamentals of Programming Languages 2/E, by E. Horowitz. A coverage of languages from the viewpoint of technical and structural concepts. Designed as a college textbook. (Computer Science Press)

The Programming Language Landscape, by Ledgard & Marcotty. Covers languages from the viewpoint of design principles and their implementation in actual languages. (SRA)

Computer Language Reference Guide 2/E, by H. Helms. Gives a concise reference overview of nine languages. (H.W. Sams)

Programming the IBM PC and XT, by C. Germain. A computer specific (IBM PC-DOS) guide to several languages, including examples and programming techniques. (Brady)

The Master Handbook of High-Level Microcomputer Languages, by C. Taylor. A beginner's guide to ten programming languages, using examples from microcomputer compilers/interpreters. (TAB)

Programming Languages: Featuring the IBM PC and Compatibles, by Steigler & Hansen. Covers twelve languages available for IBM PC computers, with examples using machine-specific compilers and interpreters. (Baen)

II. Compilers

Compiler Construction, by Barrett & Couch. A complete coverage of compilers and translation, including both the mathematical foundations and the practical aspects of designing professional compilers. An advanced textbook. (SRA)

The Theory and Practice of Compiler Writing, by Tremblay & Sorenson. An advanced textbook on developing compiler programs. (McGraw-Hill)

III. Computer Organization and Structure

Introduction to Computer Architecture, by Stone et al. A book covering a selection of topics in computer architecture, both basic and advanced, with chapters written by a number of different authors. (SRA)

Introduction to Computer Organization, by I. Tomek. A coverage of hardware organization from the logic viewpoint. (Computer Science Press)

IV. Data Structures and Computer Algorithms

Fundamental of Data Structures, by Horowitz & Sahni. A mathematically oriented textbook on data structures. (Computer Science Press)

Data Structures, by M. Elson. A beginning coverage of data structures, including sections on Lisp & SNOBOL4+ languages. (SRA)

Fundamentals of Computer Algorithms, by Horowitz & Sahni. This text covers various computer programming algorithms using the SPARKS pseudo-language and mathematical emphasis. (Computer Science Press)

V. Other Topics

Software Toolkit for Microcomputers, by Schindler et al. Selected articles from *Electronic Design* magazine, including an extensive section on languages. (Hayden)

Introduction to Operating System Design, by Habermann. A beginner's text, yet a college-level book, with examples from currently used operating systems. (SRA)

A First Course in Formal Language Theory, by Rayward & Smith. A concise coverage of this theoretical topic. (Blackwell)

The Programmer's CP/M Handbook, by A. Johnson-Laird. Programming on the assembly language operating-system level, for customizing CP/M to your specifications. (Osborne MGH)

Data Representation and Manipulation in a Computer 2/E, by Page & Wilson. Information and coding theory, including data structures and search/sort. (Cambridge)

Intro to the Theory of Automata, by Z. Bavel. An advanced text on automata and related theories for those with a theoretical computer science background. (Reston)

LANGUAGE MAGAZINES

The following magazines are specifically geared to the use and promotion of programming languages.

COMPUTER LANGUAGE
2443 Fillmore Street #346
San Francisco, CA 94115
(415) 957-9353

A magazine devoted entirely to programming languages. Includes reviews of language software, books, and programming techniques, as well as interviews and the "Exotic Language of the Month Club."

DR. DOBBS JOURNAL
2464 Embarcadero Way
Palo Alto, CA 94303
(415) 424-0600

Although not specializing in languages, this is an advanced magazine devoted to programming and it often covers various languages and programming techniques.

DIRECTORY OF BOOK AND SOFTWARE PUBLISHERS

ABACUS SOFTWARE
P.O. Box 7211
Grand Rapids, MI 49510
(616) 241-5510

ABSOFT
4268 North Woodward
Royal Oak, MI 48072
(313) 549-7111

ACADEMIC PRESS
Orlando, FL 32887
(305) 305-2000

ADDISON-WESLEY BOOKS AND SOFTWARE
Jacob Way
Reading, MA 01867
(617) 944-3700

ADVANCED COMPUTER TECHNIQUES
16 East 32nd Street
New York, NY 10016
(212) 696-3600

ALFRED PUBLISHING CO.
15335 Morrison Street
P.O. Box 5964
Sherman Oaks, CA 91413
(213) 995-8811

ALLYN & BACON
7 Wells Avenue
Newton, MA 02159
(617) 964-5530

AMERICAN PLANNING CORP.
4600 Duke Street #425
Alexandria, VA 22304
(703) 751-2574
(800) 368-2248

ANAHEIM PUBLISHING CORP.
2632 Saturn Street
Brea, CA 92621
(714) 993-3700

APPLE COMPUTER CORP.
20525 Mariani Avenue
Cupertino, CA 95014
(408) 996-1010

APPLIED SOFTWARE TECHNOLOGY
1350 Dell Avenue #206
Campbell, CA 95008
(408) 370-2662

ARTSCI
5547 Satsuma Avenue
North Hollywood, CA 91601
(818) 985-2922

ASHTON-TATE
10150 West Jefferson Boulevard
Culver City, CA 90230
(213) 204-5570

BD SOFTWARE
P.O. Box 2368
Cambridge, MA 02238
(617) 576-3828

BELLESOFT
2820 Northrup Way #150
Bellevue, WA 98004
(206) 828-7282

BENJAMIN-CUMMINGS PUBLISHING CO.
2727 Sand Hill Road
Menlo Park, CA 94025
(415) 854-6020

BERSTIS INTERNATIONAL
P.O. Box 441
Millwood, NY 10546
(914) 271-5855

BLACKWELL SCIENTIFIC
Distributed by Computer Science Press

BLAISE COMPUTING
2034 Blake Street
Berkeley, CA 94704
(415) 540-5441

BORLAND INTERNATIONAL
4113 Scotts Valley Drive
Scotts Valley, CA 95066
(408) 438-8400

BRADY COMMUNICATIONS
Bowie, MD 20715
(301) 262-3600

WILLIAM C. BROWN GROUP
2460 Kerper Boulevard
Dubuque, IA 52001
(319) 588-1451

BYTE WORKS
8000 Wagon Mound S.W.
Albuquerque, NM 87120
(505) 898-8183

CALIFORNIA SOFTWARE PRODUCTS
525 North Cabrillo Park Drive #300
Santa Ana, CA 92701
(714) 973-0440

CAMBRIDGE UNIVERSITY PRESS
32 East 57th Street
New York, NY 10022
(212) 688-8888

CATSPAW
P.O. Box 1123
Salida, CO 81201
(303) 539-3884

CGRS MICROTEK
513 Fairview Avenue
Penndel, PA 19047
(215) 757-0284

CHALCEDONY SOFTWARE
5580 La Jolla Boulevard #126
La Jolla, CA 92037
(619) 483-8513

CHILTON BECK COMPANY
Radnor, PA 19089-0230
(215) 964-4000

THE CODE WORKS
P.O. Box 6905
Santa Barbara, CA 93160
(805) 683-1585

COMMODORE COMPUTER COMPANY
1200 Wilson Drive
West Chester, PA 19380
(215) 431-9100

COMPUTER INNOVATIONS
980 Shrewsbury Avenue
Tinton Falls, NJ 07724
(201) 542-5920

COMPUTER SCIENCE PRESS
1803 Research Boulevard
Rockville, MD 20850
(301) 251-9050

COMPUTER SOFTWARE DESIGN
1904 Wright Circle
Anaheim, CA 92806
(714) 634-7012

CONSULAIR CORP.
140 Camps Drive
Portola Valley, CA 94025
(415) 851-3849

CONTROL-C SOFTWARE
6441 S.W. Canyon Court
Portland, OR 97221
(503) 297-7153

C WARE
P.O. Box C
Sunnyvale, CA 94087
(408) 720-9696

DATALIGHT
11157 8th Avenue N.E.
Seattle, WA 98125
(206) 367-1803

DIGITAL RESEARCH INC. (DRI)
P.O. Box 579
Pacific Grove, CA 93108
(408) 649-3896

DILITHIUM PRESS
P.O. Box 606
Beaverton, OR 97075
(503) 646-2713

DISC
3336 Bradshaw Road #340
Sacramento, CA 95827
(916) 363-7385

ECOSOFT
6413 North College Avenue
Indianapolis, IN 46220
(317) 255-6476

EDUWARE
28035 Dorothy Drive
Agoura Hills, CA 91301
(818) 706-0661

EINSTEIN CORP.
11340 West Olympic Boulevard
Los Angeles, CA 90064
(800) 221-3886

ELLIS COMPUTING
3917 Noriega Street
San Francisco, CA 94122
(415) 753-2483

EXPERTELLIGENCE
559 San Ysidro Road
Santa Barbara, CA 93108
(805) 969-7874

EXPERT SYSTEMS INTERNATIONAL
1150 First Avenue
King of Prussia, PA 19406
(215) 337-2300

FORTH INC.
2309 Pacific Coast Highway
Hermosa Beach, CA 90254
(213) 372-8493

GALFO SYSTEMS
6252 Camino Verde
San Jose, CA 95119
(408) 226-2377

GIMPEL SOFTWARE
3207 Hogarth Lane
Collegeville, PA 19426
(215) 584-4261

GNOSIS INC.
4005 Chestnut Street
Philadelphia, PA 19104
(215) 387-1500

GOLD HILL COMPUTER SYSTEMS
163 Harvard Street
Cambridge, MA 02139
(617) 492-2071

HARVARD SOFTWORKS
P.O. Box 69
Springboro, OH 45066
(513) 748-0390

HAYDEN BOOK COMPANY
10 Mulholland Drive
Hasbrouck Heights, NJ 07604
(201) 393-6300

HIPPOPOTAMUS SOFTWARE
1250 Oakmead Highway #210
Sunnyvale, CA 94086
(408) 738-1200

HOLT, RINEHART & WINSTON/CBS PUBLISHING
383 Madison Avenue
New York, NY 10017
(212) 599-7600

IBM SOFTWARE DIVISION
P.O. Box 1328
Boca Raton, FL 33429-1328
(305) 998-2000

ILLYES SYSTEMS
P.O. Box 2516 Station A
Champaign, IL 61820
(217) 359-6039

INFOPRO SYSTEMS
Box 849
Denville, NJ 07834
(201) 989-0570

INFORMATION UNLIMITED SOFTWARE
2401 Marinship Way
Sausalito, CA 94965
(415) 331-6700

INTERFACE TECHNOLOGIES CORP.
3336 Richardson #200
Houston, TX 77098
(713) 523-8422

INTEGRAL QUALITY
P.O. Box 31970
Seattle, WA 98103-0070
(206) 527-2918

I.P SHARP ASSOCIATES
2 First Canadian Place #1900
Toronto, Ontario, Canada M5X 1E3
(416) 364-5361

ITHACA INTERSYSTEMS
1650 Hanshaw Road
Ithaca, NY 14850
(800) 847-2088

JIB-RAY
P.O. Box 30283
1114 La Vista Road
Santa Barbara, CA 93110
(805) 682-1956

JIM E. HENDRIX
P.O. Box 8378
University, MIS 38677
(601) 234-7508

KRELL SOFTWARE
1320 Stony Brook Road
Stony Brook, NY 11790
(516) 751-5139
(800) 245-7355

KRIYA SYSTEMS
505 North Lake Shore Drive
Chicago, IL 60611
(312) 822-0624

KYAN SOFTWARE
850 Union Street #183
San Francisco, CA 94123
(415) 775-2923

LABORATORY MICROSYSTEMS
P.O. Box 10430
Marina Del Rey, CA 90295
(213) 306-7412

LAHEY COMPUTER SYSTEMS
31244 Palos Verdes Drive West #240
Rancho Palos Verdes, CA 90274
(213) 541-1200

LANGUAGE PROCESSORS INC.
400-1 Totten Pond Road
Waltham, MA 02154
(617) 890-1155

LATTICE INC.
P.O. Box 3072
Glen Ellyn, IL 60138
(312) 858-7950

LEVIEN INSTRUMENT CO.
P.O. Box 31
McDowell, VA 24458
(703) 396-3345

LIFEBOAT ASSOCIATES
1651 Third Avenue
New York, NY 10128
(212) 860-0300

THE LISP COMPANY
430 Monterey Avenue #4
Los Gatos, CA 95030
(408) 354-3668

LITTLE, BROWN & CO. PUBLISHERS
34 Beacon Street
Boston, MA 02106
(617) 227-0730

LOGIC PROGRAMMING ASSOCIATES
10 Burntwood Close
London, England SW18 5JU

LOGITECH
805 Veterans Boulevard
Redwood City, CA 94063
(415) 365-9852

LOGO COMPUTER SYSTEMS
555 West 57th Street #1236
New York, NY 10019
(212) 765-4780

LOKI ENGINEERING
55 Wheeler Street
Cambridge, MA 02138
(617) 576-0666

MACMILLAN INC.
866 Third Avenue
New York, NY 10022
(212) 702-2000

MANX SOFTWARE
P.O. Box 55
Shrewsbury, NJ 07701
(201) 780-4004

MARK WILLIAMS COMPANY
1430 West Wrightwood
Chicago, IL 60614
(800) MWC-1700

MCGRAW-HILL BOOK COMPANY
1221 Avenue of the Americas
New York, NY 10020
(212) 512-2000

M.E.C.A.
285 Riverside Avenue
Westport, CT 06880
(203) 222-1000

M.E.C.C.
3490 Lexington Avenue North
St. Paul, MN 55112
(612) 638-0600

MEDIA MATERIALS
2936 Remington Avenue
Baltimore, MD 21211
(301) 235-1766

MEGAMAX INC.
P.O. Box 851521
Richardson, TX 75085-1521
(214) 987-4931

MICOL SYSTEMS
1001 Graydon Hall Drive #2301
Don Mills, Ontario, Canada M3A 3A9
(416) 441-3752

MICRO FOCUS
2465 East Bayshore Road #400
Palo Alto, CA 94303
(415) 856-4161

MICRO MIKES
3015 Plains Boulevard
Amarillo, TX 79102
(806) 372-3633

MICROMOTION INC.
12077 Wilshire Boulevard #506
Los Angeles, CA 90025
(213) 821-4340

MICROPRODUCTS
24677 Watt Road
Ramona, CA 92065
(619) 789-6510

MICRORIM
3380 146th Place S.E.
Bellevue, WA 98007
(206) 641-6619

MICROSOFT INC.
10700 Northrup Way
Bellevue, WA 98004
(206) 828-8080

MICROSPARC
P.O. Box 325
Lincoln, MA 01773
(617) 259-9710

MICROTEC RESEARCH
3930 Freedom Drive #101
Santa Clara, CA 95054
(408) 733-2919

MICROWAY
P.O. Box 79
Kingston, MA 02364
(617) 746-7341

MILLER MICROCOMPUTER SERVICES
61 Lake Shore Road
Natick, MA 01760
(617) 653-6136

MITCHELL PRESS
915 River Street
Santa Cruz, CA 95060
(408) 425-3851

MITEK
94-074 Aaahi Place
Mililani, HI 96789
(808) 623-6361

MORGAN COMPUTING INC.
2520 Tarpley Road #500
Carrollton, TX 75006
(214) 245-4763

MOUNTAIN VIEW PRESS
P.O. Box 4656
Mountain View, CA 94040
(415) 961-4103

MYSTIC CANYON SOFTWARE
P.O. Box 1010
Pecos, NM 97552
(505) 988-4214

NETWORK CONSULTING
3700 Gilmore Way
Burnaby, BC, Canada V5G 4M1
(604) 430-3466

NEW AMERICAN LIBRARY
1633 Broadway
New York, NY 10019
(212) 397-8156

NEW CLASSICS SOFTWARE
239 Fox Hill Road
Denville, NJ 07834
(201) 625-8838

NORTHWEST COMPUTER ALGORITHMS
P.O. Box 90995
Long Beach, CA 90809
(213) 426-1893

W.W. NORTON & COMPANY
500 Fifth Avenue
New York, NY 10110
(212) 354-5500

O'HANLON COMPUTER SYSTEMS
8383 158th Avenue N.E.
Redmond, WA 98052
(206) 454-2261

ON-GOING IDEAS
RD 1 P.O. Box 801
STARKSBORO, VT 05487
(802) 453-4442

OPTIMIZES SYSTEMS SOFTWARE
1221 B Kentwood Avenue
San Jose, CA 95129
(408) 446-3099

OPTIMUM SYSTEMS
P.O. Box 6208
Beaverton, OR 97007

OSBORNE/MCGRAW-HILL
2600 Tenth Street
Berkeley, CA 94710
(415) 548-2805

PETROCELLI BOOKS
251 Wall Street
Research Park
Princeton, NJ 08540
(609) 924-5851

PHOENIX COMPUTER PRODUCTS
1416 Providence Highway #220
Norwood, MA 02062
(617) 762-5030

PLUM HALL INC.
1 Spruce Avenue
Cardiff, NJ 08232
(609) 927-3770

POLYTRON
P.O. Box 787
Hillsboro, OR 97123
(503) 684-3000

PORTABLE SOFTWARE
60 Aberdeen Avenue
Cambridge, MA 02138
(617) 547-2918

PRENTICE-HALL INC.
Business and Professional Division
Englewood Cliffs, NJ 07632
(201) 592-2000

PRO CODE
15930 S.W. Colony Place
Portland, OR 97224
(503) 684-3000

PROGRAMMER'S JOURNAL
P.O. Box 3000
Denville, NJ 07834
(201) 345-3043

PWS PUBLISHING
Statler Office Building
20 Park Plaza
Boston, MA 02116
(617) 482-2344

QUE CORPORATION
7999 Knue Road
Indianapolis, IN 46250
(317) 842-7162

RANDOM HOUSE
201 East 50th Street
New York, NY 10022
(212) 751-2600

RATIONAL SYSTEMS
P.O. Box 480
Natick, MA 01760
(617) 653-6194

RESTON PUBLISHING CO.
11480 Sunset Hills Road
Reston, VA 22090
(703) 437-8900

RR SOFTWARE
P.O. Box 1512
Madison, WI 53701
(608) 244-6436

RYAN-MCFARLAND CORP.
609 Deep Valley Drive
Rolling Hills Estates, CA 90274
(408) 662-2522

HOWARD W. SAMS & COMPANY
4300 62nd Street
Indianapolis, IN 46268
(317) 298-5400

SAS INSTITUTE
Box 8000
Cary, NC 27511-8000
(919) 467-8000

SCIENCE RESEARCH ASSOCIATES (SRA)
155 North Wacker Drive
Chicago, IL 60606
(312) 984-7000

SCOTT, FORESMAN & CO.
1900 East Lake Avenue
Glenview, IL 60025
(312) 729-3000

SENSIBLE SOFTWARE
210 South Woodward #229
Birmingham, MI 48011
(313) 258-5566

SHAW LABS
P.O. Box 3471
Hayward, CA 94540-5953
(415) 276-5953

SIERRA ON-LINE INC.
P.O. Box 485
Coarsegold, CA 93614
(209) 683-6858

SOCIETY FOR COMPUTER SIMULATION
P.O. Box 2228
La Jolla, CA 92038
(619) 459-3888

SOFTAID
P.O. Box 2412
Columbia, MD 21045-1412
(301) 792-8096

SOFTECH MICROSYSTEMS
16875 West Bernardo Drive
San Diego, CA 92127
(619) 451-1230

SOFTSYNC
162 Madison Avenue
New York, NY 10016
(212) 685-2080

SOFTWARE AND SYSTEMS TECHNOLOGY
7700 Edgewater Drive #360
Oakland, CA 94621
(415) 632-1555

SOFTWARE DYNAMICS
2111 West Crescent #G
Anaheim, CA 92802
(714) 635-4760

SOFTWARE TOOLWORKS
15223 Ventura Boulevard #1118
Sherman Oaks, CA 91403
(818) 986-4885

SOFTWARE WAREHOUSE
P.O. Box 11174
Honolulu, HI 96828
(808) 734-5801

SOLUTION SYSTEMS
335 Washington Street
Norwell, MA 02061
(617) 659-1571

SOUTHWEST DATA
3017 San Fernando Boulevard
Burbank, CA 91504
(818) 841-1610

SOUTHWESTERN DATA SYSTEMS
3017 San Fernando Boulevard
Burbank, CA 91504
(818) 841-1610

SPARRY SOFTWARE LABS
P.O. Box 632
Milford, MA 01757
(617) 473-5435

SPRINGER-VERLAG
175 Fifth Avenue
New York, NY 10010
(212) 460-1500

SPSS INC.
444 North Michigan Avenue #3000
Chicago, IL 60611
(312) 329-2400

STACKWORKS
3402 Trent
P.O. Box 2248
New Bern, NC 28560
(919) 638-4849

STELLATION TWO
P.O. Box 2342
Santa Barbara, CA 93120
(805) 569-3132

STERLING SWIFT
7901 South IH-35
Austin, TX 78744
(512) 282-6840

STOK
17 West 17th Street
New York, NY 10011
(212) 243-1444

STSC INC.
2115 East Jefferson Street
Rockville, MD 20852
(301) 984-5129

SUMMIT SOFTWARE TECHNOLOGY
40 Grove Street
Wellesley, MA 02181
(617) 235-0729

SUNBURST COMMUNICATIONS
39 Washington Avenue
Pleasantville, NY 10570
(914) 769-5030

SUPERSOFT INC.
P.O. Box 1628
Champaign, IL 61820
(217) 359-2112

SYBEX INC.
2344 Sixth Street
Berkeley, CA 94710
(415) 848-8233

SYSTAT
603 Main Street
Evanston, IL 60202
(312) 864-5670

SYSTEMS MANAGEMENT INC.
3700 Computer Drive #PB-1
Raleigh, NC 27609
(919) 878-3600

TAMARACK SOFTWARE
Tin Cup Road
P.O. Box 247
Darby, MT 59829

TANDY/RADIO SHACK
1700 One Tandy Center
Forth Worth, TX 76102
(817) 390-3300

TELECOM
1155 Meridian Avenue #218
San Jose, CA 95125
(408) 275-1659

TERRAPIN INC.
222 Third Street
Cambridge, MA 02142
(617) 492-8816

TRANSERA CORP.
3707 North Canyon Road
Provo, UT 84604
(801) 224-6550

U-MICROCOMPUTERS
300 Broad Street
Stamford, CT 06901
(203) 359-4236

UNIFIED SOFTWARE SYSTEMS
P.O. Box 2644
New Carrollton, MD 20784
(301) 552-9590

VALPAR
3801 East 34th Street
Tucson, AZ 85713
(602) 790-7141

VANDATA
17541 Stone Avenue North
Seattle, WA 98133
(206) 542-7611

VANGUARD SYSTEMS
4226 Center Gate
San Antonio, TX 78217

VOICE OPERATED COMPUTER SYSTEMS
P.O. Box 3705
Minneapolis, MN 55405
(612) 544-5712

VOLITION SYSTEMS
P.O. Box 99628
San Diego, CA 92109
(619) 270-6800

WADSWORTH INC.
10 Davis Drive
Belmont, CA 94002
(415) 595-2350

WARNER BOOKS INC.
666 Fifth Avenue
New York, NY 10103
(212) 484-3160

WATCOM
415 Phillip Street
Waterloo, Ontario, Canada N2L 3X2
(519) 886-3700

WHITESMITHS LTD.
97 Lowell Road
Concord, MA 01742
(617) 369-8499

WILMES SYSTEMS
300 North Michigan Avenue #414
South Bend, IN 46601

WIZARD SYSTEMS
11 Willow Court
Arlington, MA 02174
(617) 641-2379

XOR CORPORATION
5421 Opportunity Court
Minnetonka, MN 55343
(612) 938-0005

TABLE OF ASCII CODES

The table is arranged to show both hexadecimal and binary equivalents of the ASCII Code. In both cases, the column figures indicate the most significant digits (leftmost digits) and the row values list the least significant digits (right-most digits). Simply locate the character, and match up rows and columns to find the appropriate hexadecimal or binary code equivalent.

HEX least sig.	most sig--> BITS	0 000	1 001	2 010	3 011	4 100	5 101	6 110	7 111
0	0000	NUL	DLE	SP	0	@	P		p
1	0001	SOH	DC1	!	1	A	Q	a	q
2	0010	STX	DC2	"	2	B	R	b	r
3	0011	ETX	DC3	#	3	C	S	c	s
4	0100	EOT	DC4	$	4	D	T	d	t
5	0101	ENQ	NAK	%	5	E	U	e	u
6	0110	ACK	SYN	&	6	F	V	f	v
7	0111	BEL	ETB	'	7	G	W	g	w
8	1000	BS	CAN	(	8	H	X	h	x
9	1001	HT	EM	)	9	I	Y	i	y
A	1010	LF	SUB	*	:	J	Z	j	z
B	1011	VT	ESC	+	;	K	]	k	{
C	1100	FF	FS	,	<	L	\	l	
D	1101	CR	GS	–	=	M	]	m	}
E	1110	SO	RS	.	>	N	^	n	~
F	1111	SI	US	/	?	0		o	DEL

INDEX

Ada
- advanced capabilities, 106
- advantages/disadvantages, 122–123, 125–126
- Apple II computers, 308
  - with CP/M, 317
- arrays, 118–119
- Atari computers, 323
- bit strings, 119
- Booleans, 111, 117
- CASE structure, 114–115
- characteristics, summarized, 379
- Commodore computers, 325
- comparison operators, 111
- conditionals, 114–115
- CP/M-80, 353
- CP/M-86, 359
- data types, 108–110
- Department of Defense role, 105–106
- dot notation, 120
- exceptions, 125
- files, 120–121
- functions, 112
- hardware availability, summarized, 380
- history, 105–106
- IBM PC, 340
- input/output, 113–114
- libraries, 107–108
- loops, 116–118
- Lovelace, Ada, 106
- mathematical operators, 110–111
- multitasking, 106
- overloaded operators, 112
- packages, 107–108, 122–123, 231
- Pascal, 106
- prime numbers (sample code), 109
- procedures, 107, 115–116
- program structure, 107–108
- Radio Shack computers, 330
- real-time operations and multitasking, 106, 125
- records, 119–120
- references, 126, 381
- separate compilation, 106
- strings as arrays, 119
- team programming, 115–116, 122–123
- variables and assignment, 110

Algorithms, references, 382

APL, 127–141
- advantages/disadvantages, 128–129
- APL system, 129–130
- Apple II computers, 308
  - with CP/M, 317
- Apple Macintosh computer, 321
- Atari computers, 323
- ceiling and floor, 134–135, 137
- characteristics, summarized, 379
- combinations, 135
- Commodore computers, 325
- comparison operators, 135
- conciseness, 127, 128
- CP/M-80, 353
- CP/M-86, 360
- division by zero not a problem, 136
- exponentiation and exponential notation, 134
- functions, 131–138, 139–140
- grade point average (sample code), 131
- hardware availability, summarized, 380
- history, 127–128
- IBM PC, 340–341
- interpreted, 128
- iota, 139–140
- mathematical operators, 131–132
- matrix operations, 128, 133–134
- not ASCII code, 128
- outer product (dot jot), 133–134
- program saving/retrieval, 129
- Radio Shack computers, 330
- references, 141
- residue, 135
- scalar functions, 137
- squad, 139–140
- strings, 140
- timesharing services, 367–368
- variables and assignment, 132
- vector arithmetic, 132
- vector reduction, 136
- versions, 128

Apple computers, language availability, summarized, 380
Apple II computers
  Ada, 308
  APL, 308
  assembly language, 308–310
  BASIC, 304–306
  C, 311
  COBOL, 306
  Forth, 311–312
  FORTRAN, 306–307
  Lisp, 312
  Logo, 313–314
  Modula-2, 314
  Pascal, 307–308
  Pilot, 314
  PL/1, 314
  Prolog, 314
  SAS, 314
  SPSS, 314
Apple II computers with CP/M
  Ada, 317
  APL, 317
  assembly language, 317–318
  BASIC, 315
  C, 318
  COBOL, 315–316
  Forth, 318
  FORTRAN, 316
  Lisp, 319
  Logo, 319
  Modula-2, 319
  Pascal, 316
  Pilot, 319
  PL/1, 320
  Prolog, 320
  SAS, 320
  SPSS, 320
Apple Lisa computer, FORTRAN, 321
Apple Macintosh computer
  APL, 321
  C, 321–322
  Lisp, 322
  Logo, 322
  Pascal, 321
Artificial intelligence, 198, 199, 212–213, 262–263; *see also* Lisp; Prolog
ASCII codes, 23, 394
  APL not expressible, 128
  FORTRAN, 74
Assembly language, 142–162
  addition (sample code), 155
  addressing modes, 146–149
  advantages/disadvantages, 143–145, 159–160
  Apple II computers, 29, 308–310
    with CP/M, 317–318
  assembler programs, 152–154
  bit operations, 151, 158
  Booleans, 151, 158
  characteristics, summarized, 379
  column sensitivity, 152–153
  Commodore computers, 326
  comparison operators, 151
  complex structures unavailable, 143–144
  conditional assembly, 155
  conditionals, 150
  cross-assemblers, 152
  Forth language interpreter, source, 159–160
  hardware availability, summarized, 380
  IBM PC, 341
  instruction set (6502), 149–152
  interface to, BASIC, 30
  interrupts, 152
  loads and stores, 149
  loops (sample code), 156, 157
  cf. machine language, 3–4, 142–143
  macro assembler, 152, 154
  mathematical operators, 150, 155
  meta-assembler, 152
  microprocessor (6502), 145
  mnemonics, 143
  portability, 143–144
  pseudo-operations, 153–154
  Radio Shack computers, 330–331
  references, 160–162
  registers, 145–146
  stack operations, 151
  stack pointer, 145–146
  subroutines, 159
  subtraction (sample code), 155
  Timex/Sinclair, 376
  transfers/increments/decrements, 149–150
Assignment. *See* Variables, constants, and assignment
Atari computers
  Ada, 323
  APL, 323
  BASIC, 323
  C, 323
  COBOL, 323
  Forth, 323–324
  FORTRAN, 323
  language availability, summarized, 380
  Lisp, 324
  Logo, 324
  Pascal, 323

BASIC, 6, 19–37
  Apple II Computers, 304–306
    with CP/M, 315

Apple III computers, 320
arrays, 28–29
assembly language interface, 30
Atari computers, 323
Booleans, 24
bubble sort (sample code), 22
characteristics, summarized, 378
Commodore computers, 324–325
comparisons, 23
compilers, 20–21
conditionals, 25–26
control statements, 26–27
CP/M-80, 350–351
CP/M-86, 357–358
data types, 22–23
days of week (sample code), 85
DIM statement, 28
files, 29–30
functions, 24
GOTO statement, 21
graphics, 20, 30
hardware availability, summarized, 380
IBM PC, 332–335
input/output, 24–25, 29
limitations, 20–21
line numbers, 21
loops, 27–28
mathematical operators, 23
portability, 31
program structure, 21–22
Radio Shack computers, 328–329
records, 29–30
references, 33–37
ROM-based, 19
string handling, 28
structured programming, 21, 31
subroutines, 27
True BASIC, 31–33
Unix systems, 372–373
variables and assignment, 23
versions, 20, 29
Bell Laboratories, 163–164, 296
Binary numbers, 4, 8
Binary tree (sample code, Logo), 219
Bit operations
assembly language, 151, 158
C, 169, 182
PL/1, 249
Booleans, 8
Ada, 111, 117
assembly language, 151, 158
BASIC, 24
C, 169, 182
FORTRAN, 69
Logo, 225
Modula-2, 234
Bubble sort (sample code)
BASIC, 22
C, 165
C
advantages/disadvantages, 163–164
Apple II computers, 311
with CP/M, 318
Apple Macintosh computer, 321–322
arrays, 178–179
Atari computers, 323
bit operations, 169, 182
Booleans, 169, 182
braces, 166
bubble sort (sample code), 165
case sensitivity, 166
characteristics, summarized, 379
comments, 165
Commodore computers, 326
comparison operators, 169
conditional compilation, 183
conditionals, 173–176
CP/M-80, 353–354
CP/M-86, 360–362
data types, 166–167, 171, 172, 173
declarations, 170
dot addressing, 180
escape sequences, 173, 178
files, 183
functions, 169–171
hardware availability, summarized, 380
history, 163–164
IBM PC, 341–343
input/output, 171–173
libraries, 166, 169–170, 171–172
loops, 176–177
mathematical operators, 168–169
as middle-level language, 163, 169
newline character, 166
pointers, 182
preprocessor directives, 172, 182–183
program structure, 164–166
Radio Shack computers, 331
references, 184, 381
strings, 177–178
structures, 180–181
SWITCH structure, 175–176
unions, 181
Unix, 164, 375
variables and assignment, 168
CAI, 296; *see also* Pilot
CASE structure. *See* Conditionals and branching
CELLISM, 296
Charts. *See* Graphics
CHILI, 296
COBOL, 38–63
advantages/disadvantages, 38–39
ANSI, 39
Apple II computers, 306
with CP/M, 315–316

Atari computers, 323
characteristics, summarized, 378
class and sign conditions, 56
coding sheets, 41
column sensitivity, 41
comments, 41
Commodore computers, 325
comparison operators, 56
conditionals, 55–57
CP/M-80, 351–352
CP/M-86, 358–359
DATA DIVISION, 43–50
error handling, 55
field names, 45–46
files, 43–44, 51–52, 60–61
hardware availability, summarized, 380
IBM PC, 335–337
IDENTIFICATION DIVISION, 42–43
indexed files, 16, 58, 60
input/output, 50–53
justification, 47
level numbers, 45
mathematical operators, 54–55
PICTURE clauses, 47–50
portability, 38
printing data file (sample code), 39
PROCEDURE DIVISION, 50–51
procedures, 54
program structure, 39–43
Radio Shack computers, 329
records, 44, 45–46
references, 61–63
report writer, 59–60
self-documentation, 39, 44
sort/merge, 59
string handling, 57
table handling, 57–59
tape, 44
Unix systems, 373–374
variables and assignment, 53
versions, 39

Commodore computers
Ada, 325
APL, 325
assembly language, 326
BASIC, 324–325
C, 326
COBOL, 325
Forth, 326
FORTRAN, 325
language availability, summarized, 380
Lisp, 327
Logo, 327
Modula-2, 327
Pascal, 325
Pilot, 327
PL/1, 328
Prolog, 328
PROMAL, 328
SAS, 328
SPSS, 328

Compilers
cf. interpreters, 6
references, 382

Computer-aided instruction (CAI), 296; *see also* Pilot

Conditional assembly, 155

Conditionals and branching
Ada, 114–115
assembly language, 150
BASIC, 25–26
C, 173–176
COBOL, 55–57
Forth, 193–194
FORTRAN, 72–73
general characteristics, 12
Lisp, 205–206
Logo, 224–225
Modula-2, 237–239
Pascal, 90–91
Pilot, 244
PL/1, 253–254
SAS, 228

Constants. *See* Variables, constants, and assignment

Control statements. *See* Conditionals and branching

CORAL66, 296

CP/M-80, 349
Ada, 353
APL, 353
BASIC, 350–351
C, 353–354
COBOL, 351–352
Forth, 354–355
FORTRAN, 352
language availability, summarized, 380
Lisp, 356
Pascal, 352–353
Pilot, 356–357
PL/1, 357
RPGII, 357

CP/M-86, 349
Ada, 359
APL, 360
BASIC, 357–358
C, 360–362
COBOL, 358–359
Forth, 362
language availability, summmarized, 380
Lisp, 362
Modula-2, 363
Pascal, 359
Prolog, 363

CROSSTABS (language), 296

Crosstabs, SPSS, 279
CSSL, 296

Data processing, specialized languages, 296
Data structures, references, 382
Data types, 7–9
  Ada, 108–110
  BASIC, 22–23
  C, 166–167, 171, 172, 173
  character, 8–9
  files, 9–10
  Forth, 191–192, 196
  FORTRAN, 67–68
  lists, 9
  logical, 9
  Modula-2, 233–234
  numeric, 7–8
  Pascal, 9, 84–88
  PL/1, 249
  pointers, 10
  records, 9–10
  user-defined, 10
dBASE II, 297–298, 348–349
dBASE III, 298, 349
Dot notation
  Ada, 120
  C, 180
  Pascal, 97–98
  PL/1, 258
Double-precision numbers, 8
DYNAMO-III, 296

Education
  computer-aided (CAI), 296; *see also* Pilot
  Logo, 212–213; *see also* Logo
Educational services, 371–372
Engineering, 296
Escape sequences, C, 173, 178
Expert systems, 198, 262–263; *see also* Lisp; Prolog

Factorials (sample code)
  Lisp, 208
  Logo, 224
Fibonacci numbers (sample code, Lisp), 199
Files, 9–10
  Ada, 120–121
  BASIC, 29–30
  C, 183
  COBOL, 43–44, 51–52, 60–61
  data, 12
  general characteristics, 15–16
  Lisp, 208
  Logo, 213
  Modula-2, 237
  Pascal, 97–98
  PL/1, 259
  SAS, 287–288
Forth, 185–197
  advantages/disadvantages, 196
  Apple II computers, 311–312
    with CP/M, 318
  assignment, 192–193
  Atari computers, 323–324
  characteristics, summarized, 379
  Commodore computers, 326
  comparison operators, 193
  conditionals, 193–194
  constants, 192–193
  CP/M-80, 354–355
  CP/M-86, 362
  data types, 191–192, 196
  dictionary, 187–188
  hardware availability, summarized, 380
  history, 185–186
  IBM PC, 343–346
  input/output, 194–196
  interpreter, assembly language source code, 159–160
  loops, 193–195
  mathematical operators, 191–192
  postfix notation, 188, 190
  Radio Shack computers, 331
  references, 196–197
  stacks and stack operations, 188–190
  threaded code, 185
  Unix systems, 375
  variables and assignment, 192–193
  versions, 186
  words, 187–188
FORTRAN, 64–77
  adding two numbers (sample code), 5
  advantages/disadvantages, 65–66
  ANSI, 64
  Apple II computers, 306–307
    with CP/M, 316
  Apple Lisa computer, 321
  arrays, 75
  Atari computers, 323
  Booleans, 69
  characteristics, summarized, 378
  column sensitivity, 67
  Commodore computers, 325
  comparison operators, 69
  complex numbers, 67
  conditionals, 72–73
  consecutive numbers summing to 100, 66
  CP/M-80, 352
  data types, 67–68
  files, 75–76
  functions, 69–71

hardware availability, summarized, 380
history, 64
IBM PC, 337–338
input/output, 67, 71–72
loops, 74
mathematical operators, 68
portability, 64
program structure, 66–67
Radio Shack computers, 329–330
records, 75–76
references, 76–77
string handling, 67–68, 75
subprograms/subroutines, 70–71, 74
Unix systems, 374
variables and assignment, 68
versions, 64
WATFIV, 65, 72, 75
WATFIV-S, 65, 72–73
WATFOR, 65

Grades (sample code)
APL, 131
SAS, 285
SPSS, 277–278

Hexadecimal, 4
Hypothesis testing, SPSS, 279

IBM 370, 152, 247
SAS, 285
IBM 1130, 186
IBM PC
Ada, 340
ADAPT, 348
APL, 340–341
assembly language, 341
BASIC, 332–335
C, 341–343
COBOL, 335–337
compatibles, 377
dBASE II, 348–349
dBASE III, 349
Forth, 343–346
FORTRAN, 337–338
GAUSS, 348
language availability, summarized, 380
Lisp, 344–345
Logo, 345–346
Modula-2, 346
numeric coprocessor (8087), 333, 335, 338, 340, 341, 343, 345
Pascal, 338–339
Pilot, 346
PL/1, 347
Prolog, 347
RBase 5000, 298, 349
SAS, 347
SENSIBLE SOLUTION, 348
SNOBOL4, 348
SPSS, 347
IBM System/34, 297
ICON, 29
IF..THEN structure. *See* Conditionals and branching
Interpreters cf. compilers, 6

Lisp, 198–226
advantages/disadvantages, 199
Apple II computers, 312
with CP/M, 319
Apple Macintosh computer, 322
artificial intelligence, 198, 199
Atari computers, 324
atoms, 201
binding, 206
characteristics, summarized, 379
Commodore computers, 327
comparison operators, 204–205
conditionals, 205–206
control structures, 209–211
CP/M-80, 356
CP/M-86, 362
factorials (sample code), 208
Fibonacci sequence (sample code), 199
files, 208
functions, 201–204
hardware availability, summarized, 380
IBM PC, 344–345
input/output, 207–208
interpreted language, 200–201
lambda calculus, 199, 209–211
list orientation, 198, 199
lists, 200–201
loops (iterative or repeat structure), 209–211
predicates, 201, 204, 207
procedures (PROG structure), 210
program structure, 200, 204
quoting, 204
Radio Shack computers, 331
recursion, 198, 208–209
references, 211, 382
symbols, 201
variables and assignment, 206
versions, 199, 207
words, 200–201
Logo, 212–226
advantages/disadvantages, 213
Apple II computers, 313–314
with CP/M, 319
Apple Macintosh computer, 322
artificial intelligence, 212–213
Atari computers, 324
binary tree (sample code), 219
Booleans, 225

characteristics, summarized, 379
Commodore computers, 327
conditionals, 224–225
editor, 217
educational applications, 212–213
factorials (sample code), 224
files, 213
functions, 220–221
graphics (sample code), 213
hardware availability, summarized, 380
history, 212–213
IBM PC, 345–346
input/output, 224
lists, 221–223
loops, 218–219
mathematical operators, 217–218, 220
names, 223
procedures, 216–217
Radio Shack computers, 331
recursion, 218–219, 224
references, 225–226
REPEAT command, 216–217
sprites, 220
Turtlegraphics, 212, 213, 214–215
Unix systems, 375
variables and assignment, 217–218, 223
words, 221–223

Machine language, 3–4
cf. assembly, 142–143
see also Assembly language
Macro assemblers, 152, 154
Magazines, listed, 383
Mathematical operators
Ada, 110–111
APL, 131–132
assembly language, 150, 155
BASIC, 23
C, 168–169
COBOL, 54–55
Forth, 191–192
FORTRAN, 68
Logo, 217–218, 220
Modula-2, 235
Pascal, 88
PL/1, 250–251
Prolog, 267–268
Mathematics, specialized languages, 296
Meta-assembler, 152
Modula-2, 227–240
advantages/disadvantages, 228
Apple II computers, 314
with CP/M, 319
arrays, 239
Booleans, 234
characteristics, summarized, 379
Commodore computers, 327
comparison operators, 235
conditionals, 237–239
constants, 234–235
coroutines, 232–233
CP/M-86, 363
data types, 233–234
files, 237
functions, 235–236
greatest common denominator (sc), 233-234
hardware availability, summarized, 380
history, 227–228
IBM PC, 346
importing/exporting, 230–231
input/output, 236–237
interrupts, 232–233
libraries, 231, 232, 236, 239
linked list, 239
low-level features, 232
mathematical operators, 235
modular structure, 227
modules, 229–231
Pascal, 227–228
pointers, 239
portability, 232
procedures, 235–236
procedure variables, 233
program structure, 233
Radio Shack computers, 331
references, 240, 381
separate compilation, 231–232
side effects, avoiding (sample code), 229–231
variables and assignment, 234–235
versions, 228

Object-C, 299
Object code, 6
Object-oriented languages
Prolog, 263, 264
Smalltalk, 299
Operators, general characteristics, 11; *see also* Comparison operators; Mathematical operators

Pascal
Ada, 106
advantages/disadvantages, 79–80
Apple II computers, 307–308
with CP/M, 316
Apple III computers, 320
Apple Macintosh computer, 321
arrays, 96–97
Atari computers, 323
characteristics, summarized, 379
comments, 83
Commodore computers, 325

comparison operators, 89
conditionals, 90–91
constants, 82
CP/M-80, 352–353
CP/M-86, 359
data types, 9, 84–88
days of week (sample code), 85
declarations, 81–83
dot notation, 97–98
files, 97–98
functions, 84, 94–95
hardware availability, summarized, 380
history, 78–79
IBM PC, 338–339
input/output, 89–90
labels, 82
loops, 94
mathematical operators, 88
cf. Modula-2, 227–228
multiplication table (sample code), 81
nonstandard features, 98–99
pointers, 87
portability, 78
procedures, 91–93
program structure, 80–83
Radio Shack computers, 330
records, 83, 97–98
recursive procedures, 93
references, 99–101, 381
sets, 86
string handling, 95–96
Turtlegraphics, 99
Unix systems, 374–375
variables and assignment, 88
Venn diagrams, 86
Peripherals, 12
Pictures
COBOL, 47–50
PL/1, 259–260
Pilot, 241–245
advantages/disadvantages, 242–243
Apple II computers, 314
with CP/M, 319
Bible quiz (sample code), 244
characteristics, summarized, 381
Commodore computers, 327
comparison operators, 244
conditionals, 244
CP/M-80, 356–357
hardware availability, summarized, 380
IBM PC, 346
input/output, 242–243
labels, 244
references, 245
state capitals (sample code), 242–243
PL/1, 246–261
advantages/disadvantages, 246–247
Apple II computers, 314
arrays, 257
bit operations, 249
characteristics, summarized, 381
comments, 248
Commodore computers, 328
comparison operators, 250–251
conditionals, 253–254
CP/M-80, 357
data types, 249
dot notation, 258
files, 259
finding largest value (sample code), 248
functions, 251
hardware availability, summarized, 380
history, 246–247
IBM PC, 347
input/output, 251–252
mathematical operators, 250–251
pictures, 259–260
procedures, 254–255
program structure, 248–249
references, 260–261
strings, 255–257
structures, 257–258
timesharing, 247
Unix systems, 276
variables and assignment, 249–250
versions, 247
Program control. *See* Conditionals and branching
Program structure
Ada, 107–108
BASIC, 21–22
C, 164–166
COBOL, 39, 41–43
FORTRAN, 66–67
Lisp, 200, 204
Modula-2, 233
Pascal, 80–83
PL/1, 248–249
SAS, 285–287
Prolog, 198, 262–272
advantages/disadvantages, 263
Apple II computers, 314
artificial intelligence, 262–263
characteristics, summarized, 381
comments, 270–271
Commodore computers, 328
CP/M-86, 363
expert systems, 262–263
facts, 264–267
fifth-generation computing, 263
hardware availability, summarized, 380

history, 263
IBM PC, 347
input/output, 265–266
lists, 269
logical types, 9
logic, complex, 270–271
mathematical operators, 267–268
objects, 263, 264
program structure, 264
propositional calculus, 263
queries, 264–267
Radio Shack computers, 331
references, 271–272, 381
relations, defining, 264–265
robotics, 262–263
rules, 268–269
versions, 263, 264
Pseudocode, 79
P-system, 79
Publishers, book/software, listed, 384–393

Radio Shack computers
Ada, 330
APL, 330
assembly language, 330–331
BASIC, 328–329
C, 331
COBOL, 329
Forth, 331
FORTRAN, 329–330
language availability, summarized, 380
Lisp, 331
Logo, 331
Modula-2, 331
Pascal, 330
Prolog, 331
SAS, 332
SPSS, 332
RATFOR preprocessor, FORTRAN, 337–338
RBase 5000, 298, 349
Real-time operations, Ada, 106, 125
Robotics, 198, 262–263; *see also* Lisp; Prolog
ROM-based, BASIC, 19
RPGII, 297, 357

SAS, 284–294
advantages/disadvantages, 284–285
Apple II computers, 314
characteristics, summarized, 381
charts/graphs, 289–290
Commodore computers, 328
conditionals, 288
Data General Eclipse, 285
DATA step, 286–289
grades (sample code), 285
hardware availability, summarized, 380
history, 284
IBM 370, 285
IBM PC, 347
input/output, 288, 289–290
loops, 288
Prime series 50, 285
PROC step, 289–291
program structure, 285–287
Radio Shack computers, 332
references, 291
subroutines, 288
variables and assignment, 288–289
Scattergrams
SAS, 289–290
SPSS, 280
Scientific languages, 296
Simulation, 296
Smalltalk, 299
SNOBOL4, 296–297
IBM PC, 348
references, 382
word count (sample code), 297
Social sciences, 296; *see also* SAS; SPSS
Source code, 6
SPARKS, 382
SPEAKEASY, 296
Speciality languages, 295–296
Sprites, Logo, 220
SPSS (Statistical Program for the Social Sciences), 275–283
Apple II computers, 314
with CP/M, 320
bar charts, 278
batch processing, 276
characteristics, summarized, 381
column sensitivity, 278
command file, 277–278
Commodore computers, 328
correlation, 280
crosstabs, 279
customizing, 276
DEC Professional 350, 276–277
frequencies, 278–279
grades (sample code), 277–278
hardware availability, summarized, 380
history, 275–276
hypothesis testing, 279
IBM PC, 347
Radio Shack computers, 332
references, 282–283
regression, 281–282
scattergrams, 280
variance, analysis of, 280–281

Stack(s)
  assembly language, 151
  Forth, 188–190
  pointer, assembly language, 145–146
Statistics. *See* SAS; SPSS
String(s)
  Ada, 119
  APL, 140
  BASIC, 28
  C, 177–178
  FORTRAN, 67–68, 75
  general characteristics, 13–14
  -oriented languages, 296; *see also* SNOBOL4
  Pascal, 83, 95–96
  PL/1, 255–257
Structured programming, 21, 31
Subprograms/subroutines
  assembly language, 159
    sample code, 156
  BASIC, 27
  FORTRAN, 70–71, 74
  general characteristics, 14
  SAS, 288
  True BASIC, 33
  see also Functions; Procedures
Systems programming, 296; *see also* Ada; C; Modula-2

Tandy. *See* Radio Shack computers
Telecommunications services, 364–372
  educational, 371–372
  general timesharing services, 369–370
  language availability, summarized, 380
  popular, 366–367
  pricing, 365
  professional, 367–370
Telenet, 364
Texas Instruments Professional computers, 376
Timesharing, 365
  PL/1, 247
  services, 369–370
Timex/Sinclair, assembly language, 376
TRS-80. *See* Radio Shack computers
True BASIC, 31–33
Turtlegraphics
  Logo, 212–215
  Pascal, 99
TUTOR, 296
Tymnet, 364
Types. *See* Data types

UCSD P-system, 79
Unix, 163
  BASIC, 372–373
  C, 164, 375
  COBOL, 373–374
  Forth, 375
  FORTRAN, 374
  language availability, summarized, 380
  Logo, 375
  Pascal, 374–375
  PL/1, 376

Variance
  SAS, 289
  SPSS, 280–281
Vector operations, APL
  arithmetic, 132
  reduction, 136
Vendors, listed, 384–393
Venn diagrams, 86

9229